Serving Special Needs Students in the School Library Media Center

Greenwood Professional Guides in School Librarianship

School Library Media Centers in the 21st Century: Changes and Challenges
Kathleen W. Craver

Developing a Vision: Strategic Planning and the Library Media Specialist
John D. Crowley

Serving Special Needs Students in the School Library Media Center

Edited by CAREN L. WESSON
and
MARGARET J. KEFFE

Greenwood Professional Guides in School Librarianship

GREENWOOD PRESS
Westport, Connecticut • London

Library of Congress Cataloging-in-Publication Data

Serving special needs students in the school library media center /
edited by Caren L. Wesson and Margaret J. Keefe.
p. cm.—(Greenwood professional guides in school
librarianship, ISSN 1074–150X)
Includes bibliographical references and index.
ISBN 0–313–28697–3 (alk. paper)
1. School libraries—United States—Services to the handicapped.
I. Wesson, Caren. II. Keefe, Margaret J. III. Series.
Z675.S3S46 1995
027.6'63—dc20 94–39085

British Library Cataloguing in Publication Data is available.

Library of Congress Catalog Card Number: 94–39085
ISBN: 0–313–28697–3
ISSN: 1074–150X

First published in 1995

Greenwood Press, 88 Post Road West, Westport, CT 06881
An imprint of Greenwood Publishing Group, Inc.

Printed in the United States of America

The paper used in this book complies with the
Permanent Paper Standard issued by the National
Information Standards Organization (Z39.48–1984).

10 9 8 7 6 5 4 3 2 1

This book is dedicated to the memory of Caren L. Wesson who served as mentor and collaborator to the authors. Her endless energy and dedication to the field of education, and in particular for students with special needs, will continue to serve as an inspiration to others. We have been privileged to have shared in her life.

Contents

Illustrations

Introduction

Two primary changes in schools have magnified the importance of the relationship between the school librarian and special needs students. First, school library media specialists' roles have changed; they are not merely keepers of the library and the collection but part of the teaching staff, with an important library and information skills curriculum they are in charge of teaching and integrating with classroom curriculum. This role is especially important because of trends in education with regard to the integration of curriculum and the concept of resource-based teaching. The second change is that more and more special needs students are part of every school and every classroom, making it inevitable that the school library media specialist will teach these students, as well as the other students. The increase in this population is a result of more children being identified as special needs and the trend toward inclusion of these students in general education settings. As the hub of the school, the school library media center sets the tone for the acceptance of individual differences. (Throughout this book, *school library media specialist, school librarian,* and *librarian* are used synonymously.)

The American Library Association in 1988 described three roles for the school library media specialist: teacher, information specialist, and instructional consultant (or collaborator). The library media specialist as teacher refers to the role of formal and informal instructor in the development of skills, knowledge, and attitudes regarding the use of and access to information. Understanding the questions to ask, the resources to consult when answering these questions, and how to evaluate that information critically are strategies necessary for success today. In the information specialist role, the school library media specialist provides access to the information and resources for both colleagues and students. Also, in this role, the librarian assists in identifying appropriate resources and in interpreting their content. The third role is instructional collaborator, which includes working with colleagues in curriculum development, program implementation, and integration of information skills into the classroom curriculum.

The goal of this book is to explore how these roles operate with respect to students who have special needs: mildly or moderately disabled students classified as learning disabled, emotionally disturbed or behavior disordered, mentally retarded, hearing impaired, and visually impaired students, and severely disabled students. In addition, we have used the term *special needs* so that some discussion of students who are referred to as at risk (meaning at risk for school failure and/or for needing special education services) may be included. Finally, gifted and talented students are also in need of special instruction and therefore fit in the special needs category.

The two major educational trends with a major impact on the role of the school librarian are integration and inclusion. Integration is a curricular concept meaning that all instruction should be embedded in a meaningful context and that isolated subject areas should be merged, so that students do not simply receive splinters of information but rather knowledge that creates a meaningful whole. The second trend, inclusion, refers to the return and maintenance of students with special needs in general education classrooms. In other words, special needs students need to be included with their typical peers in general classes to the extent possible, so that they will appear in the school library not as segregated groups but as individuals within a larger class. In districts where special schools have been used to place these students, these students are now likely to be returning to their neighborhood schools and assigned to a general education classroom. In these cases, substantial assistance will be required for the inclusion to be effective for everyone involved—including the special needs students, the general education students, and the teachers.

INTEGRATION

Constructivists have criticized the traditional models of instruction in which reading, language arts, social studies, science, art, music, and math are taught as separate entities. They believe that children learn better if these subject areas are taught in more meaningful ways through integrated, thematic units. Units should be topic or theme driven, and the appropriate subject areas should be integrated into the unit as opposed to having separate time periods every day for each subject. The constructivists claim that children are less interested when the information is fragmented, and the connections among topics are lost unless teachers help students understand the concepts on a much deeper level. The topics or themes need to revolve around major concepts with larger understandings that are meaningful and important to students in their own lives; otherwise, the theme is merely a collection of activities and not a true integrated thematic unit (Routman, 1991). More important, students need to be able to apply these skills and information to the real world. It is the teacher's job to help make this connection to the real world for students—both special needs and general education students.

As a result of integration, teaching models now being used in schools are different from the traditional didactive structure. Thus, resource-based teaching, defined as the "use of multiple resources in a variety of media formats and technologies to achieve a curricular objective," has become important (Loertscher, 1988, p. 59). Resource-based teaching must be used with integrated, thematic units. This newer model of instruction calls for resources not usually available in the typical classroom. A multitude of materials in a variety of formats for teacher and student use is required; thus, resource-based instruction depends more than ever on the school library media specialist and the school library media center. Integrated instruction means more of a collaborative role for the school library media specialist as he or she assists teachers and students in identifying appropriate resources.

Another aspect of integration refers to the integration or collaboration of the library skills curriculum with that of the classroom curriculum. Students have often been heard to say that library or information skills class is boring. This topic is not exciting for students or teachers until the connection between the skill and its application is also taught.

One fourth-grade classroom teacher and the school library media specialist collaborated on a unit on dinosaurs. Before students began to research, they were taught a lesson that covered identifying information on a catalog card, reviewed call numbers, and brainstormed possible subject headings to look up related to the topic. They were then asked to locate dinosaur books themselves, thus putting the library skill immediately to a practical use. The next day, a notetaking lesson was team taught by both teachers, and students were asked to begin taking notes using the books they had retrieved from the library the previous day. As a culminating activity, students were asked to word process their reports and thus integrated computer technology learned in the library media center. After this lesson, when students were asked to apply the library information skill to an assignment, one student was quoted as saying, "Library skills are real now." This example shows a few ways the school library media specialist can affect the integrated thematic approach to teaching.

Students cannot possibly acquire all the information or content that is available to them, so the application of information skills is paramount. Students may not be able to retain all of life's information, but they should be able to retrieve, evaluate, assimilate, and utilize it when needed, especially for real-life application. Throughout this book, the movement toward more integrated instruction will be highlighted. Integrated instruction exemplifies the collaborative role for the school library media specialist highlighted in Part III.

INCLUSION

In 1986, Madeline Will, assistant secretary of education in charge of special education at the federal level, wrote an article "Educating Children with Learning Problems: A Shared Responsibility," in which she called for major change, igniting a movement that has been sweeping the country ever since. She and many other special and general educators had begun to question the efficacy of pull-out and self-contained special education classes. Part of their concern stemmed from studies examining the efficacy issue of special education. Special education students left in general education settings had as much academic gain, self-esteem, and social skill growth as the special education students who had been isolated in pull-out and special self-contained classes. Some evidence seemed to suggest that social skills and self-concepts were higher when special education students remained in general education classes. Another concern was that special needs students were not learning how to survive in a real-world setting because they were isolated in a setting with only other students like them and no broad continuum of abilities and personalities. Yet another disadvantage was that students in general education did not have the opportunity to learn about and from their special needs peers. Looking forward to the time these students would join society, the question was how educators might expect disabled and nondisabled adults to get along and understand each other when they had not been given the experiences in school to learn how to communicate and accept differences.

The idea of mainstreaming had been proposed in the early 1970s, but this model was beginning to crack under all its flaws. Mainstreaming meant that special education students were assigned to a special class, such as a self-contained learning disabilities class or a resource room, and then spent a portion of their day in the general education mainstream program. Three major flaws were inherent in this mainstreaming model. First, no one teacher was responsible for the mainstreamed students, and thus, often their time in the mainstream was not well spent. Second, some educators saw a major rift between special and general education and considered that within the public schools there were two separate systems: general and special. There were major problems with communication as basic as two teachers teaching one student math and not coordinating instruction. Ownership and responsibility for individual students was left hanging. No one seemed to take full responsibility. The general education teacher looked at the student as an extra burden instead of part of his or her caseload. The special education student was generally not included on the general education teacher's class list. Third, the stigma from being labeled and sometimes separated from peers caused problems for many students.

The system of referral, identification, and placement of special education students appears to many to be ludicrous. Many times the teacher makes the referral for special education testing; the teacher believes that the general education setting is not the best placement for this student to maximize his or her potential, and is having trouble reaching and teaching the student, who appears to have a disabling condition. The assessment procedure involves up to a dozen people. The general education teacher participates actively in assessment as well by allowing many visitors to observe in the classroom and permitting interruptions when the referred student leaves the room for assessment purposes. Following assessment, a meeting is held among the professionals, and parents are invited and encouraged to attend as well. Many times the student may not fit the definition of disabled given the criteria set by the district and state board of education. The child may be identified as a special education student, but the primary placement may still remain in the general education classroom. When a resource room or self-contained classroom placement is the program of choice by this committee, the general education teacher may still have this student in his or her classroom for the mainstreamed portion of the day. For example, the student may attend special education for only one hour of language arts instruction. The amount of time in a resource setting, which is the most frequently used placement option, varies from thirty minutes three times weekly to half a day, five days per week. Thus, after asking for assistance with this difficult-to-teach student and then proceeding through the referral and assessment process, the student often ends up remaining in this teacher's classroom for at least a portion of the day. After all this effort to help the student, this teacher is probably frustrated because little has really changed as a result of this effort.

Pull-out programs, such as resource rooms, have a host of their own problems. First and foremost is the difficulty of coordinating instruction for students in the pull-out instruction setting and in the general classroom. (This dilemma arises not only for special education resource room students but also for pull-out gifted students.) Usually a resource teacher works with fifteen to twenty students who are in classrooms with six to twelve teachers across the grade spectrum in the school. It is nearly impossible to communicate regularly about so many students with so many teachers. As a result, instruction becomes fragmented. Children may have to leave in the midst of a lesson in the general education class to go to the resource room for instruction (Pugach & Wesson, in press). They spend ten minutes packing up and walking to the resource room. When they get there, that teacher is in the middle of another lesson with a different group of students, so the arriving students wait for directions. When finished with the resource room time, they pack up materials and walk down the hallway, only to find the general education class knee-deep in a different lesson, and so the traveling students have no idea of how to catch up. For many children, pull-out programs can be counterproductive; their actual time receiving teacher-led instruction decreases due to the time required for transition, and the teachers' lessons often have no relationship to each other. Sometimes the two teachers confuse children with different explanations of the same concept. This fragmentation and lack of cohesiveness is challenging for any child but is especially problematic for a child with special needs.

The final major problem with the dual system of education—special and general—is the stigma caused by being identified as different and needing to go to specialists to be taught. They view themselves and are seen by others as being different from everyone else—and somehow not as good. They are often ridiculed and called names. They may not develop friendships with their classmates because they do not spend enough time with them to be known for their personalities and strengths. Teachers may inadvertently model a lack of understanding and frustration with the special needs students, and the other students will learn to turn away from them as well.

This dual system and resulting problems do not have to exist. There are other ways to organize schools and serve all children. One of the goals of this book is to promote a better relationship between general and special education and inclusion of special needs students in general education settings, especially the school library media center.

STRUCTURE OF THE BOOK

The roles of the school library media specialist as teacher, information specialist, and instructional collaborator in relation to students who have special needs provide the structure for the parts of this book. Part I, on the school library media specialist as teacher, highlights the teaching role as the specialist works directly with special needs students. How and what to teach are the main points of this part.

Part II focuses on the school library media specialist's role as an information specialist. It examines how the specialist can take into account the presence of special needs students when designing the library and selecting materials. The role of technology is addressed, as is the literary technique of bibliotherapy.

Part III highlights the school library media specialist's role as collaborator as he or she works with special needs students. As schools restructure in the future, the largest portion of this specialist's role will be in collaborating with other teachers. This is the way of the future in education, and there is no one more essential to this effort than the school library media specialist. This part provides guidance on the different aspects of this role as they relate to special needs students.

This book is meant to be used as a resource for school library media specialists who seek guidance with special needs students. Yet although it can assist in problem solving, it cannot replace the face-to-face communication so necessary for effective schools.

REFERENCES

Loertscher, David V. *Taxonomies of the School Library Media Program*, Illus. by Mark Loertscher. Englewood, CO: Libraries Unlimited, Inc., 1988.

Routman, Regie. *Invitations: Changing as Teachers and Learners K-12*. Toronto, Can: Irwin Publishing, 1991.

American Association for School Librarians & Association for Educational Communications and Technology. (1988). *Information power: Guidelines for school library media programs*. Chicago & Washington, DC: American Library Association & Association for Educational Communications and Technology.

Will, M. (1986). Educating children with learning problems: A shared responsibility. *Exceptional Children* Washington, D.C.: Office of Special Education and Rehabilitation Services, U.S. Dept. of Education.

I

The School Library Media Specialist's Role as Teacher

Teaching Library and Information Skills to Special Needs Students

1

Caren L. Wesson and Margaret J. Keefe

The role of school librarian has evolved from library clerk and keeper of the collection into a multifaceted school library media specialist who is viewed as an integral part of the educational process in the school, directly involved in teaching and curriculum development as well as in the organization and operation of the school library media center. As information and technology become more important, students need to learn how to access information and analyze data. Research skills and resource-based learning become a central focus of education. As resource-based learning becomes the norm, the teaching role of the librarian will grow even more. As the role of school library media specialist becomes more teaching oriented, it becomes imperative that school library media specialists become aware of the implications of the Individuals with Disabilities Education Act (IDEA) passed in 1990. This law, as well as the law that preceded it (PL 94–142, The Education for all Handicapped Children Act), mandates that students with special needs be instructed in the least restrictive environment. This chapter describes special needs students and the programs that serve them, states the rationale for including these students in library activity with their typical peers, and describes a model for instruction.

WHO ARE STUDENTS WITH SPECIAL NEEDS?

Special needs students fall into four categories: high and low-incidence disabilities, categories that refer to the prevalence of the disability; at-risk students, or those who have not been formally identified as special education students but nonetheless need extra support to be successful in a general education setting; and gifted and talented students, who demonstrate superior abilities in one or more of the following domains: cognitive, affective, physical, intuitive, and societal (Clark, 1992). Students in these categories may require some individualization in the school library. (For specific information on definitions, see particular states' special education laws, their district manuals, and general special education texts. Also see Heward & Orlansky, 1992, and Meyen, 1990).

High Incidence

High-incidence disabilities refers to students who are officially identified through an assessment process as learning disabled (LD), emotionally disturbed (ED) (or behavior disordered [BD]), or mentally retarded (MR). Different states may use alternative labels; for example, in Wisconsin, the term *cognitive disabilities* is used instead of *mentally retarded.*

A learning disabled child often has difficulty with acquiring, storing, and retrieving information, although the child has normal intelligence and fully functioning visual and auditory senses. State departments of education set criteria for determining whether a child is learning disabled, such as a discrepancy between ability and achievement, which can be determined through comparing scores on intelligence tests with those on achievement tests. Other state definitions may include the presence of an underlying processing problem; that is, the senses are functioning normally, but the processing of the information for receptive and expressive purposes is inadequate. The bottom line is that children identified as LD are not learning at the rate of improvement expected given their normal or above-normal intelligence.

Students who are identified as emotionally disturbed may have several problem behaviors, including demonstrating unusual behaviors in normal circumstances, a pervasive mood of unhappiness or depression, or chronic misbehavior, including aggressiveness and inappropriate verbalizations. Again, each state has specific criteria used to determine if a particular student is emotionally disturbed or behavior disordered (the terms vary state to state). For example, evidence of problems in two or more environments, such as home, school, and community, may be required, evidence that the behaviors are frequent, severe, or chronic may be necessary, or both.

Three facets are considered when the label mentally retarded is used: low IQ (below 70), low adaptive behavior performance, and problems identified prior to age nineteen. Adaptive behaviors are those used in normal daily life such as communication, self-care (bathing, feeding self), social skills, and use of transportation.

Low Incidence

Low-incidence special education students include children with autism, visual, and/or auditory impairments, severe and/or multiple disabilities, traumatic brain injury, and physical and other health impairments—an extremely heterogeneous group. As school library media specialists become acquainted with children in this group, specific strategies for individual students need to be shared with the librarian. Advice from their teachers and supervisors from these various special education programs is essential.

As with the high-incidence categories, students with low-incidence special needs are identified by determining whether they meet specific criteria set forth by the state department of public instruction. For example, to determine if a child is hearing impaired, an audiogram is conducted, and specific parameters for the extent of hearing loss in terms of decibels and frequencies are used to judge eligibility for special education services. Many children in this low-incidence group require adaptation of equipment and modification of instruction in order to learn. Physically disabled children may use augmentative communication tools, such as computers, language boards, and eye contact sensors in order to express themselves. Visually-impaired children require special materials, such as large-print or braille books. Most children who are visually impaired have low vision ability, but some vision; only a small percentage are totally blind. Similarly, children with hearing impairment are seldom completely deaf; rather, they have some residual hearing ability, which needs to be recognized and used.

Children who have autistic behaviors also need library privileges, though it may be difficult to discern the benefit of their activity in the library. Children with autism have very poor communication and interpersonal skills. They seem to be unresponsive to the language directed to them and seldom initiate or maintain conversations. Another group that has difficulty communicating for other reasons are students with severe or multiple disabilities. Usually children in this group have low intelligence (IQs below 40) and other physical or sensory problems, such as cerebral palsy or visual problems. These children also need multiple settings in which to learn, and among these potential sites is the school library media center. They may be learning to sit quietly while a book is being read or to make an X on the line of the checkout card, but the benefit of including them or children with autism is that they feel part of the school and their classroom community.

At Risk

Some students who have not been formally identified as needing special education nevertheless are difficult to teach in general education. Many general education students fall into this category of at-risk or gray-area students. They do not meet criteria for special education, so do not qualify and cannot receive those services. Yet their school performance is poor, as reflected in poor grades, low standardized test scores, and negative teacher perceptions, and they have poor self-concepts. Many of these students are disenfranchised from education and have little motivation to put forth academic effort. The library may be the key location for fostering interest in learning and school.

Gifted and Talented

In contrast to the other groups are gifted and talented students. If left in a traditional classroom environment where large-group, teacher-directed instruction is the mainstay, these students may soon lose interest and motivation. Some schools do not formally identify these gifted students until fourth grade and at that time special pull-out programs may begin. Other schools pair teachers and a coordinator to help bolster the curricular needs of these students.

When working with gifted students, school librarians should be aware of their varying characteristics. In the past, gifted students were identified solely on the basis of an IQ score of 140 or above. More recent definitions have broadened that perspective based on more varied criteria. Renzulli (1978) looks at above-average general abilities, a high level of task commitment, and high levels of creativity as the ingredients of giftedness. In his model, students with all three characteristics are considered gifted. There is no federal definition of giftedness, nor is there any federal mandate for gifted programs. Many states have definitions but loose requirements for programmatic implementation. Critics argue that shortsightedness with regard to serving gifted and talented students is a national tragedy with long-term political, economic, and social ramifications (Davis & Rimm, 1985). Clearly, the school library is a key environment for improving the education of gifted and talented students as this is the locale of the materials and resources they need to access as they learn independent research skills.

HOW ARE SPECIAL NEEDS STUDENTS SERVED?

There are many programmatic structures for serving students with special needs, and often discussion about these structures focuses on a continuum of services, from the general education classroom to more segregated settings to settings that are completely isolated from typical students.

General Education

The vast majority of students with special needs are schooled in general education classroom settings with their peers. Thus, the school librarian will likely teach these students as part of a large general education class, with the contact person being the general education classroom teacher. Students identified as MR, LD, or ED, and students requiring supplemental reading and math services provided by federally funded Chapter 1 funds, counseling, physical and occupational therapy, and other support services typically spend almost all their school hours in the general education setting. A growing trend is to keep them in the general education setting to the maximum extent possible. In fact, the IDEA and the Education for All Handicapped Children Act mandate placement for identified special education students in the least restrictive setting. The majority of leaders in the fields of special education and remedial reading agree that for all students to have the benefit of peer modeling and socialization in a typical setting, the general classroom setting is the best placement as long as support services are provided (Allington & Johnson, 1989).

Several different means of support of special needs students placed in general education settings are being employed. In the team teaching model, the general education teacher works in partnership with either a special education teacher or a Chapter 1 teacher in order to meet the needs of all the students in the class, both typical learners and special needs learners. Team teaching may be an all-day, every-day model or a part-time situation (e.g., one hour per day). Much discussion and negotiation go into these teams before they are undertaken. Roles and responsibilities need to be delineated, as do expectations for student academic and social behaviors. During the planning process for teaming, the teachers may decide to split the instructional responsibilities evenly, to share given their different areas of expertise, or to have one person be lead teacher while the other provides support via monitoring and guiding individual students (Pugach & Wesson, in press). Often one teacher has curricular responsibility, while the other is child centered in perspective. These two perspectives may stay permanently with a given member of the team or may be alternated between team members. With large teams, the roles may be shared. The primary goal is that all the needs of all the students are met. In addition to special education teachers' teaming with general education teachers, sometimes the Chapter 1 teacher is the partner. The traditional pull-out model has given way to pull-aside practices within the classroom itself. There are two advantages to the pull-aside model: there is less stigma associated with having the student leave the class, and the teachers (Chapter 1 and regular education) who are both instructing the student in reading or math may coordinate their lessons so that redundancy and gaps do not exist in the curriculum. With two teachers present, pull-aside may evolve into team teaching, which could benefit all children in the classroom, as well as the targeted Chapter 1 students.

A second model for serving all students in a general education setting is the use of a consulting teacher. The consulting teacher usually does not work directly with the students but may observe the students, prepare materials for them, and assist in preparing lesson plans to accommodate individual needs. Consultants meet with the teacher regularly and bring a knowledge of specific learning and behavior characteristics of the student and alternative teaching strategies to these sessions. The consultant lets the teacher take the lead in deciding how to instruct the student but provides support and advice.

The third model, a teacher assistance team, is similar to the consultant model with the exception that a group of colleagues meet to discuss the challenges of the difficult-to-teach students. These meetings tend to occur less frequently than consulting teacher meetings, but the advice may be more readily accepted by the teacher because it comes from a group of peers rather than from an expert. The team may be a group of teachers who meet on every case throughout the year or a specific group identified by the teacher solely for the specific case. The latter model is preferable and more accommodating to including the school librarian. This model primarily serves the at-risk group.

Resource Room—Partial Pull-Out

Students with special needs may go to separate classes for a portion of the day; these are often referred to as resource rooms and are taught by a special education teacher. Chapter 1 pull-out classes are actually quite similar in structure. Students usually attend the resource room for a half-hour to three hours per day. There may be one to fifteen students in the room at any time. In this setting, there are usually fewer distractions and smaller instructional groups and therefore more individualized attention. The problems with this model are the isolation and associated stigma, lack of appropriate peer models, and the difficulty of coordinating instruction between the general education teacher and the resource teacher.

Self-Contained Special Education Class

A separate class, the self-contained classroom, is taught by a special education teacher. The students spend the majority of their time in this segregated setting but may participate in general classes at their age-appropriate level for music, gym, and library. Within this structure, there is no problem with coordinating basic skill and content instruction, but the students have little contact with their typical peers and no models for academic and social skills development. Another dilemma is that often content areas such as social studies and science are seldom addressed in special classes, which makes it difficult for students who could be integrated into these content-area classes in later years because they have acquired little background knowledge.

Special Schools

Residential and special day schools are the last level of the special education continuum. Occasionally there is home tutoring if illness or school phobia is substantially problematic. Special schools are becoming increasingly rare but still exist for students who are hearing impaired, visually impaired, or emotionally disturbed. A special education–trained core of teachers and teacher assistants staff the schools. Specialized instruction, including adaptive physical education, physical and occupational therapy, art and music therapy, and other specializations are often offered in such settings. The drawbacks are the isolation, lack of appropriate models, and the teachers' loss of perception of normalcy. Parents are less and less enamored with these isolated schools because the long-term likelihood of the students' fitting into society as adults is decreased.

WHY INCLUDE SPECIAL NEEDS STUDENTS IN LIBRARY ACTIVITIES?

The library is an important setting for special needs students because of the range of skills that may be addressed given the technology, resources available, and potential skills that may be taught there. The specific skills each special needs student needs to be taught in this setting are documented in the individualized education plans (IEPs), part of the mandate found in the IDEA. The IEP lists the student's level of performance, goals, objectives, and proposed interventions to be used in an effort to help the student reach his or her potential in all areas in which special education instruction is needed. School library media specialists should play an important role in the implementation of these laws and in the movement to include special needs students. Libraries, both public and school, are excellent examples of places where integration can be readily facilitated. Inclusion means more than providing access to facilities. Physical presence in the library, especially the school library media center, is not enough. In order to include special needs students in a meaningful way, many aspects of their activity in the library should be considered; instructional strategies to help them learn skills associated with the library, selection of materials appropriate for all students, and helping students interact with each other in a positive manner.

The school library media specialist and the special education teacher can work together to teach library skills to mildly and moderately didsabled students. A team approach with joint planning by both the school library media specialist and special education teacher is important for several reasons. First, both individuals have unique information: the school library media specialist knows the library skills sequence and the teaching techniques used with general education students, and the special education teacher knows the individual students and the teaching accommodations that may facilitate learning. Another reason for working as a team is that the two can provide for generalization training for the students. Generalization refers to the ability of students to apply a skill to another person, time, setting or situation. Many students can perform a task to criteria for one teacher but do not demonstrate mastery for a second person. Transition from a special education setting to the regular classroom is often a problem for this reason. Library skills incorporate a good set of specific skills that can provide practice in transferring skills from one person to another. A third reason for the team approach is that the school library media specialist becomes one more person with whom the special needs student can interact. Many of these students have social skill deficits, which cause difficulties for them in school, work, and many social arenas. The school library media specialist can become another individual helping to foster the development of appropriate social skills. Regardless of the setting these children are in or the label they have, the school library media specialist must have some information about how to modify instruction to meet the needs of special needs students in the library.

USING THE INSTRUCTIONAL CYCLE TO TEACH SPECIAL NEEDS STUDENTS

Teaching library skills to special needs students follows the same overall model of instruction useful in teaching other skills. Two aspects of instruction must be considered: the hard work of an instructional cycle, which helps the teacher systematically identify and teach the skills necessary, and the teaching strategies that are employed.

The instructional cycle has three major steps before it repeats itself: (1) assessing the student's current proficiency level in library skills, (2) identifying performance objectives based on a hierarchy of library skills and the student's needs, and (3) specifying an instructional plan and a strategy for monitoring student progress. This cycle of test-teach-test is then repeated as other skills are targeted for assessment and instruction.

Determining the Student's Skill Level

Many young students have had little, if any, exposure to the library. For these students, the teacher and school library media specialist can assume that they begin at the first skill on the skills hierarchy. With older students, the teacher and school library media specialist must assess the students' incoming skill level using an informal inventory. (An example of an informal library and information skills inventory is found in Chapter 2.) In compiling this inventory, the first step is to ask the special education teacher to estimate the approximate grade-level library skill ability of the student.

For example, a fourth grader who reads on a second-grade level is likely to have approximately second-grade-level library skills as well. The person conducting the inventory should begin by administering some skills from one grade level lower than the estimated skill level. Beginning testing at this lower level helps ensure that the student will experience some success in the inventory. Starting with items that are too difficult may lead to frustration and failure.

The teacher or school library media specialist administering an informal library and information skills inventory may use the items suggested in Chapter 2 under the "Assessment Task" heading. One, two, or three additional items may need to be developed in order to obtain a truly accurate measure of the student's ability or to assess areas not covered in this hierarchy but viewed as important by the teacher and librarian. Two important guidelines should be followed when developing additional assessment items. First, all items should contain verbs that can be objectively evaluated. Words like *express*, *recognize*, and *know* have no visible actions that are directly observable; action words that may be used include *write*, *state*, *point to*, and *pick up*. Second, the items should be based on clearly stated and important, necessary objectives. Superfluous items place an unnecessary burden on the teacher and student and waste valuable instructional time.

Stating Objectives

To date, very little attention has been paid to library skills in the IEP. However, these skills should not be overlooked because they are useful for leisure, vocational, and academic purposes. Also, many of these skills are easily taught and therefore useful in creating successful learning experiences for the special needs student.

An objective is an operational, behavioral statement that guides instruction and provides a benchmark for evaluating student progress. It has three essential components:

1. What the learner will do (*performance*).
2. Under what conditions the learner will do this (*condition*).
3. How well it must be done (*criteria*).

Several guidelines must be kept in mind when writing objectives. First, the functional nature of the objective should be considered. The objective should be based on a task that the student is likely to perform in the future. The IEP team must predict what library skills may be helpful to the individual during the coming school years and adult life. For example, learning to use an atlas may not be important in terms of vocation but may be included as an objective for leisure purposes, such as planning vacations.

In each case, the individual student's level of functioning and future potential must be kept in mind as the objectives are written.

A second guideline is to consider the prerequisite skills and keep a task hierarchy in mind. There is no one correct sequence of library skills, but some skills should be taught before others. For example, orientation to the library media center should come before using the Dewey decimal system. Asking, "What does the student need to do to attain this objective?" will help clarify prerequisite skills. Any prerequisite skills not yet mastered should be the focus of instruction first.

Third, the criteria included in the objective should be based on the individual student. For example, the criterion of a maximum of one to two minor disruptions in a thirty-minute period for the objective on behavior in the library media center listed in Chapter 2 may be unrealistic for a student with behavior problems (emotionally disturbed or behavior disordered). A more realistic criterion may be a maximum of five minor disruptions in thirty minutes. The IEP team should collaborate in determining the criteria for individual students.

Finally, not all the skills listed in the skills hierarchy will be appropriate for all mildly or moderately disabled students. Again, functionality and current skill level should be considered when objectives are written. One to three library objectives may be written per year. (More than three would be cumbersome for the school library media specialist or teacher to monitor.) The objectives should become the focal point for instruction and play an active role in the student's school day. Lists of objectives that are filed away until the end of the school year have little bearing on day-to-day instruction.

The objectives that the IEP team develops for the student become the basis for instructional planning. The teacher and school library media specialist then work together to develop instructional procedures for teaching the specific skills to the individual student. Modifications of the school library media specialist's usual instructional procedures may be in order if the objectives are to be mastered by the special education student.

Teaching Strategies for Special Needs Students

Three components of instruction—methods, materials, and motivation—may need to be modified in order to teach the special needs student.

Methods

A school library media specialist must use principles of effective teaching in order to ensure mastery of library skills. The recent special and regular education literature has summarized variables of effective instruction. One effective instructional procedure, referred to as direct instruction, is a demonstrate-prompt-practice procedure. The school library media specialist first models the behavior the student is to learn. For example, if the objective is locating books in the library, the specialist may go to the specified section and say to the student, "I am standing in front of the picture books. These are the books you will want to look at—the picture books." Then he or she may prompt the student to come stand near them and label the section of the library: "Come stand with me in front of the picture books section. What kind of books are these? [Student responds.] Yes, these are the picture books, the books you will like best."

A second principle is to point out nonexamples to the student: "Are the picture books over here? [Librarian points to the card catalog or reference books.] No. The picture books are there." Including nonexamples will help the student discriminate between correct and incorrect responses.

A third teaching technique is to provide many prompts or clues as to what the student's behavior should be or how to practice the task. For example, when teaching the location of picture books, the school library media specialist may use a large picture and the words PICTURE BOOKS on the wall in that section of the library to prompt the student. If the student still cannot find the section, a large set of paper eyes may be put next to the picture and the librarian may tell the student to "look" for the picture (and the eyes). The long-term goal is to reduce the prompts gradually and systematically so that only the natural features of the setting are enough for the student to complete the task. Prompts range from subtle visual or verbal hints, to very direct hints, to modeling the skill, to direct physical guidance. All students can benefit from some prompting, but special needs students often need stronger prompts and the prompts faded more slowly than their general education peers.

Also, with respect to methods, the school librarian needs to keep a meaningful context in mind. A lesson on using an atlas should be tied into a broader context, such as planning a class trip (reality or fantasy) or a family vacation. Tying the atlas into the current social studies lesson is also a good idea. Being flexible and finding topics of interest to the students is important as well.

Discovery or inquiry methods may be used with special needs students as they participate in cooperative groups, large and small. The sample lesson at the end of this chapter uses inquiry and direct instruction ideas; it may be helpful for all students because most also need to hear information clearly stated. In inquiry instruction, the librarian poses questions, challenges, and puzzles to the children, who then try to come up with solutions. They learn through discovery and group processes.

A common model for school library instruction is to teach the research process directly and then let students use this inquiry-based approach. The research process is cyclical and encompasses choosing a topic; developing questions about the topic; finding sources; page finding; using the read-think-write method, and creating a final product. The final product is no more important than the process and therefore does not need to be viewed as a formal activity. Final products could be "Jeopardy"-type games, collages, crossword puzzles, a speech, or a written report.

Materials

The school library media specialist should include in the collection materials appropriate for all different students, including those who are LD, MR, and ED. Special needs students should be guided to materials and books suitable to their skills and interests. The school library media specialist should select materials for acquisition that adapt to needs of physically disabled students, such as large-print, taped books, and lightweight paperbacks placed on reachable shelves. Children who are mentally retarded need access to materials that are simple and sequential. The child who is ED may need access to materials that are emotionally nonthreatening and conclude with a sense of satisfaction. By careful selection of materials, the school library media specialist can strengthen the benefits of including special students in the school library media center activities.

Another aspect of the school library media specialist's role with respect to materials is the modification of materials used to teach library skills. Often the materials are those natural to the setting, such as the card catalog and the dictionary. When they are to be used for instruction, they may be modified by adding visual cues. For example, the card catalog drawer that the student needs may be marked with a larger label, or the drawer with the subject cards for cats may have a picture of a cat taped to it. Sometimes additional devices may be helpful, such as when the task is to locate a call number on a card. For this task, the school library media specialist may provide a blank card with a square cut out in the appropriate spot so that when the blank card is placed in front of the card in the card catalog, the call number appears through the square. This kind of prompt helps focus the student's attention.

Worksheets used for teaching a specific skill to the regular education students may need to be modified for special needs students. The task for special needs students may be shortened, or some of the answers may be provided, or the students may work cooperatively to complete the assignment. The modifications should be designed to help students complete the task, feel successful, and learn the skill. The teacher and librarian will jointly decide on the best alteration of the task for the specific student.

Motivation

Grades and teacher praise may work as motivation for most students but not for some special needs students. The key to motivating students is to be creative, ask them for input about their instruction so that the desire is inherent, and when teaching necessary skills provide a rationale for why learning the specific skill is important. When naturally existing motivators are ineffective, the librarian may need to use more highly structured behavioral programs—reinforcers such as words (praise), activities, or privileges, and items students will work to earn. The official definition of a reinforcer is an event following a behavior (the library task) that maintains or strengthens the likelihood that the behavior will be performed again. A whole range of potential reinforcers is available to a school library media specialist and should be used consistently and contingently to help teach special needs students. Simple praise and warm gestures of support are often effective. The school library media specialist may try utilizing library jobs for activity reinforcers: putting up chairs, stamping due dates, picking up books, putting on book slips and jackets, straightening up and putting away audiovisual equipment and materials. Often when weeding out the book collection, the school library media specialist has books that have been removed from the shelves. These books, as well as discarded magazines and paperbacks, may be used for concrete reinforcers or rewards. Motivational charts that record the number of words found in the dictionary or a number of "good behavior" library visits can be developed. The librarian should use artificial extrinsic reinforcers only as necessary, allowing natural, intrinsic reinforcers to work as often as possible. When artificial reinforcers are necessary, the ultimate goal is to fade those away and replace them with naturally occurring or intrinsic motivators.

Monitoring Progress of Library Skill Acquisition

After the skills to be taught and the instructional strategy have been identified, teaching can begin. The student's progress in mastering the targeted skill needs to be monitored. One means is to keep a chart of the objectives and the level of learning: exposure, mastering, maintenance, and application. The dates of assessment may be filled in on a progress monitoring chart (see Chapter 2). Periodically—once a month or more often—the student should be assessed for mastery of the objectives. With careful monitoring, the student will not be made to continue working on tasks he or she has already mastered and therefore make quicker progress. Progress checks require that the school library media specialist readminister the assessment tasks and record the prompts necessary for completion of the task or the percentage accuracy.

AN EXAMPLE OF A LESSON: TEACHING THE DEWEY DECIMAL SYSTEM

This section contains a transcript of a lesson designed to motivate and involve all children. Following the lesson are some ways this lesson may be modified or adapted to meet the needs of special learners. As an introduction to the arrangement of nonfiction books in the library and the Dewey decimal system, a librarian may tell this story to the class.

Lesson Setup

Spread a big pile of nonfiction books from each of the ten classes of the Dewey decimal system over a table in a messy pile. The first part of the lesson is conducted as a role play—a one-act show—with the librarian playing both Melville and his mother. Two hats, such as a newsboy and sunhat, may be used as prompts to clarify the voice being used.

THE MELVILLE DEWEY STORY

Once upon a time about a hundred years ago or so, there was a little boy named Melville Dewey. He was a pretty normal little boy who liked most things that little boys liked to do: fishing, playing baseball, and hanging out with his friends. But most of all Melville liked to read. A day wouldn't go by when his mother couldn't find him with his nose in a book. He loved books more than anything in the world and had quite a collection of his own.

Melville had one problem, though. Melville was a big slob. He had one of the messiest rooms on the block. It drove his mother crazy that his room was always such a mess. One day his mother went into his room.

"Melville!!! Get in this room right this very minute!! Melville, I want this mess cleaned up this instant. I can't believe it looks like this. There will be no supper tonight until this room is cleaned up. Is that understood?"

"But, MOOOM!!"

"I don't care! This room is to be cleaned up right now."

"But, MOOOOM!!!

"I will be back in a little while."

Melville was stuck. He wasn't sure where to begin cleaning up his messy room. Then he decided to clean it up the way all kids clean their rooms. He pushed all the toys to one side of the room, opened the closet door, and stuffed them in as fast as he could before they all fell out again. He attempted to make his bed, but it looked pretty lumpy when he was finished. Then he lifted the bedspread on his bed, shoved all his clothes that had been on the floor under the bed, and put the spread back down. He figured out of sight, out of mind.

"Mom, I'm ready. It's all clean."

As his mother entered the room, she was taken by surprise when she saw how clean the room was. She couldn't believe her eyes. She knew it was too good to be true.

"Well, Melville, the clothes and toys are cleaned up. The bed looks a little lumpy, but I guess it will do."

And then she saw the books all over the desk.

"Melville, I'm sorry, but these books are not put away properly. I want you to put them neatly on your bookshelf or there will be no supper."

"But, MOOOM!!"

"Melville, take care of it now!"

"But, MOOOM!! I won't be able to find them when I need them."

"Melville, I want them neatly on the shelf, and that's final!"

You see, even though they were a mess, they were spread in such a way that he could see most of the titles. Unfortunately, it was just too messy for his mother. So Melville sat staring at his books, wondering how to solve his problem. What could he do to put his books in order so that he could find the books he needed when he wanted them?

Teacher-Led Discussion

At this point, change the story into a discussion and using the Socratic method of questioning, get the class to help figure out that the best way to put the books in order is by subject.

Direct Instruction Component

After the class has discovered the organizational subject scheme of Dewey's, discuss the name of his system and using a transparency of a list of Dewey classes go through the ten categories, briefly explaining them.

Using signs with the number of each of the Dewey classes for students to hold up, have the class help Melville clean up his mess by having students sort the books and place them in a pile by the appropriate sign. When this task is complete, go through the books and discover together if they fit the ten classes on the overhead. When this part of the lesson is complete, continue the story.

When Melville had the last book on the shelf in his new organized system, he called his mother.

"Mom!! I'm finished."

His mother entered his room and looked around.

"This is quite an improvement, Melville. I'm very much impressed with the way in which you have organized your books. Your father will very much like to see this when he comes home. Now run along. You will find your supper in the kitchen waiting for you."

After Melville had left the room, his mother slowly walked over toward the closet, turned the handle, and opened the door. As the toys came tumbling out onto the floor, you could hear her all the way through the neighborhood.

"MEELLVVILLEE!!!!!!!"

Adapting the Lesson for Students with Special Needs

If this lesson is being taught to a general education class that includes some students with special needs or to a special education class, some adaptations and modifications may be considered. First, the school librarian may want to consider pairing the special needs students with general education peers. Having a buddy system throughout this lesson serves several purposes. During the storytelling portion of the lesson, the buddy may encourage listening by proximity to the special needs student, laughing at the appropriate times and fostering listening by eye contact with the school librarian. When the students are categorizing books, the buddy may assist the special needs student and even provide verbal hints as necessary.

Overall, the school librarian should include the special needs student actively whenever possible. Making sure the student is sitting close to the librarian and that all the materials are clearly visible is helpful. Giving special eye contact and verbal comments and praise as often as possible is a good idea. Comments such as, "You're being a good listener," and questions such as, "How do you think Mrs. Dewey felt when she saw his room was clean?" will help keep the attention focused. For all children, using voice inflections and changes as well as large gestures will help them to stay glued to the story.

Other prompts may also be useful. For example, making sure that the books the special needs student will categorize clearly fit into a specific category and even include the key word in the book title may help the student succeed. Another good prompt is to ensure that the call number is written in large type so that no visual disability will hinder success. Generally the librarian should be watchful of any possible straying of attention and pull in any student whose attention begins to wander.

CONCLUSION

The suggestions presented here are meant to be illustrative and serve as catalysts for teacher–library media specialist teams to promote the teaching of library skills to special needs students. The ideas will need to be personalized for the individual student. Each student's performance should be the guidepost for evaluating the effectiveness of the techniques that are tried. If the student has not mastered a skill given one teaching technique, another instructional procedure should be used. Only through trial and error and closely monitoring student performance can the best ways for teaching special needs students be identified. When a special needs student masters use of the library, the door to a wonderful world of learning is revealed. This door can be readily opened with the help of the teacher and library media specialist.

REFERENCES

Allington, R. L., & Johnson, P. (1989). Coordination, collaboration and consistency: The redesign of compensatory and special education interventions. In R. E. Slavin, N. L. Karweit & N. A. Madden (Eds.), *Effective programs for students at risk* (pp. 320–354). Boston: Allyn & Bacon.

Clark, B. 1992. *Growing up gifted: Developing the potential of children at home and school*. New York: Macmillan.

Davis, G. A., & Rimm, S. B. (1985). *Education of the gifted and talented*. Englewood Cliffs, NJ: Prentice-Hall.

Heward, W., & Orlansky, M. (1992). *Exceptional children: An introductory survey of special education*. (4th ed). Columbus, OH: Merrill.

Karnine, D., Silbert, J., & Kameenui, E. J. (1990). *Direct instruction reading*. Columbus, OH: Merrill.

Meyen, E. (1990). *Exceptional children in today's schools*. (2nd ed). Denver: Love Publishing.

Pugach, M., & Wesson, C. (1990). Supporting the participation of exceptional students in today's classrooms. In E. Meyen (Ed.), *Exceptional children in today's schools* (pp. 75–106). Denver: Love Publishing.

———. (In press). Teachers' and students' views of team teaching of general education and learning-disabled students in two fifth grade classes. *Elementary School Journal*.

Renzulli, J. S. (1978). What makes giftedness? Reexamining a definition. *Phi Delta Kappan* 61: 180–184.

2 Assessing Library and Information Skills of Special Needs Students

Margaret J. Keefe and Caren L. Wesson

The assessment of skills is an ongoing process by which teachers determine if they have taught and if students have mastered various objectives. Each time teachers assess student skills, they are also examining and reevaluating their own teaching strategies to determine to what extent the strategies should be modified or enriched and thus ensure better results the next time.

Teachers use a variety of formats to assess students' skills, ranging from formal tests to basal mastery tests and curriculum-based assessment. A new trend is toward authentic assessment and portfolio assessment, methods that have resulted from concerted effort to make the connection between teaching and assessment more direct and useful with respect to instructional planning.

The teaching role of the library media specialist comes into play when the librarian evaluates and assesses student progress and mastery of skills. Specifically, the library media specialist needs to evaluate the acquisition of library skills or what this chapter will refer to as library and information skills. Traditionally, library skills referred to identifying information on a catalog card and classifying books with the Dewey decimal system. With the dawning of the information age, it has become imperative for students to acquire skills that enable them to access information not only by locating and retrieving it but also by analyzing, synthesizing, and evaluating it.

Library and information skills need to be assessed and evaluated continually, whether the teacher is assessing the regular education or the special needs student. Often the assessment criteria may need to be adapted for the special needs student to ensure success, but the general list of objectives should be the same.

METHODS OF ASSESSMENT

Teachers and educators have been assessing and evaluating students since the dawn of education with a variety of tools: standardized achievement tests, basal mastery tests, curriculum-based assessments, criterion-referenced tests, performance-based assessments, and portfolio assessments.

Standardized or *state academic achievement* tests are the means by which many schools determine yearly what students have achieved in all subject areas. These tests are also referred to as norm-referenced tests, meaning that students can be compared to others at the same age or grade level. Many of these tests have a section on reference skills, which may have been taught in the classroom as well as in the library media center. There are two dangers in using these tests as a means of assessing student skill level. One is that teachers often teach to the test, and the end result is students who can parrot memorized information but not necessarily apply or generalize these skills. The other problem is that these tests do not often align with the district curriculum and thus are not a true indicator of whether students have learned what they have been taught.

Basal mastery tests are tools prepared by a particular publisher to coordinate with that publisher's basal texts. Reading basals often intertwine reference skills throughout the text and then test them in the chapter or unit tests. These instruments, like the standardized and norm-referenced tests, are indicators of lower-level thinking. Again there is a danger of teaching to the test, with too much time spent on isolated skills, working in workbooks or on worksheets, and not enough time on teaching thinking skills and problem solving. Students learn the acquisition of facts by rote instead of concepts and ideas (Henrikson, 1992).

Criterion-referenced assessments measure the specific achievement of one student against a preset criterion. Many school districts have developed criterion-referenced tests that coordinate with their curriculum. Some of these tests come in the paper-and-pencil, multiple-choice format that is tabulated on a computer. That students can reiterate the correct answer by filling in a circle does not mean that they have learned the skill or skills and can apply them in the classroom or in real life.

Criterion-referenced assessment need not be a paper and-pencil task, however. This format can also be an informal test that a teacher devises to ascertain whether a student has mastered a skill. The teacher determines the criterion for the task, as well as to what extent the student should be able to accomplish it —in other words, the percentage of the time or how many times a student should be able to perform this skill. Teachers use a variety of indicators that can determine mastery, such as simple observation and a recording of that observation.

A new trend in student assessment is *performance-based assessment*, which requires students to demonstrate what they have learned through a variety of formats in a natural context (Henrikson, 1992). Evaluation is based on what the student can actually do, such as reading aloud a passage, writing a composition, designing an experiment, preparing an oral presentation, building a model or diagram, or locating a book on the library shelf. These measurements are much more authentic than the other tools and more likely to be true indicators of what students have learned.

Another way to document or record student performance is through the use of *portfolios*, "a systematic and organized collection of evidence used by the teacher and student to monitor growth of the student's knowledge, skills, and attitudes" (Vavrus, 1990, p. 48). The purpose of a portfolio is to document student progress over time. In this way, a teacher may get a more complete picture of the student's progress. A portfolio can be compared to a videotape as opposed to a snapshot, as it involves more action (Wesson & King, in press).

A significant important component of a portfolio is that students can help determine what goes into the portfolio and are also expected to write a self-evaluation pinpointing what has been learned and how the learning took place, as well as what should be learned next. Both student and teacher can see the progress made and better understand the student's strengths and weaknesses. Self-evaluation, a higher-level thinking skill that we want all students to achieve, is also included in portfolios. The student's reflective writing about what he or she learned and how it was learned is an important component of the portfolio.

The library media specialist is responsible for evaluating and assessing student progress with regard to library and information skills. He or she must determine which format for testing is best suited to determine student learning and application of these skills and fit the evaluation tool into an integrated curriculum when collaborating with classroom teachers.

USING THE LIBRARY AND INFORMATION SKILLS INVENTORY

Determining Skill Level

The first step in teaching and assessing a library and information skill is to understand what the student already knows and whether he or she can already use a particular skill in the library media center. This determination can be made by observation: the teacher asks the student to perform a task and then observes to what extent the student completes the intended task. Specific library and information skills assessment tasks are outlined in Figure 2.1, a skills inventory.

Figure 2.1
Informal Library and Information Skills Inventory

***SLMS = school library media specialist. **LMC = library media center.**

Skill	Grade Introduced	Assessment Task	Objective
I. Citizenship			
A. Behavior in the LMC	K	*SLMS: 1) Asks student to state how they should behave in the **LMC. 2) Observes the student's behavior during a 15-30 minute visit to the LMC. Student: 1) Talks quietly, walks, and respects others. 2) Does not cause any disruptions in the LMC.	1) Given a direction to state appropriate LMC behavior, the student will say that quiet voices, walking, and respecting others is appropriate all the time. 2) Given 30 minutes in the LMC, the student will behave appropriately with a maximum of 1-2 minor disruptions (loud talk or run).
B. Care and handing of books	K	SLMS: 1) Asks student to use a bookmark to mark the location when removing a book from the shelf, page through, and return it to its proper place. Student: 1) Uses a bookmark to mark the location, removes a book from the shelf, pages through and returns it to its proper place with the binding facing out without damaging the pages or binding.	1) Given a bookmark, the student will mark the location of a book when removing a book from the shelf, page though, and return it to its proper place with the binding facing out and without damage 100% of the time.
C. Borrowing books	K	SLMS: 1) Asks student to check out his or her book. Student: 1) Writes name on book slip (if applicable), takes book to checkout desk, and waits while book is checked out.	1) Given a student-selected book, the student will follow the proper procedure for checking out the book 100% of the time.

D. Returning books	K	**SLMS**: 1) Asks student to show you how to return a library book. 2) Asks student what to do if the book is overdue, damaged, or lost. **Student**: 1) Returns book to proper location and on time. 2) States that he/she would talk to the SLMS if the book is overdue, lost, or damaged. Student states that a fine will be paid in these circumstances (if applicable).	1) Given a library book, the student will return it to the proper place and on time 100% of the time. 2) Given a question about overdue, lost, or damaged books, the student will state the policy/penalties with 100% accuracy.
II. Location of LMC Sections A. Primary books B. Fiction books C. Nonfiction books D. Reference E. Card & Automated catalogs F. Magazines G. Computers/ Equipment H. AV materials/Games	 K 2 1 2 2 K K 2	**SLMS**: 1) Asks student to show where their age and ability appropriate books are located, as well as the reference shelf, magazines, card & automated catalogs, computers, equipment, AV materials and games. **Student**: 1) Goes to the correct section in the LMC given the direction.	1) Given directions to find their age- and ability-appropriate books and the reference shelf, magazines, card & automated catalogs, computers, equipment, AV materials and games, the student will go to the correct section of the LMC for each type of material 100% of the time.
III. Kinds of Books			
A. Fiction & Nonfiction	2	**SLMS**: 1) Gives the student 10 books and asks him/her to group them into 2 piles: fiction and nonfiction. 2) Asks student to define fiction and nonfiction. **Student**: 1) Places the books into piles of fiction and nonfiction. 2) States that "fiction" books are make-believe, not based on true life and "nonfiction" are factual books based on true information or happenings.	1) Given 10 books and directions to separate them into 2 piles of fiction and nonfiction, the student will do so with 100% accuracy. 2) Given the directions to define "fiction" and "nonfiction," the student will state (or write) the correct response with 100% accuracy.

Figure 2.1 (continued)

Skill	Grade Introduced	Assessment Task	Objective
B. Reference	2-3	SLMS: 1) Gives student 15 books and asks him/her to group in 3 piles: fiction, nonfiction, and reference. 2) Asks student to define the term "reference." Student: 1) Places books in the 3 piles: fiction, nonfiction, and reference. 2) Defines "reference."	1) Given 15 books and directions to separate them into piles of fiction, nonfiction, and reference, the student will do so with 100% accuracy. 2) Given directions to define "reference" books, the student will state (or write) the definition accurately 100% of the time.
C. Biography	2-3	SLMS: 1) Asks student to define "biography." Student: 1) Defines "biography" as a book which is based on fact about a person or persons.	1) Given the directions to define "biography," the student will state (or write) the definition with 100% accuracy.
IV. Arrangement of Books A. Fiction	1-2	SLMS: 1) Asks student how fiction books are arranged. 2) Asks student to locate a specific fiction book, given the author and title. Student: 1) States that fiction is organized in alphabetical order by the author's last name. 2) Locates a specific fiction book, given the author and title.	1) Given the question, "how are fiction books arranged?", the student will state (or write) the correct response with 100% accuracy. 2) Given 5 authors and titles, the student will point to the books in their proper location 100% of the time.
B. Nonfiction	2-3	SLMS: 1) Asks student how nonfiction books are arranged. 2) Asks student to place books in piles.	1) When asked how the nonfiction books are organized, the student states (or writes) by subject according to the Dewey Decimal System with 100% accuracy.

		according to the 10 classes of the Dewey Decimal System. 3) Gives the student a nonfiction call number and asks him/her to locate it on the shelf. **Student**: 1) States that nonfiction books are organized by subject according to the Dewey Decimal System. 2) Places books in piles according to the 10 classes of the Dewey Decimal System. 3) Points to a specific book on the nonfiction shelf, given its call number.	2) Given 20 books, the student will place the books in the correct pile according to the 10 classes of the Dewey Decimal System. 3) Given 10 Dewey Call Numbers, the student will point to the correct books on the nonfiction shelf with 80% accuracy.
C. Reference	2-3	**SLMS**: 1) Asks student to locate a reference book when given a nonfiction call number with an **R** above it. **Student**: 1) Locates a reference book in the reference section when given a reference call number.	1) Given a reference call number, the student will locate the book on the reference shelf with 100% accuracy.
D. Biography	2-3	**SLMS**: 1) Asks student where biographies are located. 2) Asks student how biographies are arranged. 3) Asks student to point to a specific biography on the shelf. **Student**: 1) Points to section of the LMC where biographies are located. 2) States that biographies are located in the 900 section using the number 921 and the first 3 letters of the last name of the person the book is about. (This will change from library to library.) 3) Points to a biography on the shelf, given the call number.	1) Given the directions to locate the biography section, the student will point to that section 100% of the time. 2) Given the directions to explain the biography arrangement, the student will state the correct response with 100% accuracy. 3) Given 2 biography call numbers, the student will point to the books on the shelf.
V. Equipment A. Cassette Recorders B. Record (if still used)	 1 2	**SLMS**: 1) Asks student to use the piece of equipment, watch for proper sequence of steps, and correct use of equipment.	Given equipment and materials (e.g., cassette recorder and cassette), the student will use the equipment correctly 100% of the time.

Figure 2.1 (continued)

Skill	Grade Introduced	Assessment Task	Objective
C. Filmstrip Viewers D. Filmstrip Projector E. Computer F. CD ROM G. VCR H. Video Camera	2 2 K 3 2 4	**Student**: 1) Pushes buttons, turns knobs, inserts materials in proper space, and in correct order.	
VI. Card and Automated Catalog A. Arrangement B. Catalog Cards	2-3	**SLMS**: 1) Asks student to locate an author, title, and subject card in the card catalog and record the information, e.g., call number, title, author, illustrator, publisher, and copyright date. 2) Asks student to locate a title, author, and subject in the automated catalog and record the information. **Student**: 1) Locates and points to the correct cards in the card catalog, given a title, author, and subject, and records the information. 2) Locates and displays on the computer the correct information, given a title, author, and subject, and records the information.	1) Given an author, title, and subject, the student will locate and point to the card in the catalog and record the information with 100% accuracy. 2) Given an author, title, and subject, the student will locate them in the automated catalog and record the information with 100% accuracy.
VII. Parts of a Book A. Title page 1. title 2. author 3. illustrator 4. publisher 5. place of publication 6. copyright date B. Table of Contents C. Index D. Glossary E. Bibliography F. Appendix	3 3-4 3-4 3-4 3-4 3-4	**SLMS**: 1) Asks student to show you the individual book parts, e.g., "Show me the table of contents." 2) Shows the student a book part and asks him/her to name it. 3) Asks the student to define each book part. **Student**: 1) Opens the book to the designated book part. 2) States the name of each book part, when displayed. 3) States the definition of each book part.	1) Given directions to locate a book part, the student will open the book to the stated part 100% of the time. 2) Given a book part, the student will correctly state the name of the part 100% of the time. 3) Student will state (or write) the definition of each book part with 100% accuracy.

<u>**VIII. Using Parts of Books**</u> A. Table of Contents B. Glossary C. Index	3-4	<u>**SLMS**</u>: 1) Asks student to use the table of contents to locate a specific chapter on a specific page. 2) Asks the student to open the book to the glossary and copy a specific definition. 3) Asks the student to look up 5 terms in the index and open the book to each page referred to by the index. <u>**Student**</u>: 1) Uses the table of contents by opening the book to a specific chapter and page. 2) Opens the book to the glossary and copies a specific definition. 3) Looks up 5 terms in the index and opens to each page referred to in the index.	1) Given a book, the student will look at the table of contents, find the name of a specific chapter, and then open to the page where that chapter begins with 100% accuracy. 2) Given a book, the student will open the book to the glossary and copy a specific definition with 100% accuracy. 3) Given a book, the student will pick out 5 terms in the index and open the book to each page where those terms are located with 100% accuracy.
<u>**IX. Reference Materials**</u> A. Dictionaries	2-3	<u>**SLMS**</u>: 1) Asks student to look up a specific word in a dictionary and write the definition, as well as the guide words on that page. 2) Asks student to define the term "dictionary." <u>**Student**</u>: 1) Looks up a specific word in the dictionary and writes the definition as well as the guide word on that page. 2) States (or writes) the definition of the term "dictionary."	1) Given a dictionary and 5 words, the student will open the book to the correct pages, copy the definitions and the guide words with 100% accuracy. 2) Given the directions to define the term "dictionary," the student will state (or write) the definition with 100% accuracy.
B. Encyclopedias	2-3	<u>**SLMS**</u>: 1) Asks student to state the definition of the term "encyclopedia" and how they are organized. 2) Ask student to look up a term in the encyclopedia by choosing the correct page, reading the excerpt, answering 5 questions about the excerpt and returning the volume to its proper place.	1) Given the directions to define the term "encyclopedia," the student will state (or write) the definition and how they are organized in alphabetical order with 100% accuracy. 2) Given a set of encyclopedias and a subject to research, the student will choose the correct volume, open to the correct page, read the excerpt, answer 5.

Figure 2.1 (continued)

Skill	Grade Introduced	Assessment Task	Objective
		3) Asks student to look up a specific subject in the index of the encyclopedia set, write down the page number and volume where it can be found, open to that volume, and answer 5 questions about that subject. **Student**: 1) States (or writes) the definition of the term "encyclopedia" and how they are organized in alphabetical order. 2) Does all the SLMS asks in question #2 above. 3) Does all the SLMS asks in question #3 above.	questions about the excerpt, and return the volume to its proper place with 80% accuracy. 3) Given a subject to research, the student will look up the subject encyclopedia index, write down the volume and page number where the information can be found, open to the correct volume, read the excerpt, answer 5 questions and return the volume to its proper place with 80% accuracy.
C. Atlas	4	**SLMS**: 1) Asks student to define the term "atlas." 2) Asks student to locate a map in an atlas, given a geographical location. **Student**: 1) States (or writes) the definition of the term "atlas." 2) Locates a map in an atlas of a given geographical location.	1) Given the directions to define atlas, the student will state (or write) the definition with 100% accuracy. 2) Given an atlas and a specific geographical location, the student will open the atlas to the correct page with 100% accuracy.
D. Almanac	4	**SLMS**: 1) Asks student to define the term "almanac." 2) Asks student to locate a statistical or factual answer in the almanac, given a specific question. **Student**: 1) States (or writes) the definition of "almanac." 2) Locates the factual answer in an almanac, given a specific question.	1) Given the directions to define the term "almanac," the student will state (or write) the definition with 100% accuracy. 2) Given an almanac and a specific factual question, the student will locate the answer with 100% accuracy.

E. Magazine Guide 1. Children's Magazine Guide 2. Reader's Guide (if applicable)	4-5	<u>**SLMS**</u>: 1) Asks student to identify the bibliographic information in a magazine guide entry. 2) Asks student to locate a magazine article using the guide. <u>**Student**</u>: 1) Identifies by stating or writing the bibliographic information in a magazine guide entry. 2) Locates a magazine article using the magazine guide, given a subject.	1) Given an example of a magazine guide entry, the student will identify by labeling the information with 100% accuracy. 2) Given a subject, the student will locate a magazine article on this topic using the magazine guide.
F. Biographical & Geographical Dictionaries	4-5	<u>**SLMS**</u>: 1) Asks student to locate an answer in a biographical and geographical dictionaries, given a specific question. <u>**Student**</u>: 1) Locates an answer to a specific question using the biographical and geographical dictionaries.	1) Given specific questions, the student will locate the answers using the biographical and geographical dictionaries.
G. CD ROM Encyclopedia & Online Telecommunications (if applicable)	4-5	<u>**SLMS**</u>: 1) Asks student to locate an article in a CD ROM encyclopedia and via online telecommunications, given a specific topic. <u>**Student**</u>: 1) Locates an article on a given topic in a CD ROM encyclopedia and via online telecommunications.	1) Given a specific topic, the student will locate the topic in the CD ROM encyclopedia and via online telecommunications.

Figure 2.1 (continued)

Skill	Grade Introduced	Assessment Task	Objective
H. Selecting Reference Materials	6-8	**SLMS**: 1) Asks student to state (or write) which reference material is best to use to find information, given a list of questions. **Student**: 1) States (or writes) which reference material is best to use to find information, given a list of questions.	1) Given a list of 20 questions, the student will state (or write) in which reference material the answers could best be located with 80% accuracy.
X. Research Process	3-4	**SLMS:** 1) Asks student to select a topic and write a list of questions pertaining to that topic. 2) Asks student to locate and read sources; writing notes from each source on notecards or on a notechart. 3) Asks student to organize these notes into outline form. 4) Asks student to write a rough draft. 5) Asks student to prepare a final product. **Student:** 1) Selects a topic and writes questions pertaining to the topic. 2) Locates and reads sources, and writes notes. 3) Organizes notes in outline form. 4) Writes a rough draft. 5) Prepares a final product.	1) Given directions to select a topic and write a list of 5 questions pertaining to that topic, the student will do so. 2) Given sources in the LMC and notecards or a notechart, the student will read the sources and write notes, including the answers to the 5 questions. 3) Given written notes, the student will organize them in outline form using at least 5 main headings with 2 levels. 4) Given the outline, the student will write a rough draft with an introduction, 3 supporting paragraphs, and a conclusion. 5) Given the rough draft and several options of presentation, such as oral, written, poster, etc., the student will prepare a final product.

The inventory can be used to assess students in the acquisition of skills in the library media center. It may be applied to regular education students as well as those with special needs; the recommended grade levels are merely suggestions for the average student. When assessing the special needs student, the library media specialist may need to adapt the grade level to suit these students.

Setting Student Objectives

Once the skill level of a special needs student has been determined, the next step is to establish objectives for library and information skills. These objectives should be incorporated into the individualized education plan (IEP) process and integrated with the curriculum areas.

That the inventory in Figure 2.1 is organized in a hierarchical fashion does not mean that it must be followed in sequential order, especially when the library media specialist is integrating these skills with classroom skills. Integrating library and information skills with classroom curriculum may prove to be the most authentic way to assess library and information skills, because the application of these skills will be evident and thus have more meaning for students. Library media specialists may find it best to teach and assess a particular library and information skill in the inventory when its application is immediate in a classroom project. For example, teaching Children's Magazine Guide (section IX.E in the figure) when students are asked to research endangered animals for a reading or science class project may prove to be timely and thus successful.

Monitoring Student Progress

The library media specialist needs to monitor student progress continually, especially for special needs students who may get lost in the mainstream. A checklist of the skills in the inventory such as the progress monitoring chart in Figure 2.2, may prove to be a resourceful and easy method to monitor progress. The checklist in the figure has a column for exposure, one for mastery, one for maintenance, and, most important, one for application or generalization of the skill. Dates when these skills are demonstrated may be filled in on the chart.

Generalizing of Library and Information Skills

The library media specialist must ensure that students have generalized particular library and information skills across time, setting, people, and place. In other words, that students should be able to apply the skill to a different time or setting when that skill is needed. For example, after learning the skill of fiction call numbers, will the student remember that the

Figure 2.2
Progress Monitoring Chart

Name______________________

Progress Monitoring Chart

	Skill	Exposure	Mastery	Maintenance	Application
Citizenship	IA. Behavior IB. Care of books IC. Borrow books ID. Return books				
Location	IIA. Locate primary IIB. Locate fiction IIC. Locate nonfiction IID. Locate reference IIE. Locate card catalogs IIF. Locate magazine IIG. Locate computers IIH. Locate AV				
Define Kinds of Books	IIIA. Fiction and nonfiction IIIB. Reference IIIC. Biography				
How books are arranged	IVA. Fiction IVB. Nonfiction IVC. Reference IVD. Biography				
Equipment	VA. Cassette player VB. Record VC. Filmstrip viewer VD. Filmstrip projector VE. Computer VF. CD ROM VG. VCR VH. Video camera				
Card and Automated Catalog	VIA. Arrangement of Catalogs VIB. Catalog cards				
Parts of a book	VIIA. Title page (1-6) VIIB. Table of contents VIIC. Index VIID. Glossary VIIE. Bibliography VIIF. Appendix				
Using parts of book	VIIIA. Table of contents VIIIB. Glossary VIIIC. Index				
Reference material	IXA. Dictionaries IXB. Encyclopedia IXC. Atlas IXD. Almanac IXE. Magazine guide IXF. Biographical & geographical dictionaries IXG. CD ROM encyclopedia & on-line IXH. Selecting reference materials				
Research	X. Research process				

first three letters of the author's last name is the call number of a fiction book? If they remember this, will they then apply it by finding books by Dr. Seuss on the SEU shelf of the fiction section?

PORTFOLIO ASSESSMENT

Teaching within the context in which a skill may be used in real life will show students why they need to learn this particular skill. For example, when studying a reference book, such as the atlas, the library media specialist might ask students to list times when they might use an atlas, such as vacation traveling, keeping up on world news, or taking a business trip. Another example is the skill of alphabetizing, needed in many aspects of real life from using the card catalog and the encyclopedia to reading a telephone book or television guide.

Portfolio assessment is a good means by which to assess application. A portfolio is an organized collection of materials that documents the progress of an individual student. The idea of portfolios is not new; they have been used in art, writing, modeling, architecture, and other fields for a long time. Educational portfolios may include a variety of materials, most typically papers written by the student but also audiotapes, videotapes, or pictures of completed three-dimensional projects. Both teacher and student have input concerning the content of the portfolio, and both should include a summary of what was learned, how the material was learned, and how each feels about the progress that was made, as well as goals for future learning. A school librarian may want to chat with the teachers or look through various literacy portfolios kept by the classroom teachers as a means of understanding the popularity of books and authors. Most literacy portfolios contain lists of books read, lists of authors and books to read in the future, summaries of some books read, a summary of strategies used when reading, and strategies that need to be learned. The lists of books read and books to read in the future may be helpful as the librarian plans to order books in the future. For the librarian's purposes, the most important type of portfolio is a research process portfolio.

Research process portfolios may be collected over a number of years, thus containing research products from first through sixth grades, the junior high years, or the high school years. Classroom teachers have primary responsibility for managing the research portfolio, but librarians should peruse them approximately two to three times a year because their contents may provide inspiration for experiments, potential topics for library research, completed research papers, and pictures of displays of research such as a poster from a science fair. Another important feature of a research process portfolio is documentation of each step in the research process. The student:

1. Writes out a list of potential topics.
2. Selects a topic and writes a list of preliminary questions about the topic.
3. Reads sources and compiles notes.
4. Completes a reference card for each source used.
5. Expands questions and finds three sources for each question.
6. Organizes notecards to develop an outline.
7. Writes a rough draft.
8. Edits the draft with the librarian or teacher.
9. Prepares the final product.

For a scientific research project in which the student collects data, a similar sequence of steps may be followed. The student:

1. Lists possible ideas for an experiment (either social or scientific).
2. Chooses the experiment and writes a hypothesis.
3. Designs means for comparing or describing the outcomes of the experiment and methods for conducting the experiment. This will become the methods and materials section of the report.
4. Conducts the experiment and collects the data.
5. Analyzes data and makes conclusion (results section).
6. Considers the outcome of the study and its importance and relevance as well as weakness in the study itself.
7. Summarizes all of these features in a final product, such as a report or poster.

Elements related to these steps may be included in the research process portfolio. The portfolio should also include the student's own description of what was learned through the research process, a reflection that provides insight into what aspects of the process the student did well and what aspects could use improvement. For example, the student may think that his or her system for collecting and organizing data was inefficient and seek to improve that aspect of the project.

A CASE STUDY

Charlie's family is new to the district. His mother reports that he was in an LD resource room in the old district and in the fifth grade, but his teacher told her he was reading on the third-grade level. The teacher has filed a referral for special education testing to begin, but in the meantime the school librarian wants to begin working with Charlie in the library. She decides to use an informal library and information skills inventory to find out what skills he knows and does not know.

The librarian takes him around the library and tells him where the different materials are located; then she asks him to give her a similar tour so she can determine if he remembers the different locations. Once he completes her tour successfully, she begins to probe about other skills. She asks him to explain the differences among reference books, fiction, nonfiction, and biographies. Charlie does know that fiction and nonfiction are based on truths or nontruths, but he has no idea what a reference book or biography is. She then asks him if he knows how to check out and return books and how he should behave when he is in the library. He answers all of those questions satisfactorily.

As their conversation proceeds, she finds that he is a charming boy with a great sense of humor. She thinks his biggest problem is that he is not a very good reader, but his visual and perception skills seem fine since he was able to give her a nice tour of the library after one exposure to the setting. She excuses him from the library and directs him to return to class. She then records on the progress monitoring form that he has been exposed to and has mastered sections I and II. She circles section III to indicate that these objectives are next to be taught. She will not start a portfolio until section III is mastered because use of these materials is necessary for the research process to be taught. She is looking forward to working with this delightful boy.

CONCLUSION

Assessment is a necessary component of the instructional process. A librarian who is not sure what skills a child has learned is not able to teach effectively. Certainly no child needs to spend time relearning material he or she has already mastered; there is too much to learn and too little time. Assessment may also be viewed as a reinforcer for the librarian because it illuminates the results of all the efforts made as the library and information skills curriculum is taught. Integrating the portfolio model and the informal skills inventory in order to monitor all the progress a student is making in the library is the most effective way to assess. Through collaboration with the classroom teacher, this goal can be fully met.

REFERENCES

Henrikson, D. (1992). Student assessment. *Teacher Today* 7(4): 1–4.

Loertscher, D. (1988). *Taxonomies of the school library media program*. Englewood, CO: Libraries Unlimited.

Vavrus, L. (1990). Put portfolios to the test. *Instructor* 100(1): 48–53.

Walker, H., & Montgomery, P. (1983). *Teaching library media skills*. Littleton CO: Libraries Unlimited.

Wesson, C., & King, R. (in press). Portfolio assessment for the exceptional education classroom. *Teaching Exceptional Children*.

Fostering an Appreciation of Literature in Special Needs Students

3

Margaret J. Keefe and Caren L. Wesson

One of the main goals of the school library media specialist is to help all students develop a love of books and a sense of joy about reading. Worlds of information and wonder are opened to students who buy into the notion that reading is enjoyable and useful. Every child deserves exposure to a wide variety of literature, as it is a vehicle through which they learn language and an awareness of culture—their own as well as that of others. In today's global society, exposure to and an understanding and appreciation of other cultures are imperative. All teachers routinely foster literature appreciation; however, the school library media specialist's role in the development of well-rounded, well-read students is unique. The techniques set out in this chapter for school library media specialists to use when fostering literature appreciation in children with special needs can be modified for special populations as well.

READING ALOUD

No one is ever too old to be read to. Many teachers read aloud to their classes, fostering a joy of books through the listening and mental pictures the students develop.

Children need to hear language before they can say it, read it, and then write it. Thus, the more children are read to in school and at home, the stronger will their use of language be. Children of all ages want and need to be read to. Being read to helps develop a visual imagination that is sometimes lost in today's world of video and computers. Jim Trelease (1989) gives an example of a young boy in *The New Read-Aloud Handbook*. While being read to from a pictureless novel, this young boy asked to see the illustrations. He did not know how to create the pictures in his own mind because he was so accustomed to television's creating them for him. He was, says Trelease, "going blind in his mind's eye." Developing their imagination, expanding their world, and strengthening their language and culture is the goal of reading aloud to children.

At an early age, children need to hear short readings, analogous to commercials, so that by the time they reach school, they have a strong language base and a richness of experiences on which to draw. They then can tolerate and even enjoy listening to longer passages and begin to learn to read on their own. Learning to read may be painstakingly slow for some children, unless they have had the experience of being read to from which to generalize learning to read.

Schools of thought about how children learn to read have proliferated. In reality, each learns to read in his or her own way. The two current primary schools of thought can be summarized as bottom-up or top-down reading. Bottom-up means beginning with isolated fragments, letters, and sounds and putting those together in chains of sounds that link together into words. Often special needs students who have difficulty learning to read are given workbooks, skill sheets, and flashcards to improve their reading skills. Sometimes they begin to think that reading is merely a series of skill-oriented tasks, and they miss out on the beauty and richness of literature.

The top-down approach, which is related to the whole language movement, proposes keeping the meaning whole. Beginning readers do not look at letters initially. Instead they read whole, meaningful, yet brief passages, such as a two-line silly poem. The teacher reads the poem to the students; they read it aloud together several times. They often use large class-sized copies and individual copies for read-aloud practice. After some time, they may begin to look at words that repeat. Trelease (1989) compares reading to baseball spring training. It is important and has a purpose, and yet a true love of baseball is learned only on a trip to a professional ballpark with hotdogs, peanuts, and all the magic that a game provides. Ultimately the goal is to develop students who read with ease across a wide variety of topics and genres of literature.

In order to get to this point, students need more than one adult reading to them. Not only is having another individual read important for the generalization of the idea that there are lots of good books but also for establishing the idea that there are many adults who read to us. Ideally parents read aloud daily. Another guaranteed source of reading aloud is the school library media specialist, who is connecting children to libraries as a place to obtain the wonderful books to which they have been exposed. Reading aloud is also a form of showing caring; it is a means by which attention can be given. Children know that adults who read to them are interested in them and care about them, because they are sharing not only the story but also a bit of themselves. The school library media specialist has a special role; he or she has more resources available and is more knowledgeable about the selection of books to read. Also important here is that the manner in which the reading is done may be unique. The library media specialist may be more dramatic or creative than teachers or parents because this task of reading aloud is one in which he or she specializes. Reading aloud to children will widen their horizons and help to ensure that they do not get stuck on one style of book or one author.

Techniques of Reading Aloud

Most library media specialists know the basics about making reading aloud an enjoyable experience for most children, including those with special needs. An important component to the art of reading aloud is the use of dramatics: voice changes and inflection, body language, and the use of pauses that build suspense. The use of dramatics is sure to capture the undivided attention of the audience, especially students who may be easily distracted. The librarian should be cognizant of giving special needs students extra eye contact. Other gimmicks such as changing voice volume and speed are also effective with special needs students. The use of voice inflection, dramatics, music, and sound effects on tape is especially critical for visually impaired students (Marshall, 1981).

Visual cues may promote or enhance a book, especially for hearing-impaired students. These cues might include pictures, posters, flannelboard cutouts, puppets, props, or objects to be touched (Marshall, 1981). Hats, capes, jackets, or aprons that hold props such as flowers, puppets, or models can make the reading aloud attractive and interesting. Asking students to guess the title by displaying an object beforehand is a way to invite students to a read-aloud session. Using a flashlight for scary books, balloons for happy books, and a handkerchief for a tale of woe are some ideas for providing visual cues (Carletti, Girard & Willing, 1991). If puppets or props are used, making sure these items come into close proximity with the special needs students helps maintain their attention.

Giving special needs students an explanation of the story beforehand will help them better understand what is happening. When reading aloud from a book, showing the pictures before reading a page and keeping the book in close proximity to the children are also beneficial. These techniques will promote student participation and interaction. With special needs students, it is important to allow for interruptions and questions so that they can have the opportunity to interact and thus develop and practice use of language. In the discussion of the story, during or after, special needs students may need more time to think through their responses to questions (Marshall, 1981).

Selecting Books to Read Aloud

Selecting books that lend themselves to theatrics is an important decision for the school library media specialist. A wealth of great children's books is available, so there is no reason for anyone to read any book that bores children. Sometimes it is difficult to know whether the children will find a new book interesting. Testing the new material on classes that do not include special needs children allows an evaluation to be made. The best advice is to use only high-interest books with special needs children.

Primary grades

Books that use a great deal of figurative language, such as onomatopoeia, yield high interest. Words in the story that represent sounds become real when read aloud with dramatics and enthusiasm. Some good examples of these type of stories are those by Jim Aylesworth, such as *Country Crossing* and *Hanna's Hog*, and Peter Spier's *Gobble, Growl, Grunt*, both excellent for younger children in preschool or the early primary grades.

Another consideration might be books that use a great deal of repetitive language and present highly predictable stories. Repetition and predictability build language and thus facilitate beginning reading skills. *The Very Hungry Caterpillar* by Eric Carle is a good example of a book that uses these two concepts. The reading aloud of this story can be enhanced with the use of a sock puppet, made with a green sock with two small eyes sewn on and accompanied by food made of felt with slashes cut in the middle. The story can be dramatized by placing the felt food pieces over the puppet and onto the reader's arm, as if the caterpillar were eating the food. Younger children love to hear this story again and again as they watch the puppet, and eventually they are able to relate the story themselves. Another favorite repetitive book is *I Know an Old Lady Who Swallowed a Fly* by Rose Bonne. This book has also been put to music so the students may first read and then sing. (See the end of this chapter for lists of books to read aloud to this age group.)

Picture books should be used with all ages of special needs students, as well as general education students, as they are easily understood and enjoyable. They have a simple story structure and concise language that open themselves up to group discussion (Carletti, 1991). Stories with few puns, metaphors, and abstract ideas are the wisest choice. Humorous situations, such as the Frog and Toad stories by Arnold Lobel, are more likely to be understood and appreciated by special needs students than puns. Books with a singular concept and an identifiable beginning, middle, and end are also suggested (Marshall, 1981). *The Story of Jumping Mouse* by John Steptoe, a picture book of a Native American folktale, features an easily identified sequence of events as it explains the birth and existence of many creatures and teaches a moral at the same time. Like so many other classic picture books, it is suitable for all ages.

Intermediate Grades

When reading aloud to third through sixth graders, dialogue is an important component, since dialogue enables the person reading aloud to build dramatics. *Bunnicula* by James Howe consistently uses dialogue that may be read dramatically, especially the dialogue between Harold, the dog, and Chester, the cat. Also beneficial are stories in the realistic genre, because students can relate to the language of the story. Judy Blume's *Tales of a Fourth Grade Nothing* and *Superfudge* are excellent examples of stories that speak to students in language they hear in their daily lives and thus can easily relate to. This aspect is especially important for special needs students, who may need familiar language to catch their interest. For students with learning disabilities who struggle in school, *Do Bananas Chew Gum?* by Jamie Gilson is a good novel to listen to as they can easily relate to the character. This book is also good for general education students because it imparts to them a sense of what it feels like to have a learning disability. (See the reading list at the end of this chapter for more ideas on books to read aloud to intermediate students.)

All children, even young ones, love to be read to from a novel. As the chapters unfold, the listeners feel as if they are becoming part of that story. Because special needs students often lack the ability or attention span to make it through a novel on their own, having novels read aloud to them is a way to entice them into attempting to read one on their own. One novel that consistently captures the interest of younger and older children but has simple vocabulary is *The Boxcar Children* by Gertrude Warner. This book was written in the early 1950s and continues in a series that is still being written today. A terrific high-interest story to read aloud is *Hatchet* by Gary Paulsen, the story of a young boy who suddenly finds himself in the wilds of Canada with only a hatchet to survive. Once this book is begun, students beg to listen until the end. *Julie of the Wolves* and *My Side of the Mountain*, both by Jean Craighead George, are also survival stories that spark the interest of all children.

Nonfiction

Reading aloud nonfiction to special needs students can entice them into checking out this type of book on their own. Some nonfiction books may be too difficult for special needs students to read themselves and yet the concepts may be easily understandable. Having students bring in objects or models to touch and handle that are related to the topic that is being read to them connects the information for them—for example, a butterfly net when reading a book about butterflies, an anthill box when reading about insects, or a model of the space shuttle when reading about space exploration. The Magic School Bus series by Joanna Cole is a delightful set of books that give a great deal of information in a fun, exciting, and attractive way for children. Isaac Asimov's Library of the Universe series is another fine example of good nonfiction books to share with students. In the social studies area, Jean Fritz's biographies are told in a story format that is appealing to children and yet are very realistic in their approach to history. The New True Books are easily readable books, which students may check out and read on their own. Sharing nonfiction books in the library media center is another way to extend the curriculum from the classroom into the library.

Seasonal activities

Holidays lend themselves to special reading activities. For example, during the week before Halloween, the librarian or a guest may dress up as a "Reading Witch" and read for each class in costume using a variety of materials, including poetry and scary stories. *Scary Stories to Tell in the Dark* and its two sequels by Alvin Schwartz and *When the Lights Go Out: 20 Scary Stories to Tell* by Margaret Read MacDonald are favorites of all ages of school-children. These books rarely make it back to the shelf before they are checked out again. *Ghost Poems* and *Witch Poems*, selected and illustrated by Trina Schart Hyman, are also widely loved. Plastic spider rings cost about a penny per student and help make a lasting impression of these stories and poems. For kindergartners and first graders, *Cranberry Halloween* by Wende and Harry Devlin is a good read-aloud book. Sharing and eating grand-mother's cranberry bread after the story and distributing the recipe is a way for students to carry the story home with them.

Thanksgiving is a time for the pilgrim or Native American to appear to read to the children. Here too a wide variety of material is available, including *Molly's Pilgrim* by Barbara Cohen, *Brother Eagle, Sister Sky* by Susan Jeffers, and *The Legend of Scarface: A Blackfeet Indian Tale* by Joe Page Edwards.

Other holidays too provide good opportunities for a unique reading event. An elf, a bunny, and a cupid all entertain and further the joy of reading for the students.

For children who are older, these events may be flipped: the children become the special characters who visit the school to read to the younger students. Thus, these activities can be useful across age groups. Small squads of students from the higher grades can prepare brief dramatic readings to present to the younger students, benefiting both age groups.

Special Read-Aloud Programs

A special reading-aloud portion of the library program brings in other readers to add variety and interest. For example, a Wisconsin librarian has a rocking chair in the library that she sits in to read aloud. Every year she has a special "Rock 'n' Reading Week" during which she brings in local celebrities to read aloud to the children. Her list of guests varies each year, and widely too: local sports talent, television personalities, school board members and school district officials, college professors, firefighters and police officers, and husbands and wives of the school staff members, as well as staff members who normally do not read to the children, such as the cooks, the janitors, and the security officer. This week is special to the children, who usually write thank-you notes and complete follow-up activities on the book. Many of the guests come with a book they have found in the bookstore and donate the book to the library.

Trelease (1989) recounts the story of Boston's inner-city Lewenberg Middle School, which had a poor academic reputation until Thomas P. O'Neill became principal. He developed a program whereby each teacher was assigned a homeroom to read aloud to each day, so that every sixth, seventh, and eighth grader heard an adult read every day. Another project involved Stephen Lewenberg, legal counsel for Honeywell Corporation and the grandson of Solomon Lewenberg, for whom the school was named. Lewenberg was invited for several ceremonial assemblies and took such an interest in the school and the reading program that he agreed to come every Friday morning on his way to work and read to a sixth-grade class. Lewenberg students have the highest reading scores in Boston, and a waiting list to get into this school continues to grow.

STORYTELLING

Storytelling is another wonderful and exciting way to expose children to literature. As stories are told from memory, the ideas, images, values, and emotions are translated and preserved.

Storytelling is the oldest form by which civilizations have passed on their history and culture (Cassady, 1990). Anyone who wants to share an experience, who likes being with people, and who has a bit of the entertainer in them can tell a story. Storytelling as entertainment is much more intimate than a theatrical performance because interaction with the audience is an integral part of the event. Every time a story is told, it changes, grows, and adapts to the audience (MacDonald, 1986).

Storytellers should choose stories that they personally enjoy and then consider other aspects of it: Will it mean something to the audience? Does it have language appropriate for the intended audience? Does it have good description, dialogue, repetition, and rhythm? Is it tellable? In other words, are the plot and action of the story simple and the characters interesting (Cassady, 1990)? The best tales to tell are those with simple language and not filled with flowery and heavily descriptive writing (MacDonald, 1986).

The simpler the language and the more repetitive it is, the easier it will be to memorize and the more interesting it will be for the audience.

Choosing familiar stories, such as *The Three Little Pigs* or *Jack and the Beanstalk,* is a good way to begin storytelling. As children delight in the medium of storytelling, the school library media specialist might expand to stories similar to known ones that can be compared and contrasted, and then on to new tales that will enlighten and charm. *The Gunny Wolf,* a tale similar to *Little Red Riding Hood,* and *Jack and the Robber* are wonderful telling tales that use familiar characters and sounds with a great deal of action and repetition. They are found in Margaret Read MacDonald's *Twenty Tellable Tales,* an excellent source for stories and techniques for telling them.

Many of the ideas already noted for reading aloud—pacing, pitch, speed, and volume of voice—pertain as well to telling a story. For visually-impaired students, this medium is especially important to build language. The pleasant sound of the voice heard and the mental picture the story creates are important for this special needs group. Mentally disabled students require literal stories with a simple story line and vocabulary, and humor needs to be obvious. The simple structure of folktales, with an identifiable beginning, middle, and end is perfect for this group. Emotionally disturbed children with short attention spans need to be told the story slowly, and it is wise to involve them as much as possible in the story.

For students with hearing impairment, the visual presentation is crucial. Props or posters are helpful with this group. A few other suggestions are to make tremendous use of facial expressions and body movement, speak slowly in a moderate tone, and keep sunlight to the storyteller's back, so that there are no shadows on the face. To facilitate the lip readers, women can use lipstick, and men can refrain from wearing a mustache. Flannel-board figures or shapes on the overhead projector to demonstrate the story visually are especially beneficial for students with hearing impairment and other students as well. Choosing stories with a great deal of action is a sure-fire way to capture their interest. That the storyteller can always adapt a story to suit the age or ability of the audience is the beauty of storytelling with special needs students (Baker & Green, 1977).

Children should be invited to participate and perform in this medium. Encouraging them to become storytellers themselves will help develop many valuable skills, such as improving the use of oral language, improving listening skills, stimulating creative imagination, enhancing public speaking abilities, improving sequential memory, and improving visualization skills (Kinghorn & Pelton, 1991). Learning to be a storyteller is a process. Kinghorn and Pelton's *Every Child a Storyteller* presents a variety of ideas to encourage and develop this art form in children. Learning the art of storytelling is a wonderful way for special needs children, often slow or reticent to express themselves, to learn how to share their oral language and creativity.

BOOKTALKS

A booktalk is, as the name suggests, a brief talk about a book. The purpose is to entice others into reading it. One format is sharing a single title immediately after it has been read; others are discussing a single author's various books or sharing multiple books that cover the same theme, especially beneficial when a classroom teacher is teaching an integrated thematic unit, as it is an ideal time for collaboration between the school library media specialist and the classroom teacher.

The booktalk theme need not necessarily be the central theme of the books discussed. The two merely need to be related somehow. For example, if the theme is elephants and the children are first, second, and third graders, *The Story of Babar* by Jean de Brunhoff and *Horton Hatches the Egg* by Dr. Seuss might be incorporated into a booktalk theme with several nonfiction books, such as *Jane Goodall's Animal World: Elephants* by Miriam Schlein and *Elephants* by Michael Bright. If the booktalk theme revolves around the topic of space, a big subject covering a variety of concepts, the books chosen need only be related loosely by the larger idea. With third, fourth, and fifth graders, the school library media specialist might share such fiction books as *Stinker from Space* by Pamela F. Service and *The Fallen Spaceman* by Lee Harding, along with several nonfiction books such as *Seeing Earth from Space* or *Journey to the Planets*, both by Patricia Lauber, or *Rand McNally Children's Atlas of the Universe*. Booktalks are not unlike commercials; the purpose is to give the children a little taste of a book and hope that they will run out and read it.

A booktalk technique is to use a personal approach by relating the story to a personal experience or a current event. Students might also be encouraged to share their own similar personal experiences. Using quotations from the book is another technique, being sure to use the book itself so that students will see the book cover and remember it. A third technique to entice children is to read the first sentence of the book. One school library media specialist uses this method when booktalking on Beverly Cleary and asks the students if they can guess from which Cleary book she is reading. When the book being shared has seen heavy use and thus is not in good physical shape or is not on the shelf, it might be wise to use large, colorful, attractive remakes of the original cover as a visual aid. Booktalks to special needs students can feature tangible objects or puppets to arouse interest. When doing a booktalk to a large group, it is best to share a variety of books, so that there is something for everybody (Bauer, 1983).

No more than five minutes should be spent on any one title. Just enough information to pique student interest should be given, so the children will want to get a copy of the book. Overall, a booktalk session should last no longer than a half-hour, with no more than ten titles discussed.

ALTERNATIVE BOOK REPORTS

Teachers often require book reports as a way of holding children accountable for their reading activity and to entice fellow students to choose books read by peers. The time-honored book report, however, is highly structured and often lacking in imagination. Newer versions make the idea of reading and sharing the book with others more exciting.

One structure for student sharing of information about books is a literature circle of three to four students who get together once or twice weekly to update each other about what each has been reading. The members form a circle (for face-to-face interaction), with each one taking about five to six minutes to tell the others about what is happening in the book he or she is reading. (Someone who has recently completed a book may need more time to share.) After sharing by each member, the other circle members ask questions about the book. Where does it take place? Who else is a character in the book? How much time has passed since the first event in the book and where you are now? Part of the goal of the literature circle is to give the students multiple opportunities to hear about a number of books and thereby develop a list of books and authors they may want to read. Another point is that it is not important to document every book read with a report.

When special needs children are involved in literature circles, teachers need to establish a comfort level so that all the students understand that not every book each student discusses has to be on grade level. All students should feel free to read from a variety of levels, from independent easy-readers to difficult books. Each child should be pushed to keep his or her reading range wide.

Another structure for sharing books read is a book club. All children in the club read the same book and discuss it when the club meets. They start by covering the basics—setting, characters, chronology of events, and plot—and then move on. What part moved them? Which character is their favorite, and for what reasons? If they had been a specific character in the book, would they have acted in the same way? Following their discussion, they may expand their activities, for example, by putting together a skit, a rap, or a dramatic reading to share their book with classmates.

For children with special needs, the book club may be a structure in which the other students read aloud to the student who needs that type of assistance. As the first group reads a specific book, one of their goals may be to take turns reading aloud, and as they read aloud they could tape-record so that eventually many of their favorite books would be available on tape for other groups.

Biographies can be translated into interesting book reports as well. Imagine each child with a posterboard with a place for their face cut out of the center. The area around the face hole can be used to transform the student into the character from the book. Draw on a hat, a necktie, or a blouse. Add some pertinent facts, such as date of birth, date of death, major accomplishments, and significant events. Older students can dress in costume as the person about whom they have read. One group of students that read biographies did some unusual activities to demonstrate what they had learned about the famous people about whom they had read. A boy who read a book on Georgia O'Keeffe executed a painting in the style of the artist; a child who read about Mozart learned a piece on the piano by the composer.

Students at one school who were asked to put together a list of possible alternative formats for book reports came up with writing and performing skits and plays; doing a commercial in any form—television (video), radio (audio), or billboard (poster); writing newspaper and magazine articles or advertisements using Children's Writing and Publishing Center (a computer software word processing program by Learning); preparing a timeline of events using the Timeliner computer program (Tom Snyder Products); visualizing the story in a diorama; writing the next chapter to the book; creating a mobile with story elements or characters; illustrating a sequential cartoon sketch; writing a poem about a scene or character in the book; or rewriting the story from the point of view of a different character (such as Jon Scieszka does in *The True Story of the Three Little Pigs*). When students can share a book in a medium that they enjoy or at which they excel, the products prove rewarding for those producing and those with whom they share their stories, whether the students be special needs, general education, or gifted.

A schoolwide activity that may be implemented through the school library media center is a schoolwide database of the most popular books read by students in the school. The students themselves can input the information into the computer by filling out a form on their favorite books. The information is then accessible when they come to look for a book to read. A buddy system can assist special needs students in putting the information into the computer on their favorite stories. Children's Book Week in November might be a good time to kick off this program.

Children's Book Week in November and National Library Week in April are ideal times to implement schoolwide reading programs that special needs students can be part of and share with their schoolmates. One school had a Where's Waldo? contest where everyone was the winner. Students were asked to read at least one picture book or one chapter a day during the week. Then they were to fill out a form on a construction paper "shoeprint" with the title, author, and a brief description of the story or chapter. The "shoeprints" were then displayed around the school "searching for Waldo," beginning at the library media center and concluding behind the principal's door, where a giant poster of Waldo was mounted. There are a multitude of ideas for displaying how many books students have read around the school: worms, kites, flower gardens, trains, and fish are but a few. The important part is to include the special needs students with the general education students in a program that belongs to all of them and generates excitement in literature.

PUPPETRY AND CREATIVE DRAMATICS

Incorporating puppetry and creative dramatics into the library media program or the classroom promotes participation by students and develops their appreciation for literature. Children learn through play and thus learn literature by "playing it" themselves. Librarians are well versed in published plays, skits, and puppet shows and can offer a wealth of resources to students and teachers.

Library media specialists who seek to use puppetry or creative dramatics with students need to exhibit confidence to students, who will then be likely to respond and thus participate themselves. The location should be comfortable to the librarian, and the stories and props should be familiar. With dramatics, the librarian must start out with a great deal of structure in a smaller space; as children become more involved, they can move beyond the boundaries. Keeping control is also imperative, especially with special needs students, who often lack self-control. Developing a signal such as clapping hands or a drumbeat that asks students, when they get overexcited in their participation, to bring their attention back to the teacher is beneficial (Champlin, 1980).

The library media specialist may be the sole performer. When using puppets, he or she may use a script, stage, and several puppets to do a performance or merely sit down with a puppet and improvise. Using a puppet of Clifford, the big red dog, as a means of communicating with students after watching a video of a Clifford story and talking about what they had seen in the video or what they know about Clifford is a simple way to combine puppets and drama. Children delight in the pretending aspect of this "play acting." When first utilizing dramatics, the librarian may read a story that is very familiar and emphasize the character's voices or actions with exaggerated meaning or memorize a short story or poem to act out. The modeling of these forms of dramatics is an important first step.

As students become accustomed to this form of literature, they may be asked to participate. First, they may participate in the form of sound effects, such as giggling in *The Funny Little Woman*, and then move on to choraling the lines, as in *Brown Bear, Brown Bear* by Bill Martin, Jr. Eventually more active and individual forms of participation may be utilized. After listening to a story or watching a video of a story, such as *The Three Billy Goats*, volunteers can reenact the story. Familiar folktales that use repetitive action are best to use when first attempting this activity. Stories such as *Why Mosquitoes Buzz in People's Ears* by Verna Aardema or *I Know an Old Lady Who Swallowed a Fly* by Rose Bonne have built-in dramatics and repetition.

Bauer's *Presenting Reader's Theater: Plays and Poems to Read Aloud* is an excellent source for stories that children can read aloud and dramatize, as well as ideas on how to encourage these dramatics. Importantly, children should not be forced to participate. They will participate when they feel ready, especially after watching the librarian and other students.

Another way to proceed with drama and puppetry in the school library media center is to have the students write the play or puppet show cooperatively. Often rewriting a classic story is a good first step in this type of writing. For example, instead of the Gingerbread Man, the main character may be the dougnut girl rolling down Main Street as opposed to through the fields. Older intermediate students may rewrite a fairy tale in play form, possibly in a common modern dialect, create the puppets, and then perform the puppet show for younger students. To integrate the curriculum, this activity can be planned with the art teacher, and perhaps when the students are studying folklore in reading class.

When special needs students participate in the drama and puppetry activities, the librarian needs to be especially mindful of their individual strengths and weaknesses. These students may not be helpful in writing the script but may excel in puppet or scenery making. Perhaps collecting noisemakers to accompany the show may be the task assigned to the child with special needs. Other children with special needs may be great at creating the dialogue and story line but unable to do the physical writing. A peer can assist, or a tape recorder may be used. Like every other activity, the better the teacher knows the student, the better is the decision about the student's role. The goal is to ensure that everyone is given the opportunity to participate.

POETRY

Children probably spend more time reading poetry than adults do because of their exposure to such authors as Shel Silverstein and Jack Prelutsky. This renewed interest in poetry is also spreading its wings to some of the traditional poems of the past. Many teachers and librarians have taken this opportunity to expose children to a wide variety of poetry and to use it in many different ways.

Poetry lends itself to all the methods of enjoying literature discussed in this chapter with: listening, singing, chanting, impromptu choral reading, body movement, dance, and dramatization (Larrick, 1991). It can be enjoyed in a large group, with a partner, or alone in a quiet corner.

One way to involve students is through the use of music. They first identify some of their favorite songs whose words remind them of a poem. Younger students may see the rhyme and patterns more easily when they look for the poetry in music with its rhythms. With older secondary students, the teacher might share music by such artists as Simon and Garfunkel, John Cougar Mellencamp, and Eric Clapton to illustrate how poetry is used in our everyday lives. This is especially beneficial to those who have difficulty reading to share poetry, and thus literature through music, contemporary or more traditional, is useful. Children can add sound effects. If the poem is about a boat in the water, a small tub of water may be used for a water sound or a triangle instrument may be rung each time the poem says "snow."

CONCLUSION

School library media specialists have a wealth of materials at their fingertips and a big bag of tricks for presenting literature in a captivating and entertaining manner. The activities described in this chapter will help students learn where to go for a good book, how to find a good book, and how to read that book and get the most from it. School library media specialists also want students to develop a comfort level with the library itself. Teaching them to use the library as a resource for literature in later school years and in adulthood is one of the long-range goals for school library media specialists.

REFERENCES

Baker, A., & Greene, E. (1977). *Storytelling: Art and technique*. New York: R. R. Bowker.

Bauer, C. (1983). *This way to books*. New York: H. W. Wilson.

———. (1987). *Presenting reader's theater: Plays and poems to read aloud*. New York: H. W. Wilson.

Carletti, S., Girard, S., & Willing, K. (1991). *The library/classroom connection*. Portsmouth, NH: Heinemann.

Cassady, M. (1990). *Storytelling step by step*. San Jose: Resource Publications.

Champlin, C. (1980). *Puppetry and creative dramatics in storytelling*. Austin, TX: Nancy Renfro Studios.

Kinghorn, H., & Pelton, M. (1991). *Every child a storyteller: A handbook of ideas*. Englewood, CA: Teacher's Ideas Press.

Larrick, N. (1991). *Let's do a poem: Introducing poetry to children*. New York: Delacorte Press.

MacDonald, M. (1988). *When the lights go out: 20 scary tales to tell*. New York: H. W. Wilson.

———. (1986). *Twenty tellable tales*. New York: H. W. Wilson.

Marshall, M. (1981). *Libraries and the handicapped child*. London: André Deutsch.

Sierra, J. (1991). *Fantastic theater: Puppets and plays for young performers and young audiences*. New York: H. W. Wilson.

Trelease, J. (1989). *The new read-aloud handbook*. New York: Penguin Books.

BOOKS TO READ ALOUD TO PRIMARY STUDENTS (GRADES K-2)

Aardema, Verna. *Why mosquitoes buzz in people's ears*. Illus. Leo & Diane Dillon. New York: Dial, 1975. (folklore)

Allard, Harry. *Miss Nelson is missing*. Illus. James Marshall. Boston: Houghton Mifflin, 1977. (school)

Asch, Frank. *Bear shadow*. Englewood Cliffs, NJ: Prentice-Hall, 1985. (animal fantasy)

Ayelsworth, Jim. *Country crossing*. Illus. Ted Rand. New York: Atheneum, 1991. (country sounds)

______. *Two terrible frights*. Illus. Eileen Christelow. New York: Atheneum, 1987. (animal fantasy)

______. *Hanna's hog*. Illus. Glen Rounds. New York: Atheneum, 1988. (folklore)

Blume, Judy. *Freckle juice*. Illus. Sonia O. Lisker. New York: Macmillan, 1971. (family)

Bond, Michael. *A bear called Paddington*. Illus. Peggy Fortnum. Boston: Houghton Mifflin, 1958. (animal fantasy)

Bonne, Rose. *I know an old lady*. Music by Alan Mills. Illus. Abner Graboff. Chicago: Rand McNally, 1961. (folklore)

Booth, Barbara D. *Mandy*. Illus. Jim Lamarche. New York: Lothrop, Lee & Shepard, 1991. (hearing impaired)

Brunhoff, Jean de. *The story of Babar*. New York: Random House, 1960. (animal fantasy)

Burton, Virginia Lee. *Mike Mulligan and his steam shovel*. Boston: Houghton Mifflin, 1967. (city life)

Carle, Eric. *The very hungry caterpillar*. New York: Philomel, 1969. (repetitive language)

Cleary, Beverly. *Ramona Quimby, age 8*. Illus. Alan Tiegreen. New York: William Morrow, 1981. (family)

______. *The mouse and the motorcycle*. Illus. Louis Darling. New York: William Morrow, 1965. (animal fantasy)

Cohen, Barbara. *Molly's pilgrim*. Illus. Michael J. Deraney. New York: Lothrop, Lee & Shepard, 1983. (Thanksgiving)

Cohen, Miriam. *When will I read?* Illus. Lillian Hoban. New York: Greenwillow Books, 1977. (slow learner)

Cole, Joanna. Magic School Bus series. Illus. by Bruce Degen. New York: Scholastic. (science, school)

dePaola, Tomie. *Strega Nona*. Englewood, NJ: Prentice-Hall, 1975. (folklore)

Devlin, Wende, and Harry. *Cranberry Halloween*. New York: Four Winds Press, 1982. (Halloween mystery)

Hyman, Trina Schart. *Ghost poems*. Ed. Daisy Wallace. Sel. and illus. Trina Schart Hyman. New York: Holiday House, 1979. (poetry)

______. *Witch poems*. Ed. Daisy Wallace. Sel. and illus. Trina Schart Hyman. New York: Holiday House, 1976. (poetry)

Joosse, Barbara. *Mama, do you love me*? Illus. Barbra Lavallee. San Francisco: Chronicle Books, 1991. (Eskimos)

Keats, Ezra Jack. *The snowy day*. New York: Viking Press, 1962. (African-American, city life)

Lee, Jeanne M. *Silent Lotus*. New York: Farrar, Strauss & Giroux, 1991. (hearing impaired)

Levi, Dorothy Hoffman. *A very special friend*. Washington, DC: Kendall Green Publications, 1989. (hearing impaired)

Lionni, Leo. *Alexander and the wind-up mouse*. New York: Random House, 1969. (animal fantasy)

———. *Little Blue and Little Yellow*. Toronto: George J. Molead, 1959. (colors)

Lobel, Arnold. *Frog and Toad all year*. New York: Harper & Row, 1979. (animal fantasy)

———. *Days with Frog and Toad*. New York: Harper & Row, 1979. (animal fantasy)

———. *Frog and Toad are friends*. New York: Harper & Row, 1976. (animal fantasy)

Martin, Bill Jr. *Brown Bear, Brown Bear*. Illus. Eric Carle. New York: Henry Holt & Co., 1983. (repetitive language)

———. *Chicka-chicka boom boom*. Illus. Lois Ehlert. New York: Simon & Schuster Books for Young Readers, 1989. (alphabet)

Martin, Bill, Jr., & John Archambault. *Knots on a counting rope*. Illus. Ted Rand. New York: Henry Holt & Co., 1987. (blind)

Mayer, Mercer. *There's an alligator under my bed*. New York: Dial Books for Young Readers, 1987. (animal fantasy)

Muldoon, Kathleen M. *Princess Pooh*. Illus. Linda Shute. Niles, IL: Albert Whitman & Co., 1989. (physically disabled, wheelchair bound)

Numeroff, Laura Joffe. *If you give a mouse a cookie*. Illus. by Felicia Bond. New York: Harper & Row, 1985. (animal fantasy)

Osofsky, Audrey. *My buddy*. Illus. Ted Rand. New York: Henry Holt & Co., 1991. (muscular dystrophy)

Rabe, Berniece. *The balancing girl*. Illus. Lillian Hoban. New York: Dutton Children's Books, 1981. (physically disabled, wheelchair bound)

———. *Where's Chimpy?* Photo. Diane Schmidt. Niles, IL: Albert Whitman & Co., 1988. (Downs' syndrome)

Russo, Marisabina. *Alex is my friend*. New York: Greenwillow Books, 1992. (physically disabled, dwarf)

Scieszka, Jon. *The true story of the three little pigs*. Illus. Lane Smith. New York: Viking Kestrel, 1989. (folklore)

Seattle, Chief. *Brother Eagle, Sister Sky: A message from Chief Seattle*. Illus. Susan Jeffers. New York: Dial Books, 1991. (biography, Native American)

Seuss, Dr. *Horton hatches the egg*. New York: Random House, 1940. (animal fantasy)

Spier, Peter. *Gobble, growl, grunt*. Garden City, NY: Doubleday, 1971. (animal sounds)

Steptoe, John. *The story of Jumping Mouse*. New York: Lothrop, Lee & Shepard, 1984. (folklore, Native American)

White, E. B. *Charlotte's web*. Illus. Garth Williams. New York: Dell, 1952. (animal fantasy)

———. *Stuart Little*. Illus. Garth Williams. New York: Scholastic, 1945. (animal fantasy)

Zion, Gene. *Harry by the sea*. Illus. Margaret Blah Graham. New York: Harper & Row, 1965. (animal fantasy)

BOOKS TO READ ALOUD TO INTERMEDIATE, MIDDLE SCHOOL OR JUNIOR HIGH STUDENTS (GRADES 3–8)

Aiello, Barbra, & Jeffrey Shulman. *Secrets aren't always for keeps*. Illus. Loel Barr. Frederick, MD: Twenty-first Century Books, 1988. (The Kids on the Block series about special needs children)

Atwater, Richard. *Mr. Popper's penguins*. Illus. Robert Lawson. Boston: Little, Brown, 1938. (fantasy)

Blume, Judy. *Tales of a fourth grade nothing*. Illus. Roy Doty. New York: Bradbury Press, 1972. (family)

______. *Superfudge*. New York: E. P. Dutton, 1980. (family)

Burnett, Frances Hodgson. *The secret garden*. Illus. Shirley Hughes. New York: Viking Kestrel, 1988. (orphan)

Burnford, Sheila. *The incredible journey*. Illus. Carl Burger. Boston: Little, Brown, 1961. (animal adventure)

Byars, Betsy. *Summer of the swans*. Illus. Ted CoConis. New York: Viking Press, 1970. (mental retardation)

Carrick, Carol. *Stay away from Simon*. Illus. Donald Carrick. Boston: Clarion Books, 1988. (mental retardation)

Cassedy, Sylvia. *M. E. and Morton*. New York: Thomas Y. Crowell, 1987. (slow learner)

Catling, Patrick Skene. *The chocolate touch*. Illus. Margot Apple. New York: William Morrow & Co., 1979. (fantasy)

Christopher, John. *The white mountains*. New York: Collier, 1988. (fantasy)

Clifford, Eth. *The man who sang in the dark*. Illus. Mary Beth Owens. Boston: Houghton Mifflin, 1987. (blind)

Dahl, Roald. *Charlie and the chocolate factory*. Illus. Joseph Schindelman. New York: Alfred Knopf, 1964. (fantasy)

______. *James and the giant peach*. Illus. Nancy Elkholm Burkett. New York: Alfred A. Knopf, 1961. (fantasy)

DeClements, Barthe. *Sixth grade can really kill you*. New York: Viking Kestrel Books, 1985. (nonreader)

Eager, Edward. *Half-magic*. Illus. N. M. Bodecker. New York: Harcourt, Brace & World, 1954. (fantasy)

Evernden, Margery. *The kite song*. Illus. Cindy Wheeler. New York: Lothrop, Lee & Shepard, 1984. (elective mute, death of mother)

Fleischman, Sid. *The whipping boy*. Illus. Peter Sis. New York: Greenwillow Books, 1986. (fantasy)

Fritz, Jean. *Will you sign here, John Hancock?* Illus. Trina Schart Hyman. New York: Coward, McCann, 1976. (biography)

Gardiner, John Reynolds. *Stone fox*. Illus. Marcia Sewall. New York: Thomas Y. Crowell, 1980.

George, Jean Craighead. *My side of the mountain*. New York: Dutton, 1959. (survival)

______. *Julie of the wolves*. Illus. John Schoenherr. New York: Harper & Row, 1972. (survival)

Gilson, Jamie. *Do bananas chew gum?* New York: Lothrop, Lee & Shepard, 1980. (learning disabilities)

Gould, Marilyn. *The twelfth of June*. Philadelphia: J. B. Lippincott, 1986. (cerebral palsy)

Greenwald, Shelia. *Will the real Gertrude Hollings please stand up?* Boston: Little, Brown, 1985. (learning disabilities)

Hahn, Mary Downing. *Wait till Helen comes*. Boston: Clarion Books, 1986. (ghost story)

Hall, Lynn. *Just one friend*. New York: Charles Scribner's Sons, 1985. (learning disabilities)

Hamilton, Virginia. *The house of dies drear*. Illus. Eros Keith. New York: Macmillan, 1968. (mystery)

Harding, Lee. *The fallen spaceman*. Illus. John & Ian Schoenherr. New York: Harper & Row, 1980. (fantasy)

Henry, Marguerite. *Misty of Chincoteague*. Illus. Wesley Dennis. Chicago: Rand McNally, 1947. (horse story)

Howe, James and Deborah. *Bunnicula*. Illus. Alan Daniel. New York: Atheneum, 1979. (animal fantasy)

League, Sam. *The king of hearts' heart*. Boston: Little, Brown, 1987. (brain damage)

Levy, Marilyn. *The girl in the plastic cage*. New York: Ballantine Books, 1982. (scoliosis)

Lewis, C. S. *The Lion, the witch and the wardrobe*. Illus. Pauline Baynes. New York: Macmillan, 1950. (fantasy)

MacLachlan, Patricia. *Sarah, plain and tall*. New York: Harper & Row, 1985. (historical fiction, family, death)

MacDonald, Margaret Read. *When the lights go out: 20 scary stories to tell*. Illus. Roxanne Murphy. New York: H. W. Wilson, 1988.

Nielson, Shelly. *Autograph, please, Victoria*. Milwaukee, WI: Chariot Books, 1987. (learning disabilities)

O'Brien, Robert C. *Mrs. Frisby and the rats of NIMH*. Illus. Zena Bernstein. New York: Atheneum, 1971. (animal fantasy)

O'Dell, Scott. *Island of the blue dolphins*.Boston: Houghton Mifflin, 1960. (survival, historical fiction)

Paterson, Katherine. *The Great Gilly Hopkins*. New York: Thomas Y. Crowell, 1978. (foster children)

———. *Bridge to Terabithia*. Illus. Donna Diamond. New York: Thomas Y. Crowell, 1977. (death)

Paulsen, Gary. *Hatchet*. New York: Bradbury Press, 1987. (survival)

Robinson, Barbara. *The best Christmas pageant ever*. Illus. Judith Gwyn Brown. New York: Harper & Row, 1972. (poverty, behavior disorder)

Rodgers, Mary. *Freaky Friday*. New York: Harper & Row, 1972. (fantasy, family)

San Souci, Robert D. *The legend of Scarface: A Blackfeet Indian tale*. Illus. Daniel San Souci. New York: Trumpet Club, 1978. (folklore, Native American)

Schwartz, Alvin. *Scary stories to tell in the dark*. Illus. Stephen Gammell. Philadelphia: J. B. Lippincott, 1981.

Service, Pamela F. *Stinker from space*. New York: Charles Scribner's Sons, 1988. (fantasy, science fiction)

Van Allsburg, Chris. *Jumanji*. Boston: Houghton Mifflin, 1981. (fantasy)

Voight, Cynthia. *Dicey's song*. New York: Fawcett, 1987. (orphans)

———. *Izzy, willy-nilly*. New York: Atheneum, 1986. (absent limb)

Warner, Gertrude Chandler. *The boxcar children*. Illus. L. Kate Deal. Niles, IL: Albert Whitman, 1977. (orphans)

Wilder, Laura Ingalls. *Little house in the big woods*. Illus. Garth Williams. New York: Harper, 1961. (historical fiction, family)

4 Vocational Instruction in the Library Media Center

Deborah Jilbert

Vocational training is the cornerstone to a successful transition from school to employment for special needs students. As society moves toward a service-oriented economy, vocational skills become essential to these students. Employable vocational skills provide a sense of recognition and self-respect to the individual. Work gives students a chance to gain job experience in an environment that is carefully monitored and has a safety net to accommodate those who need more guided practice. Providing a wide range of work training sites gives special needs students an opportunity to meet future success by getting them in touch with both their abilities and limitations (Clark & Kolstoe, 1990; Harrington, 1982).

The federal Individuals with Disabilities Education Act (IDEA) requires that the individual education plans (IEPs) include for students beginning no later than age sixteen a statement of needed transition services. These services are:

> a coordinated set of activities for a student, designed within an outcome-oriented process, which promotes movement from school to post-school activities, including postsecondary education, vocational training, integrated employment (including supported employment), continuing and adult education, adult services, independent living, or community participation. The coordinated set of activities shall be based upon the individual student's needs, taking into account the student's preferences, and interests, and shall include instruction, community experience, and the development of employment and other postsecondary adult living objectives, and when appropriate acquisition of daily living skills and functional vocational evaluation. (sec. 602(a) (19))

This law requires schools to provide and expand their vocational training sites.

Just as important are prevocational skills—such as responsibility for actions, initiative, care of materials, punctuality, and task completion, which need to be presented to students as early as the upper elementary grades and continuing through high school. Harrington (1982) notes that these skills may be more important to adult occupational adjustment than specific job training. Training in prevocational skills may take place in strictly academic settings as well as social and vocationally related situations.

The school's library media center (LMC) is an excellent location for vocational training for special needs students. It is ideal for students already at school taking classes, virtually eliminating transportation requirements. It provides as well a unique opportunity for the special needs staff and the employer to collaborate for the benefit of the student, on a daily basis if necessary. For example, if the student needs additional assistance with a task, the special needs teacher and the librarian can work together with him or her. The curriculum that the special needs teacher uses can be adapted to meet the demands of the required job.

Another advantage to using the LMC as a job training site is the variety of work possibilities; cleaning, filing, checking materials in and out, sorting materials, operating audiovisual equipment, repairing books, answering the telephone, and locating materials for patrons. In addition to learning one or more of these specific skills, the special needs student can develop job readiness, communication, and job keeping skills. Students who master these skills can become employed in a variety of workplaces, including public libraries, bookstores, and businesses such as law firms, hospitals, churches, colleges, and large corporations, which may have their own libraries on the premises. Organizations without a library would be appropriate as well if their jobs presented similar duties and tasks to those of the library.

VOCATIONAL ASSESSMENT

Task Analysis

Vocational assessment begins with task analysis of a specific job. It involves looking at a specific job task, breaking down into detail the competencies, and then determining what skills are needed to complete the task. The task needs to have a major goal or standard—something that is observable or measured—that is clearly stated for the special needs learner and the person evaluating him or her. The standard needs to be stated as a performance that is deemed appropriate for successfully completing the task (Howard, 1980). The necessary skills and competencies need to be pinpointed for each task. The skills can be identified by looking at the specific job description and in consultation with the special needs teacher

Figure 4.1
Task Analysis of Computer Work

DUTY	Computer Work-Updating and maintaining the material file in the library.
PREREQUISITE SKILLS	1. Can verbally state library procedure for checking in and out materials. 2. Ability to sequence material alphabetically. 3. Able to operate the library computer.
STANDARDS	All material that comes into the LMC needs to be kept track of. The data include titles, authors, publishers, copyright date, and case numbers.
CONDITIONS	1. Computer 2. Data to input 3. Reference chart
PERFORMANCE GUIDE	1. Gather incoming material from the mailroom. 2. Separate teacher-ordered material from the library-ordered material. 3. Distinguish what type of material it is. 4. Enter all the necessary information into the computer (title, call numbers, etc.). 5. Input material that has been returned. 6. Check for overdue material. Generate a notice for user.

Source: Model Adapted from V-TECS Catalog (V-Tecs Catalogue Vocational-Technical Education Consortium States).

and library staff. Prerequisite skills are helpful for the special needs student to have but not necessary in order to begin to learn the task (Sarkees & Scott, 1985). Clearly, the student may learn some of these skills while in the vocational training program.

The job task needs to be broken down into a series of small steps, with the number of steps depending on the ability level of the student. Then the task should be written in performance terms to assist the special needs student in completing it. The steps should be short, very specific, and listed in sequence, enabling the student to successfully complete the task (Weisgerber, Dahl & Appleby, 1981).

Another important component of task analysis is conditions of the performance—the specific tools, equipment, and work aids related to task performance. The condition section helps to organize the special needs student, so he or she can gather all the necessary materials before beginning the task.

To show how task analysis works in the library media center, we will look at the job description of library clerk (the description is taken from the *Dictionary of Occupational Titles* (DOT):

Figure 4.2
Task Analysis of Sorting Materials

DUTY	Sorting the material and placing it back on the shelves or in the files.
PREREQUISITE SKILLS	1. Able to describe Dewey Decimal System verbally. 2. Ability to sequence material alphabetically. 3. Ability to recognize number sequence. 4. Able to locate specific sectors in the LMC.
STANDARD	All material that comes into the LMC needs to be placed in its designated area.
CONDITIONS	Map of the LMC Returned material Reference chart
PERFORMANCE GUIDE	1. Gather returned material. 2. Separate material according to books, films, periodicals, papers, etc. 3. Separate fiction, nonfiction, and reference material. 4. Arrange material according to the Dewey Decimal System. 5. Return materials to specific areas.

Source: Model Adapted from V-TECS Catalog (V-Tecs Catalogue Vocational-Technical Education Consortium States).

Compiles records, sorts and shelves books, and issues and receives library materials, such as books, films, and phonograph records: Records identifying data and due date on cards by hand or by using photographic equipment to issue books to patrons. Inspects returned books for damages, verifies due-date, and computes and receives overdue fines. Reviews records to compile a list of overdue books and issues overdue notices to borrowers. Sorts books, publications, and other items according to classification code and returns them to shelves, files, or other designated storage area. Locates books and publications for patrons. Issues borrower's identification cards according to established procedures. Files cards in catalog drawers according to system. Repairs books, using mending tape and paste and brush. Answers inquiries of nonprofessional nature on telephone and in person and refers persons requiring professional assistance to librarian (library). May type material cards or issues cards and duty schedules.

The job description sets out many duties that the library clerk performs. It is then necessary to break the job down into separate tasks. Figures 4.1 through 4.3 are task analyses on three different ability levels. The special needs student is capable of doing some or all tasks; however, the number

Figure 4.3
Task Analysis of Cleaning the Library Media Center

DUTY	Cleaning and Straightening the LMC
PREREQUISITE SKILLS	1. Able to identify various sections of the library. 2. Able to perform cleaning procedures. 3. Able to match the cleaning tools to tasks.
STANDARD	The LMC needs to be kept clean and orderly.
CONDITIONS	Cleaning supplies, rags, vacuum, polish, etc. List of items that need cleaning List of procedures
PERFORMANCE GUIDE	1. Dust tops, sides, and bottoms of shelves. 2. Dust books. 3. Pick up discarded materials and place in the returned materials location. 4. Straighten tables and chairs. 5. Pick up and throw away trash. 6. Vacuum carpet, during off hours. 7. Straighten materials on the circulation desk.

Source: Model Adapted from V-TECS Catalog (V-Tecs Catalogue Vocational-Technical Education Consortium States).

of steps required in the task analysis will need to be determined by the student's ability and special needs, library media staff, and the facility itself.

Vocational Assessment of LMC Tasks

Vocational assessment is a process of collecting information that aids special needs students as they start their work experience. It provides a means of comparing each student's skills to the actual job skills needed in order to meet with success on the job. This assessment can be used as a tool for establishing expected behaviors on the job and for making any modification necessary to meet with success (Gugerty & Crowley, 1982).

One of the most widely used vocational assessment approaches is that of situational evaluation. This technique uses observation skills to record work habits the learner is expected to perform while doing the required task on the actual job site or in a simulated worksite. The major benefit of this approach is that the learner is observed and evaluated in a realistic group setting rather than in isolation. Rating scales and behavior charts are most often used. The rating takes place while the learner is on the job site (Sarkees & Scott, 1985).

The situational evaluation has several advantages. First, it is an actual work setting or simulated work setting, so the evaluator observes not only how well the learner does the task but how the learner interacts with co-workers. Second, the learner is given immediate feedback, allowing him or her to make adjustments quickly. Another advantage is that each time the learner is evaluated, the data are charted; both employee and employer can see the progress that has been made. The final advantage of this type of assessment, and perhaps the most important, is that it can evaluate other aspects of work success that cannot be taught in a classroom, such as initiative, dependability, social interaction, and interpersonal relationships (Dunn, 1973).

Figures 4.4, 4.5, and 4.6 are three examples of a vocational situational assessment. All are set up for the evaluator to use on a daily or weekly basis, include a rating scale for easy assessment and scoring, and record a total score, to use in tracking improvement in the student. Figure 4.4 assesses job readiness skills, helpful for the student to have before starting the job, although he or she does not need to have all of these skills. The assessment of job readiness skills, as with communication and job keeping, is ongoing. Figure 4.5 details the communication skills essential to getting and keeping a job. At some point, these skills may need to be demonstrated to the student through specific situations. An example is use of the telephone; the student may know how to use the telephone when talking with a peer but may be unsure of protocol in a more formal situation. Figure 4.6 delineates job keeping skills that allow the student to stay employed and become a productive, independent member of society. The assessment of all of these skills can be done with the special needs instructor and based on previous contact with the student through library instruction and interviewing. These skills will be developed through direct instruction and honed through more instruction and guided practice. Many will be obtained as the student is working at the job.

TEACHING VOCATIONAL SKILLS IN THE LMC

Individual special needs students learn at varying rates or through different instructional techniques. Because the methods that the library media specialist uses to present information to these learners may make the difference between success and failure, he or she needs to call on a variety of instructional techniques to address the individual differences of these students (Sarkees & Scott, 1985). Various forms of input, including visual, auditory, and tactile will facilitate their progress. A school library media specialist must use principles of effective teaching to ensure mastery of the

Figure 4.4
Job Readiness Skills Assessment Chart

Directions to the Evaluator: Each day that you assess the student for job readiness skills, rate each of the following subskills. Base your ratings on the global impression you have after a day of observing the student. Total the scores and look to see raised scores over time.

0 = Never 1 = Seldom 2 = 50% of the time 3 = Usually 4 = Always
No = not observed

Job Readiness Skills

Dates of Evaluation										
Displays a good self-image										
Responds appropriately in social situations										
Has personal and professional goals										
Demonstrates self-motivation and self-management										
Displays honesty in personal and work situations										
Knows and understands own values, accepts others' values										
Respects the rights and property of others										
Follows oral directions correctly										
Follows written directions correctly										
Total score on job readiness skills										

required skills. Many skills must be directly taught through a demonstration, prompt, and practice procedure (Wesson & Keefe, 1989).

If the skill or job being taught is manual, such as cleaning shelves in the library, the direct approach may require hand-over-hand assistance; the instructor actually guides the movements of the student. Such assistance is referred to as prompting. Several levels of prompts may be used, including hand-over-hand, slight touch, verbal (telling), and visual (showing, pointing). The last two are used routinely; the first are used only when necessary

Figure 4.5
Communication Skills Assessment Chart

Directions to the Evaluator: Each day that you assess the student for communication skills, rate each of the following subskills. Base your rating on the global impression you have after a day of observing the student. Total the score and look to see raised scores over time.

0 = Never 1 = Seldom 2 = 50% of the time 3 = Usually 4 = Always
No = not observed

Communication Skills

Dates of Evaluation										
Asks questions when unsure of procedure										
Communicates with co-workers										
Communicates with those in authority										
Follows oral directions pertaining to the job										
Follows written directions pertaining to the job										
Speaks clearly, in a pleasant tone										
Uses and communicates on the phone properly										
Accepts praise										
Sees (understands) criticism as a way to make improvement										
Makes requests by saying please, thank you										
Writes or prints legibly										
Computer literate										

and are faded as soon as possible because the goal is to work toward independence.

For higher-level tasks, demonstration or direct instruction may be an effective technique for introducing a new skill. Direct instruction is an approach whereby the teacher consistently provides demonstration, guided practice, and feedback (Wallace & McLoughlin, 1988). The library media specialist first models the behavior for the student, a process that encompasses verbal exchanges between the student and the instructor (Wesson & Keefe, 1989). Direct instruction shows the student how to

Figure 4.6
Job Keeping Skills Assessment Chart

Directions to the Evaluator: Each day that you assess the student for job keeping skills, rate each of the following subskills. Base your ratings on the global impression you have after a day of observing the student. Total the score and look to see raised scores over time.

0 = Never 1 = Seldom 2 = 50% of the time 3 = Usually 4 = Always
No = not observed

Job Keeping Skills

Dates of Evaluation										
Complies with attendance policy										
Practices punctuality										
Uses a time card correctly										
Uses breaktime appropriately										
Cooperates with co-workers										
Does tasks without asking										
Keeps work station clean										
Recognizes and corrects errors										
Retains work skills										
Works at appropriate speed										
Recognizes and deals with stress on the job										
Displays flexibility										
Adapts to changing demands of the job										
Works as a team member										
Demonstrates interest and enthusiasm in the job										
Manages time efficiently and effectively										
Total score on job keeping skills										

perform the task while explaining the procedure. The student needs to be guided through the task until complete understanding is gained. Direct instruction may involve thinking out loud; the teacher or librarian says everything he or she is thinking out loud to the student when completing the task. In the following example, the library media specialist is teaching the student how to enter data into the computer:

Library media specialist: First, I need to gather all the material to be entered from the basket. What is the first thing I do?

Student: Get the material from the basket.

Library media specialist: The next thing I need to do is bring up the file on the computer by using the enter key. What key brings the file up?

Student: Enter key.

This exchange continues until the procedure is complete. The student then practices several times with the instructor's guidance.

Visual prompts are effective with special needs learners. For example, a map of the library media center can be used in sorting and replacing materials, assisting the student in locating where to replace library items. A list of procedures in a cleaning task analysis, which includes the order that the jobs should be completed in and on what days, could be arranged in a quick reference format. It is helpful to the student if there is a central location for visual prompts—a corner or desk that the student can go to gather them.

Job shadowing is another helpful technique. The student follows a person around to watch how the job is done. As the student shadows, the person being shadowed verbally explains what he or she is doing and why. After the student is able to describe verbally how the task is done, he or she starts simple tasks while being closely supervised.

Special needs students should be talked to like anyone else. They may need to hear instructions more than once, but they will be able to do the task. These students may make errors due to misunderstood directions (as opposed to carelessness), and they may be distractable, so gaining their attention before giving them any instructions is imperative. All of the procedures and techniques outlined here are time-consuming. Working as a collaborative team with the special needs staff will reduce the amount of time, and once these plans are set up, less time will be required.

CASE STUDY

Annie is an eighteen-year-old senior high school student who is quiet and somewhat withdrawn and has trouble communicating with most adults. She has been in special classes or resource rooms since fifth grade.

Annie reads at a sixth-grade level and has a math achievement level of ninth-grade. She is very interested in school, and with the exception of a study hall during which time Annie goes to the special education classroom, Annie is totally mainstreamed. Annie enjoys being in the library, and she envisions working in the library as an adult, an appealing job prospect. At the beginning of her senior year, Annie signed up for the special needs vocational education co-op class. The job placement was in the LMC at her school as a library clerk.

Before Annie began the actual job, she became familiar with the job responsibilities. She shadowed the library clerk for a few days. Then the job was task analyzed, and Annie began the sorting and placement-of-material task. She had some trouble remembering the Dewey decimal system, so a prompt with the number system listed on it was made up for her. This proved to be a very helpful prompt; eventually she was able to work without it. Through the situational vocational assessment and interaction with the staff, Annie was able to improve her communication skills.

Throughout the work experience program, the librarian helped Annie document the skills that she acquired through checklists and videotaping. This documentation enabled Annie to develop a job skills portfolio. With a diploma and portfolio, Annie was able to obtain a job working in a local hospital in its in-house library.

CONCLUSION

Using the school library media center as a vocational training site is an exciting concept with many advantages. Having a work site on campus permits the special needs student to be seen in a different light, breaking down the barriers and stereotypes associated with the special needs label. The student is now seen as capable and productive.

According to the *Wisconsin Career Information System Occupations Handbook* the number of library clerk positions is expected to increase locally and nationally by the year 2000. School library work experience opportunities for the special needs learner allows the student to aim higher for future employment opportunities.

REFERENCES

Clark, G., & Kolstoe, O. P. (1990). *Career development and transition education for adolescents with learning disabilities*. Needham Heights, MA: Allyn and Bacon.

Dunn, D. (1973). *Situational assessment: Model for the future.* Menomonie, WI: University of Wisconsin.

Gugerty, J., & Crowley, C. (1982, Winter). Informal vocational assessment for special needs students. *Journal for Vocational Special Needs Education*, 16–18.

Harrington, T. F. (1982). *Handbook of career planning for special needs students.* Rockville, MD: Aspen Publication.

Howard, M. (1980). *Puzzled about educating special needs students? A handbook on modifying vocational curricula for handicapped students.* Madison, WI: Wisconsin Vocational Studies Center.

Sarkees, D. M., & Scott, J. L. (1985). *Vocational special needs* (2d ed.). Homewood, IL: American Technical Publishers.

U.S. Department of Labor. (1991). *Dictionary of occupational titles* (4th ed.). Washington, DC: Author.

Wallace, G., & McLoughlin, J. A. (1988). *Learning disabilities concepts and characteristics* (3d ed.). Columbus, OH: Merrill Publishing.

Weisgerber, R. A., Dahl, P. R., & Appleby, J. A. (1981). *Training the handicapped for productive employment.* Rockville, MD: Aspen Publication.

Wesson, C. L., & Keefe, M. (1989, Winter). Teaching library skills to special education students. *School Library Media Quarterly,* 71–77.

II

The Role of Library Media Specialist as Information Specialist

5 Selection of Materials for Special Needs Students

Lula Pride and Lois Schultz

Many school library media specialists are accustomed to a traditional role as materials selector, with full responsibility for library purchases and budget decisions. Teacher and student needs are assessed by the librarian, who selects, orders, and processes all library materials. This independent and isolated role is changing with the impact of school reform and the increasing inclusion of students with special needs. In many schools, the movement toward full inclusion is under way, and students with disabilities are now regular users of school libraries. With the increase in inclusion, school librarians must modify traditional methods of material selection. As an information specialist, the school librarian is responsible for developing a collection of materials in various formats that will serve the needs of the professionals in the building who are now facing new challenges with new students, as well as *all* of the students they teach. The school library media specialist has the responsibility for providing materials that meet the intellectual, emotional, and physical needs of students with differing abilities as well as their teachers and ensuring full physical and intellectual access to the library and its collections for all students and teachers. Focusing on the role of librarians as they help transform schools into inclusive settings, this chapter will address what the school library media specialist needs to know in order to select materials for students and professionals, as special needs students move into general education settings.

USING LIBRARY RESOURCES TO BREAK DOWN ATTITUDINAL BARRIERS

As information specialist, the school librarian functions as a clearinghouse for information about disabilities, including the local, regional, and national agencies that provide information and services. Knowing where to find resources in all formats for the school library collection, including information for parents, is a major strength of the school librarian. Additionally, school counselors, psychologists, and special education teachers might recommend books for parents that could be added to the collection, and parents themselves may have some ideas for books. The school librarian is in a key position in the school to advocate for students with disabilities by promoting disability awareness and sensitivity. He or she can promote a shared agenda with the rest of the faculty for serving special needs students. The librarian can participate in curriculum planning by recommending assignments on famous persons with disabilities, diseases, and book reports on titles (fiction and nonfiction) that portray persons with disabilities in a favorable manner. Library materials for faculty and students should include information on disability etiquette and appropriate language. Books and other materials in the collection about various disabilities could be used to prepare the student body for acceptance of a student who has disabilities. Many activities could be featured, from fiction and nonfiction reading assignments to educational puppet programs using "disabled" puppets such as Kids on the Block.

The librarian can help to break down attitudinal barriers by providing books and pamphlets about disabilities that answer questions many students have about disabilities. An important goal of this type of activity done in advance of the student's arrival is to attempt to divert any feelings of pity, so the new student will be seen in a "can do" rather than a "can't do" framework.

In the summer of 1990, Mary Raczinski, librarian at Edison Middle School in Wheaton, Illinois, was informed that a student with multiple disabilities would be arriving in the middle school the following February. She called the reference librarian at Project SLICD (Statewide Library Information for Caregivers of the Disabled, a disability information service) to discuss resources for use in the next six months as she introduced disability awareness to faculty and students. She requested a list of the names of famous persons with disabilities who led successful lives. The SLICD librarian recommended appropriate titles on disabilities, fiction and nonfiction, that Raczinski could request on interlibrary loan and then order for her collection. The resources included videos such as The People You'd Like to Know series (*Encyclopedia Britannica*) and *Regular Lives* (WETA TV, Washington, DC), which depict students with disabilities in everyday settings. The school librarian had adequate time to order and process these materials before the student arrived. Then she worked with colleagues in the school to plan for the arrival of the thirteen–year-old student, who had cerebral palsy and used a wheelchair. During the fall, students at all levels were required to write a report on the life of a famous person who had a disability. Other schoolwide programs were conducted as part of this agenda to increase disability awareness and sensitivity. As a result of this foresight, the student's assimilation into the school went smoothly.

Teachers may want to read *No Pity* (Shapiro, 1993) in order to develop the mind-set that students with disabilities are included in general education classes and in society as a whole because they have basic civil rights that have only recently been addressed (Americans with Disabilities Act of 1990).

COLLECTION DEVELOPMENT

The library media specialist, working in partnership with colleagues, is responsible for selecting materials for all students. In order to ensure that special needs students have appropriate access to library resources, a team of administrators and teachers needs to review the school library's collection development policy with the library media specialist.

Collection Development Policy

The collection development policy has three components: (1) include materials for professionals, to provide them with background information to serve children with special needs; (2) set forth the criteria for collecting materials so as to foster sensitivity and awareness about disabilities; and (3) describe criteria for selecting items new to the collection that will be used by children with special needs.

Material Formats

All material formats—books, videos, software, audiotapes, and others—should be collected as needed, based on individual student requirements. The selection of well-designed, current materials will improve overall collection quality and timeliness and will serve the needs of many students with disabilities.

Assistive Equipment

Aside from computer software and hardware, other assistive technology may be needed to serve the educational needs of students with various disabilities. Assistive devices include portable amplifiers and assistive listening devices (such as FM loops and headsets), captioned videos (for students with hearing impairments), descriptive videos (for students with visual impairments), and television sets equipped to decode these captions. High-tech and low-tech devices for students with vision impairment include audiocassette recorders, magnifiers, braillers, and print-enlarging computers. Talking computers, such as the Kurzweil reading machine, are also available. (Technology is discussed in Chapter 8.)

Resources for Parents

The library media specialist serves as a clearinghouse for supportive resources for parents as well as teachers and students. An up-to-date file of area organizations and support groups for parents of children with disabilities is an important resource for the school librarian to maintain. These organizations are usually pleased to cooperate with schools by providing informational pamphlets and speakers for classroom and schoolwide programs.

Professional Collection

A basic professional collection includes titles to help the regular classroom teacher understand the language of special education and guides to help locate books, magazines, assistive equipment, and other resources. Many comprehensive guides are available; the titles listed below are highly recommended for school librarians and general educators who are serving special education students:

Children with Disabilities: A Medical Primer, 3d ed., by Mark Batshaw (Ed.) (Baltimore: Paul H. Brookes, 1992). This basic reference work reviews the causes and characteristics of disabilities that affect young children. Chapters on cerebral palsy, autism, and other disorders are descriptive and clear. The introductory section on genetic abnormalities and normal child development is well written and informative. This overview is useful for parents and professionals.

Encyclopedia of Special Education (New York: Wiley, 1986) is an essential basic reference for media specialists, teachers, and parents who need information on special education laws and procedures, disabling conditions, diagnostic terms, and other topics of interest.

Exceptional Children (published bimonthly, official journal of the Council on Exceptional Children, $40 per year). The journal publishes articles and reviews of books for children, parents, and professionals. A major journal in the field, this should be one of the first purchases for any new professional collection. Council for Exceptional Children, 1920 Association Drive, Reston, VA 22091–1589: (305)–384–6869.

Exceptional Parent magazine provides articles of interest to special educators and parents of children with disabilities. Features include news articles, book reviews, and current issues. Write for the Exceptional Parent Press catalog. 605 Commonwealth Avenue, Boston, MA 02215; (617)–536–8961.

Meeting the Needs of People with Disabilities: A Guide for Librarians, Educators, and Other Service Professionals, by Ruth A. Vellman (Phoenix: Oryx, 1990), provides a detailed overview of people with disabilities and includes extensive chapters on school libraries and special education. Extensive listings of support agencies and resource materials make this essential in any professional collection.

Moore, Corey. *A Reader's Guide for Parents of Children with Mental, Physical, or Emotional Handicaps*, 3d ed. (Rockville, MD: Woodbine House, 1990). Written by a parent and updated twice, this "list of lists" is a basic source for information about disabilities, public policy, and advocacy, and serves as a guide to journals, magazines, newsletters, and directories about disabilities. It is an important tool for librarians, teachers, and parents in selecting books on special needs and also includes a comprehensive referral list, "Where to Write for More Information."

Negotiating the Special Education Maze: A Guide for Parents and Teachers by Winifred Anderson, Stephen Chitwood, and Diedre Hyden, 2d ed. (Rockville, MD: Woodbine House, 1992). A step-by-step guide to the special education system, this handbook provides an introduction to special education for parents. Updated to include the 1990 amendments to Public Law 94-142, this book covers special education from preschool early intervention programs to age eighteen and career education. The authors are transition specialists at the Parent Educational Advocacy Training Center described later in this chapter.

In addition to these general materials, librarians may have on hand materials useful for their specific schools. There are many elements to consider when selecting materials for students with disabilities; no one list of criteria can possibly cover every type of material in every format for every need.

CRITERIA FOR MATERIAL SELECTION

General Criteria

Materials should be selected in all types of formats: videos (both signed and closed captioned), audiocassettes, books, kits comprising materials in several formats, toys, games, computer software, puppets, children's and young adult magazines in alternative formats, and the appropriate equipment to make these materials accessible. Children with differing abilities have various learning styles. The school librarian must look for quality in all types of formats just as when selecting any other materials for the collection. He or she should be as practical as possible and think about all the ways an item may be used and the learning needs it will meet.

Manipulative Materials

The specific learning need may suggest use of a manipulative item, such as a game, toy, or puppet, for development of fine motor skills, for social skills development, or as an aid to self-expression. Items should be safe to use, easily cleaned, and durable enough to withstand a great deal of handling. The number of pieces to track and how the item(s) will be stored, are additional considerations.

Audiovisual Materials

Criteria for selecting audiovisual materials include good-quality production with clarity of picture and sound, a reasonable pace of presentation of ideas and information, length, accuracy of content, and appropriateness for various age, interest, and cognitive levels.

Books and Magazines

Literary style and quality in printed materials are important, but there are other criteria that are also critical to keep in mind when selecting for students with special needs. High-interest materials on popular topics (holidays, sports, biographies of celebrities, animals, dinosaurs, science fiction, etc.) both meet the needs and interests of those with disabilities and provide opportunities for these students to feel that they can have success with reading and be able to share interests by being informed about topics that are popular with their peers. Materials with clear pictures and photographs, clear type, plenty of white space on the page, and accurate and current content are essential.

Books should be selected from a wide range of formats to meet a significant need for those with differing abilities. Children with physical disabilities often have to expend so much intellectual, emotional, and physical energy in coping with the disability that their reading skills fall behind. Students with special needs who have difficulty reading will find the most success with books in special formats. High interest–low vocabulary materials, with brief text on a first-to fourth-grade level and many clear illustrations or photographs, are especially important. Predictable picture books, wordless picture books, picture books in an oversized format ("big" books), large print, signed stories, books on sign language, books on tape, and books in braille are all important formats to consider, both fiction or nonfiction, to meet the varying interests and skill levels of those with differing abilities.

Creativity is a key element. By assessing the existing collection and looking for materials that can be adapted or used in a variety of ways, the school librarian will discover new uses for materials already on hand. For example, predictable books, books with photographs, books with paper architecture built in, captioned videos, and books on tape can be used for a variety of special-needs purposes. Margaret Kleinpeter, resource person for special education in the Iberia Special Services Center, Iberia Parish, Louisiana, offers tips for selection as she prepares this parish-wide program to move toward full inclusion. She suggests that librarians look for the following key phrases in reviews in selection journals to alert them to suitable materials: *straightforward, simple text; accessible style; numerous photos; double-page spread and few lines of text; illustrations convey the story well; pictures provide many visual clues;* or *for readers who aren't ready for long chapters.* "The reviews may show that a book has good full color photos and/or good layout or formatting. These are key elements I find in making a book more usable to special needs users (and everyone else)" (Kleinpeter, 1993). Knowing the learning need, the purpose(s) for the item, how it might be used, by whom it will be used, and how often it will be used are important components of selection for children with special needs. Any new item purchased should be worth the price and time and effort of students who use it.

Selecting Materials to Increase Acceptance of Students with Disabilities

Faculty and students need to be aware of various disabilities and be sensitive to those with differing abilities. Probably there are many materials in the collection already that can be used to foster awareness and sensitivity. Students with disabilities may also benefit from these materials as they discover ways in which others have managed their disabilities and their abilities.

Criteria for Nonfiction about Disabilities

Materials should give current, accurate information at an accessible reading level. The writing style should be clear, unsentimental, and use accepted disability terms. Unacceptable terms include using the disability to label a person, such as saying, "Susan, the epileptic," or "John, the paraplegic." Another unacceptable phrase is "confined to a wheelchair." Antiquated terms such as *imbecile, moron, gimp, retard,* and others are also red flags that the material is inappropriate. Illustrations should be accurate and clear and follow the text. The book should help remove stigmas and stereotypes about individuals who are challenged with disabilities.

Criteria for Fiction about Disabilities

A criterion to consider is quality, just as would be used in the selection of any type of fiction for young people. The person or persons with disabilities should be portrayed as real people with full personalities. The character's abilities, rather than the disability, should be the focus. It is important to check reviews for literature that has plausible settings and characters with realistic relationships, conflicts, and problem-solving episodes.

With a set of criteria in hand, the librarian can seek out selection sources that list available materials.

TRADITIONAL SELECTION SOURCES TO FIND MATERIAL FOR SPECIAL NEEDS STUDENTS

Once the criteria have been developed for the collection development policy and this policy has been approved by the administration, the next important step is to locate materials appropriate for students with special learning needs, and for building an awareness about individuals with disabilities.

The following traditional library selection sources are good places to start to expand the collection for inclusion. Teachers with a special education background can provide expertise when planning what to select to address the individual education plans of students with disabilities.

The Best: High/Low Books for Reluctant Readers, by Marianne Laino Pilla (Libraries Unlimited, Englewood, CO.: 1990). This is a guide to 374 leisure reading books for reluctant young readers and students reading below grade level. Entries are numbered, listed alphabetically by author with title and subject indexes. Full ordering information is cited, plus number of pages, grade/interest level, and reading level. Each book is annotated with a brief content note, and some have a comment about format (illustrated with photographs, short chapters, etc.). This is a useful resource when assessing an existing collection to spot high interest/low vocabulary titles and as a source for collection expansion.

Best Books for Children, 4th ed: Preschool Through Grade 6, by John T. Gillespie and Corrinne J. Nadel (New York: Bowker, 1990); *Best Books for Junior High Readers*, by John T. Gillespie. (New York: Bowker, 1991); *Best Books for Senior High Readers*, by John T. Gillespie (New York: Bowker, 1991). These annotated basic lists of high-quality fiction and nonfiction titles are guides to collection analysis and development and serve as good sources for books about disabilities. Books are arranged by numbered entries, so the index is the key in each of these sources. There will be some difficulty tracking titles to fit specific needs, however, due to the complex indexing. Searching for disabilities by topic alphabetically is advisable, but if just the term *disabilities* is checked, it will tell the reader to see individual disabilities, such as *dyslexia, learning disabilities*, and *physical handicaps*. A sample check for fiction under *physical handicaps—fiction* cited one entry—a novel about paralysis. But when checking *disabilities*, another entry is cited—a novel about cerebral palsy and not the novel on paralysis. These three standard lists are a good place to begin a search for books that will help develop awareness and sensitivity toward those with differing abilities, but it is best to search any and all topics.

The Best Years of Their Lives: A Resource Guide for Teenagers in Crisis, comp. Stephanie Zviron (Chicago: American Library Association, 1992). This annotated list of nonfiction, with related fiction and video titles for teens, is a guide to materials to help adolescents cope with change and various stress situations. To find titles on disabilities, a subject search in the index yields topics such as *exercise* (includes *exercise for physically challenged*), *family relationships* (includes *with physically challenged parents*), *parents (physically challenged)*, *physically challenged*, and *sports injuries*.

The Bookfinder 4: When Kids Need Books. Annotations of Books Published 1983–1986, by Sharon Spredemann Dryer (American Guidance Service, Circle Pines, MN 1989). Arranged alphabetically by author, this numbered and annotated list is a guide to books to help children deal with problems. The index of subjects guides the reader to the various topics, from *amputee, blindness*, and *handicaps*, to *visual impairment* and *wheelchair, dependence on*. Under *handicaps* four titles are cited. Then various handicapping situations are listed, some with a *see* reference. All subject areas need to be checked and the numbered annotations cited need to be read to determine if specific titles fit a particular need.

Booklist (published twice monthly, American Library Association). This standard reviewing journal contains critical reviews of books and other materials for all ages and features special lists of materials in various formats on current issues and topics, (e.g., "Children with Special Needs: Video Resources," November 1, 1991, pp. 548–550. If each school library cannot afford a subscription, an effort should be made for purchase somewhere in the district so that each media specialist has access to reviews for new books and audiovisual materials.

The Elementary School Library Collection: A Guide to Books and Other Media, 18th ed. (Brodart, Williamsport, PA, 1992). This is an extensive guide to all types of materials: filmstrips, videos, audio recordings and cassettes, magazines, kits, computer software, and CD-ROM programs for preschool to sixth grade. Arranged by Dewey classification for reference and nonfiction, and alphabetically by author in the "easy fiction "sections, this source ranks selections according to phase of collection building. Phase I is "core" or first purchase; phase II is a continuing development priority, and phase III encompasses special items that are recommended if needed. Not only is this useful for collection analysis and purchase, but the full annotations help guide the librarian to items in all formats that suit special interest and ability level needs for students with disabilities. The thorough subject index guides the librarian to books about disabilities to expand resources on fostering awareness and sensitivity.

Portraying Persons with Disabilities: Fiction. An Annotated Bibliography of Fiction for Children and Teenagers, 3d ed., by Debra Roberts (New York: Bowker, 1992). This valuable guide in the selection process updates Bowker's *Notes from a Different Drummer* (1977) and *More Notes from a Different Drummer* (1984), the landmark sources for children and young adult books about disabilities. Annotated entries cover titles published between 1982 and 1991. The introduction provides background on awareness and sensitivity and sets out selection criteria for fiction about persons with differing abilities. Arranged by topical chapters, the book is fully indexed by title, author, and subject, making it useful in several ways. Specific disabilities can be checked in the index. One of the introductory chapters is a good source for background information about disabilities. Full descriptive and evaluative annotations will help in the selection process.

Portraying Persons with Disabilities: Nonfiction, 2d ed., by Joan Brest Friedberg, June B. Mullins, and Adelaide Weir Sukiennik, (New York: Bowker, 1992). This annotated bibliography of nonfiction for children and teenagers updates the authors' earlier work, *Accept Me As I Am* (1985). The four major sections cover nonfiction for children and teenagers dealing with physical problems, sensory problems, cognitive and behavior problems, and various disabilities. Within each section, books are listed alphabetically by author, with full ordering information, reading level, and review sources. Full content information is given, followed by a critical analysis of the work. Books cited are indexed by author, title, and subject. The introductory sections are excellent for background information. The authors provide a foundation for collection development with the first chapter on the criteria for selection. The second chapter provides a historical perspective of the social issues, attitudes, and trends concerning disability. A timeline of events that have influenced persons with disabilities is included. A third chapter contains a bibliography of reference books on various disabilities and on persons with disabilities, useful as a guide in developing a good reference collection about disabilities for students, staff, and parents.

School Library Journal (published monthly). Along with feature articles on library service to youth in schools and public libraries, this periodical contains reviews of children's and young adult books, professional books, audiovisual materials, and computer software. This source, useful for all areas of selection for children and young adult collections, annually features the recommended lists developed by committees from the divisions of the American Library Association. For example, one very useful list appeared in the March 1993 issue, "Recommended Books for Reluctant Readers 1993" (Young Adult Library Services Association, 1993). Articles often address issues such as inclusion (e.g., in October 1992, "CD-ROM and At-Risk Students: A Path to Excellence," in which the author stated, "CD-ROM technology is a great equalizer, bringing success to all students, regardless of their prescribed ability levels").

SPECIALIZED SELECTION SOURCES

Materials for Students with Visual Impairment

Students with visual impairment benefit from materials in various formats, including braille, large print, and audiocassettes. Braille materials are available from several locations; the primary supplier is the National Library Service, which also provides Library of Congress Talking Books. Local public libraries provide access information for this service, which can also locate braille books for students. Seedlings, a private company, publishes braille editions of popular children's books (Seedlings: Braille Books for Children, P.O. Box 2395, Livonia, MI 48151–0385, 800–777–8552 or 313–427–8552).

Large-print (or large-type) books are necessary school library materials for students with visual impairment. Very few publishers produce large-print children's books, however, and their listings of titles are limited. It is very helpful for parents and teachers to have a listing of large-print publishers on hand. Two popular publishers of these books for children are Cornerstone Books (100 Pine Avenue, Holmes, PA 19043, 800–345–8112) and G. K. Hall (70 Lincoln Street, Boston, MA 02111, 800–343–2806 or 617–423–3390).

A large-print dictionary and other basic reference books with large, clear type are building blocks of a large print collection. Some magazines, such as *Reader's Digest*, are available in large print. Print-enlarging equipment, such as a Visualtek machine or print-enlarging software for computers, makes the library collection accessible to anyone with low vision.

Audiocassettes are available for all levels and range from read-along kits to unabridged recordings. Books on tape for the general public are increasing in popularity and are available in condensed versions or in full text. The unabridged editions are popular at all levels and can be used with the printed text as a read-along. Audio books are popular with children and young adults and can be quite useful for encouraging reluctant readers. For a complete listing of audio books, consult the annual publication *Words on Cassette* (New Providence, NJ: Bowker). This definitive bibliography of spoken word audiocassettes is available at most public libraries. Three popular publishers or suppliers of recorded books are:

Books on Tape, Box 7900, Newport Beach, CA 92658, (800)–626–3333, (714)–548–5525.

Recorded Books, 270 Skipjack Road, Prince Frederick, MD 20678, (800)–638–1304, (301)–535-3000). Publishes a children's and young adult catalog.

Weston Woods, 389 Newtown Turnpike, Weston, CT 06883, (800)–243–5020, 203–226–3355.

Audio magazines are also available. *Boomerang* (Listen and Learn, 123 Townsend Street, Suite 636, San Francisco, CA 94107) is a one-hour audiocassette magazine for children ages six to ten and is good for children with dyslexia or visual impairment.

The school librarian should have on hand a listing of supplemental services for persons with visual impairment, such as tape recordings of textbooks on demand, braille transcribing, and volunteer radio reading services, which provide radio broadcast of local newspapers. These services can be located through the American Printing House for the Blind (1839 Frankfort Avenue, P.O. Box 6085, Louisville, KY 40206–0085, 502–895–2405) and the American Foundation for the Blind (15 West Sixteenth Street, New York, NY 10011, 800–AFBLIND, 212–620–2000). Another good resource for locating local services is the state office for rehabilitation services.

Materials for Students with Hearing Impairment

Books on sign language and stories in signed English are available from Gallaudet University Press (800 Florida Avenue, N.W., Washington, DC 20002, 202–651–5488). A source for books on deafness and videos for learning sign language is the National Association for the Deaf (814 Thayer Avenue, Silver Spring, MD 20910, 301–587–1788), which also produces a newsletter, *NAD Broadcaster*.

Free loan, open-captioned videotapes are available from Captioned Films/Videos (5000 Park Street North, St. Petersburg, FL 33709, 800–237–6213 voice/TDD). This program is funded by the U.S. Department of Education.

Computers

Computer hardware and software are discussed in a later chapter. For a complete listing of up-to-date resources, consult the annual computer feature (usually in October) in *Exceptional Parent* magazine. Several clearinghouses are available to help locate hardware and software for students with special needs:

ABLEDATA, a national clearinghouse for technology information for people with disabilities (800–344–5405).

Apple Office of Special Education (800–732–3131, ext. 275).

IBM National Support Center for Persons with Disabilities (800–IBM–2133).

Trace Research and Development Center (5151 Madison Center, University of Wisconsin, 1500 Highland Avenue, Madison, WI 53705, 608–262–6966).

Directories

These specialized directories focus on resources for people with disabilities and are very useful for locating unusual materials.

Assistive Technology Sourcebook (Washington, DC: RESNA Press, 1990) includes the full spectrum of disability technology and serves also as a one-volume resource and referral guide. Various disabilities, such as hearing impairment, are described and discussed. Assistive equipment, current treatment, and support networks are listed for each.

Complete Directory for People with Disabilities: Products, Resources, Books and Services (Grey House Publishing, distributed by Gale Research), a one-stop annual sourcebook for individuals and professionals covers four major areas (institutions, products, media, and programs) and is indexed in three ways (entry/organization name, disability/need, and geographics index of institutions and organizations). This useful directory would be a good district-wide purchase.

Self-Help Sourcebook—Finding and Forming Mutual Aid Self-Help Groups, 4th ed. Denville, NJ: (American Self-Help Clearinghouse, St. Clares-Riverside Medical Center. This listing of over 600 national and local groups is a useful tool for teachers and parents. At ten dollars, it is a bargain. It leads to supportive resources for all parents.

Other Resources for Parents and Teachers

The following resources can help parents and teachers locate useful information:

Association for the Care of Children's Health (7910 Woodmont Avenue, Suite 300, Bethesda, MD 20814, 301–654-6549). ACCH focuses on support for parents and families. *ACCH Network* is a quarterly newsletter with information and networking for families of children with special needs. The *Parent Resource Directory* ($5, annual) lists over 400 names of parents who are available to provide peer support for families of children with various disabilities. The quarterly journal, *Children's Health Care*, includes book reviews.

Guidelines for Establishing a Family Resource Library, 2d ed., by Barbara Steele and Carolyn Williams (Bethesda: ACCH, 1986) is a useful guide for librarians who are providing support to parents.

Beach Center on Family and Disability (University of Kansas Bureau of Child Research, 4138 Haworth Hall, Lawrence, KS 66045, 913–864–4950). This center conducts research and training and disseminates information relevant to families who have members with developmental disabilities or serious emotional disturbances or who are technology dependent. The quarterly newsletter is free.

BOSC: Books on Special Children (Box 305, Congers, NY 10920–0305). This newsletter is published by a distributor of books about children with disabilities. It includes news of new products, as well as information on books for children, teachers, and parents.

Paul H. Brookes Publishers (P.O. Box 10624, Baltimore, MD 21285–0624, 800–638–3775 or 402 West Pennsylvania Avenue, Towson, MD 21204, 410–337–9580). This publisher's catalog is an important resource for special educators and includes titles of interest to parents and professionals.

HEATH Resource Center, American Council on Education (One Dupont Circle NW, Washington, DC 20036–1193). Publishes *HEATH Resource Directory* (single copies free).

Learning Disabilities Association of America (4156 Library Road, Pittsburgh, PA 15234, 412–341–1515). LDAA is a membership organization of professionals and parents; it publishes materials and sponsors events. The newsletter, *LDAA Newsbriefs*, is available free.

National Lekotek Center (2100 Ridge Avenue, Evanston, IL 60204, 708–328–0001). Lekotek is a program of toy-lending libraries, featuring planned, professionally directed interaction between parent and child. A booklet, *How to Start a Lekotek*, is available on request.

National Center for Learning Disabilities (381 Park Avenue South, Suite 1420, New York, NY 10016, 212–545–7510, fax 212–545–9665). This organization is dedicated to helping people with learning disabilities. Services include national information and referral, educational programs and products, and legislative advocacy. Teacher training and parent education are priorities. *Their World* (annual, $10) highlights articles and resources of current interest and includes stories about the ways adults and children cope with learning disabilities. The "Resourceful Parent's List" is outstanding. The magazine also includes student book reviews and NCLD book recommendations for children and adults.

National Center for Youth with Disabilities (University of Minnesota, Box 721–UMHC, Minneapolis, MN 55455, 800–333–6293 or 612–626–2825). NCYD provides fact sheets on disabilities as well as a newsletter, *Connections*.

National Information Center for Children and Youth with Handicaps (P.O. Box 1942, Washington, DC 20013, 703–893–6061). NICHY is an excellent resource for clearly written basic information on disabilities. Write to request a free set of information sheets.

Orton Dyslexia Society (Chester Building, Suite 382, 8600 La Salle Road, Baltimore, MD 21204, 301–296–0232 or 800–ABC-D123). This parent and professional membership organization publishes materials to help teachers, parents, and students understand dyslexia.

Parent Educational Advocacy Training Center (208 South Pitt Street, Suite 300, Alexandria, VA 22314, 703–836–2953). PEATC, available in five states, provides advocacy training for parents. PEATC, via the NEXT STEPS teams, is comprised of parent and professional volunteers. These teams offer support and education to prepare parents for their child's transitions through the educational process. Transition planning is available for parents of young children as they learn to navigate the special education process. PEATC staff coauthored the Woodbine House book, *Negotiating the Special Education Maze*, discussed earlier in this chapter. To locate nearby parent advocacy training programs, contact the Federation for Children with Special Needs Technical Assistance for Parents Programs (95 Berkeley Street, Suite 104, Boston, MA 02116, 617–482–2915).

Woodbine House Publishers (5615 Fisher's Lane, Rockville, MD 20852, 800–843–7323) publishes a series of books about disabilities, the Special Needs Collection.

WHAT TO DO ABOUT FUNDING

Funding is always an issue for librarians as they select and order materials. Below are three budget levels and ideas for how to consider students with special needs regardless of budget. Good relationships with colleagues who make financial decisions are helpful. Informing the individuals of the benefits of the dollars spent in the library is a wise use of time.

No Cost

With a minimal impact on the budget, the media specialist can recommend a collection development policy with two components: (1) criteria for materials that foster sensitivity and awareness and (2) criteria for selecting items new to the collection that will be used by students with special needs.

Weed the collection, watching for materials about people with disabilities that are medically or philosophically out of date and/or negative in tone. Dispose of old, poorly illustrated volumes. Next, identify materials that can be adapted for special needs use (well designed, clearly illustrated, large type, etc.). Locate and publicize local and national networks and resources of interest to parents and teachers. Ask for pamphlets and informational materials, and get on their mailing lists for newsletters.

Low Cost

Build a collection of books on tape and read-along kits for all ages, abilities, and interests. Make tape players available in the library. While reading reviews and preparing orders, select current fiction about persons with disabilities in order to break down attitudinal barriers within the school. Look for positive images. Select current nonfiction that will help learning disabled students to cope, adjust, and learn good study habits. Look for hot topics, high/low books for reluctant readers, and books that are clearly illustrated. Add high-interest nonfiction suitable for all reading levels. Look for clearly written text and photographic illustrations. Concentrate on popular topics, such as animals, holidays, sports, and biographies.

A Generous Budget

In addition to the above recommendations, add computer hardware and software with appropriate assistive components, such as screen enlarging software, adaptive keyboards, and scanners. Purchase CD-ROM equipment and materials such as encyclopedias, reader advisory guides, and learning games. Create or expand the computer software collection with multimedia (interactive) software for high interest and accessibility. Subscribe to several professional and parenting journals, and build a professional collection that includes the specialized resources listed in this chapter.

CONCLUSION

School librarians must become aware of their new role in the inclusive school environment. Professional media specialists, trained in materials selection, offer critical skills for locating resources. Being part of the planning process for inclusion, working with teachers and parents, using existing materials creatively, and knowing how to locate specialized resources, the school library media specialist can provide a collection that supports the needs of all students. Many of the resources recommended in this chapter are available at little or no cost. All that is needed are imagination and an open attitude.

REFERENCES

Kids on the Block, Inc. 9385–C Gerwig Lane, Columbia, Maryland 21046, (310) 290–9095, (800)–368–KIDS. Kids on the Block puppet programs have been designed to enable enthusiastic individuals and groups around the world to teach children about disabilities, differences, and areas of social concern. Community-based groups operate the puppet programs in all fifty states.

Kleinpeter, Margaret (1993, January). Personal letter.

Lucas, L., & Karrenbrock, M. H. (1993). *The disabled child in the library: Moving into the mainstream.* Littleton, CO: Libraries Unlimited.

Mendrinos, R. B. (1992). CD-ROM and at-risk students: A path to excellence. *School Library Journal 38*(10): 29–31.

Shapiro, J. P. (1993). *No pity: People with disabilities forging a new civil rights movement.* New York: Times Books.

Young Adult Library Services Association. Recommended books for reluctant readers 1993. *School Library Journal 39*(3): 131.

6

The School Library Media Specialist's Role in Bibliotherapy

Robert P. King

Children enter public schools today with emotional and social problems that heretofore were not evident. America's children and youth are facing ever-increasing pressures and temptations from the media and entertainment industry, as well as experiencing the general erosion of community and family fabric. These social forces that impinge on the development of children have to date manifested themselves in the highest recorded rates of behavioral and emotional problems in our schools and neighborhoods. The most visible and readily available institution to address these problems head on is the school. Educational and psychological experts alike agree that the school's role in the 1990s is far more complex and varied than teaching the three Rs. The school library media specialist plays an increasingly important role in working with special and general educators as part of a treatment team to help students who are having situational stress as well as those who exhibit resistant, chronic behavioral problems. One extremely rich and promising methodology that has a long and varied history in library science is bibliotherapy. Increasingly bibliotherapy applications are being used with general and special education students as an important treatment methodology to ameliorate emotional and behavioral problems, while also serving as a springboard for healthy developmental growth. These applications have shown to be effective with a wide variety of students and problems across the K–12 curriculum. This chapter will define bibliotherapy, its goals and hoped-for outcomes, as well as methodologies to implement the procedures with students in both individual and small group formats.

HISTORICAL BEGINNINGS TO CURRENT APPLICATIONS

Bibliotherapy has a rich and extensive history in the United States. Its roots are firmly planted in the medical model, dating back to the turn of the nineteenth century. In its simplest form, bibliotherapy and its philosophical underpinnings are rooted in the notion that reading under guided instruction can serve as an adjuvant therapy to affect emotional problems and personality change. Hospital librarians were originally instrumental in compiling lists of recommended reading materials in concert with physicians. Notable in these early efforts were staff members at the Menninger Clinic and Veterans Administration hospitals (Brown, 1975).

Berry (1978) provides a useful conceptualization of contemporary bibliotherapy by distinguishing between clinical bibliotherapy and educational-humanistic therapy. Helpful in this distinction is the notion that clinical bibliotherapy is actually a psychotherapy designed for clinically identified "sick" clients. The model that this chapter subscribes to is the educational-humanistic approach, in which students are on a guided journey of self-discovery and self-actualization as part of their development (Berry, 1978). The educational approach does not adhere to a medical model approach of defining "sickness" and effecting a cure. Rather, this approach conceptualizes behavior on a continuum of psychological and emotional development. Difficulties that students manifest in schools are best thought of as being malleable to guidance; bibliotherapy is a methodology that encourages internal locus of control and insight. It is an extremely optimistic approach to remediating school-related problems while contributing to psychologically healthy development.

In its simplest form, bibliotherapy is defined as "storybook guidance" (Schultheis, 1972); a more comprehensive definition is "a family of techniques for structuring interaction between a facilitator and a participant based on mutual sharing of literature" (Pardeck & Pardeck, 1990, p. 228). The literature records a number of alternate terms, such as *literatherapy*, *biblioeducation*, and *bibliocounseling*, which reflect essentially the same constructs. A unifying principle underlying the various definitions, terms, and authors is the belief by those who practice these procedures that *reading* is the fundamental vehicle for effecting change.

Goals inherent in the application of bibliotherapeutic techniques are the promotion of life adjustment, promotion of psychological maturity, and the fostering of character development (Brown, 1975). Riordan and Wilson (1989) describe outcome benefits of bibliotherapy as "gaining understanding or solving problems relevant to a person's therapeutic needs" (p. 506). Calhoun (1987) states that "change in attitude, behavior, or self is manifested through the reading of selected and monitored literature" (p. 939).

Inherent in the bibliotherapeutic approach with children and youth is the assumption that development of a healthy self is a critical building block of this adjuvant approach. As a child progresses through the Piagetian stages of growth, they become more equipped cognitively and emotionally to understand the world. In a sense, they progress to look outside themselves for solutions to life's problems or identify or emulate role models as they enter adolescence. Self is developed as a result of interaction with others, either directly or vicariously through reading or media. As a child enters adolescence, social interactions become more complex, as does the necessity of having an increasingly sophisticated problem-solving repertoire to cope with the myriad of challenges facing youth today. As the self develops, a skill that strengthens empathy is referred to as social role taking, that is, the ability to understand a situation from the perspective of someone else. In a sense, this is to know what it is like to walk in someone else's shoes. By embracing literature in the bibliotherapeutic process (guided and monitored), the student looks outside himself or herself for answers, thus internalizing solutions from another's perspective that could then be useful for solving one's own problems. Promoting empathy through identification with a character is a step in the right direction to enhance a student's self-concept and, more important, to develop a psychologically well-adjusted individual who cares not only for himself but for others.

Pardeck and Pardeck (1990) have also identified several positive outcomes of bibliotherapeutic applications inclusive of helping the student become more accepting of his or her problem, developing new solutions to solving a problem, as well as increasing empathic skills by seeing similarities with his or her and others' problems. Universal in reviews and single-study applications of bibliotherapeutic techniques is the generally agreed-upon benefits of greater reading comprehension and an increase in appreciating literature.

Bibliotherapeutic applications have a long and noble history. Emerging as a bona-fide adjuvant therapy in the helping professions of medicine, library science, psychology, and social work in the early to mid-twentieth century, later applications of these procedures were evident with counselors and educators in schools. The psychological underpinnings of the process of bibliotherapy have strong linkages to psychotherapeutic outcomes. It is generally agreed that the process of bibliotherapy was grounded in psychodynamic theory, drawing on stages following identification with the character or story, allowing the reader to relax, knowing that he or she is not alone with a particular problem or life situation. This is the *catharsis* effect; the reader has reason to have hope, thus reducing tension. Next, the reader develops *insight* or an understanding of his or her own motivations or problem-solving skills as a result of this catharsis. Lastly, it is hoped that the reader will apply or *transfer* these insights to measurable behavior that will benefit him or her and others (Brown, 1975, pp. 27–60).

This prevailing psychotherapeutic paradigm dominates the literature and will serve as the focal point because it involves the use of trained bibliotherapists. The psychotherapeutic methodology when applied to educational settings is referred to as psychoeducational techniques. There is evidence that the field of contemporary bibliotherapy suffers from confusion with respect to classification of procedures that fall under the rubric of bibliotherapy, lack of clearly defined dependent measures (e.g., self-concept), and lack of systematic comparative research (Lenkowsky, 1987). Hinseth (1978) provided a case that greater research is needed to determine the psychological precepts from psychological theories other than the psychodynamic model to provide a better match between a particular type of therapy and specific type of bibliotherapy. Thus, although the field of bibliotherapy is evolving like many other disciplines, these empirical growing pains in no way dismiss the rich repository of studies that attest to its impact on children and youth.

CLASSROOM APPLICATIONS SPANNING THE FORMATIVE YEARS

Bibliotherapeutic applications span the K–12 curriculum and are applied to a variety of problems from both a treatment perspective and a preventive stance. Professionals who work with children and youth are well in tune with the fluctuation of children's behavior, especially during the transcendence period of middle school and the challenges that face high school youth. Whether the student's concern is transitory due to social or familial relationships, uncertainties about the future, or coping with a life crisis, all of these are reason to consider the judicious use of bibliotherapy to assist the student in resolving the dilemma. Special needs students who have an established history of social and emotional problems are also prime candidates for benefiting from bibliotherapy applications.

Early school application of guided reading for students has been well articulated for general education students (Russell & Shrodes, 1950) and special needs students (Barbe, 1964). More widespread applications, including manuals with specific strategies (Pardeck & Pardeck, 1984; Rubin, 1978; Schultheis 1972; Schultheis & Pavlik, 1976; Zaccaria, 1978; Zaccaria & Moses, 1968), have been used as well. Increasing evidence in professional journals of bibliotherapeutic applications with special needs populations has documented the growing trend of bibliotherapy. Several authors advocate bibliotherapy with learning disabled students (Gerber & Harris, 1983; Lenkowsky & Lenkowsky, 1978), emotionally disturbed and/or autistic students (D'Alessandro, 1990; Olsen, 1975; Russell & Russell, 1979; Wallick, 1980), and students classified as socially isolated (Nickolai-Mays, 1987). Other special needs applications include enhancement of coping skills for physically impaired students (Hopkins-Best & Wiinamaki, 1985) and blind students (Roberts, 1984). More recently, Adderholdt-Elliot and Eller (1989) have argued for its application with gifted and talented students.

There is mounting evidence for the efficacy of bibliotherapy techniques to help students adjust to life crises, from both a personal and family perspective. Pardeck (1990) recommends the use of the bibliotherapeutic process for both prevention and treatment of adolescent chemical dependency, and Manning and Manning (1984) recommend its use for children whose parents are chemically dependent. Further, evidence exists for its usefulness in helping children cope with home difficulties, such as divorce and separation (Pardeck & Pardeck, 1987; Sheridan, Baker & de Lissovoy, 1984; Winfield, 1983), adjusting to stepfamilies (Coleman & Ganong, 1990), and adjusting to foster care and adoption (Pardeck & Pardeck, 1987), as well as assisting children who have been abused (Pardeck, 1990; Pardeck & Pardeck, 1984; Watson, 1980).

This list illustrates the widespread applicability and usefulness of bibliotherapy procedures as an adjuvant technique designed for implementation by trained bibliotherapists—school librarians, teachers, and counselors. Evidence in the literature mounts as to its ever widening utility as a therapy adjunct to assist students in coping and further developing their character and healthy personalities. Nevertheless, a cautionary note is in order: researchers have found methodological problems with many empirically based studies conducted in both school- and clinic-based sites as well as problems with the conceptual framework that comprises contemporary bibliotherapy (Lenkowsky, 1987; Riordan & Wilson, 1989). Perhaps Ouzts (1991) best summarizes the state of the art by describing bibliotherapy as an emerging discipline. It is not a panacea for all of life's problems that children and adolescents are likely to face. Rather, it is a heuristically rich, psychologically well-grounded, multifaceted set of techniques that has wide applicability as an adjunct therapy useful for librarians, teachers, and counselors. When librarians become trained in the generally accepted procedures that undergird bibliotherapy, they will have a rich and powerful helping tool to guide their day-to-day practice in working with general and special educators, school counselors, and psychologists.

ROLE OF SCHOOL MEDIA SPECIALIST IN STUDENT ASSESSMENT

The field of library science experienced an exponential growth spurt in the 1980s due to the ever-changing advance of technology. With these technological advances came new duties and responsibilities that have placed the school librarian at the hub of the school's information network. The role of the librarian has never been more important than now, and it is likely to grow in importance and status.

Students today carry with them a great deal of stress, emotional problems, and challenges, which may manifest themselves in overt, acting-out behavior or, conversely, withdrawal or sullenness. Psychologists and educators have long known that students will report home and/or community problems to a trusted teacher or other school staff member. The librarian who works with students over multiple years may indeed be the adult to whom the child turns for assistance.

How should the school librarian determine if a particular student has a problem for which bibliotherapy would be beneficial? Brown (1975) suggested discussion with other teachers and school staff, examination of school records, and talking with the student directly or with his or her peer group. Other tips include observation of the student's behavior in multiple school settings, discussion with the student's parents, and examination of written work. Hendrickson (1988) also recommends close collaboration with the student's parents because some thematic topics might be interpreted as controversial; also, there should be full disclosure of the purposes and goals of the bibliotherapy sessions, as well as provision of a list of the book(s) that comprise the curriculum.

For students already identified as needing special educational services, the most efficient means to identify the proper area for beginning bibliotherapy is to contact the student's primary special educator. Recent educational reforms, such as the Regular Education Initiative, integrated mainstreaming, and full inclusion, have created a changing educational theater where the exceptional needs student receives a large amount of his or her education in mainstream, general education settings. These service delivery models are designed to maximize social and instructional opportunities for special needs students while concurrently reducing negative effects often present with special education labels, segregated classrooms, or "pullout" instructional settings. Collaborative relationships with the special educator as a member of a multidisciplinary team are clearly recommended. These joint efforts should be acknowledged and written into the student's individualized education plan (IEP) to value the efforts as well as subject the procedure to monitoring and evaluation.

Another commonly used informal assessment procedure is to develop an incomplete sentence inventory for students. Questions related to school, peers, subject matter, self-esteem, or the act of reading can prove useful as a guidepost to orient the student and bibliotherapist. Another strategy is to have the student fill out a self-esteem inventory. These instruments have proved to be valid and highly reliable when used properly to identify students whose self-concept is low. Several excellent commercially available instruments exist, such as the Self-Esteem Index (Brown & Alexander, 1991) and the Coopersmith Self-Esteem Inventories (Coopersmith, 1981). These instruments are typically administered by the student's special education teacher, school counselor, or school psychologist.

Assessment of students' interests is also important, for it allows the bibliotherapist to make informed starting point decisions. The educator typically uses informal assessment techniques to draw out from the student aspects of his or her home life and goal aspirations. Knowing a student's interests can offer the bibliotherapist insights into the motivational structures that govern a child's behavior. A collaborative effort between the school library specialist and the multidisciplinary team members will facilitate compiling information on a student's interests.

INDIVIDUAL OR GROUP APPLICATIONS

The school librarian must consider whether to use an individual or group bibliotherapeutic approach. Warner (1989) has differentiated the goals of the two approaches. Individual bibliotherapy is prescriptive in nature, designed to ameliorate currently identified problems for a student. The more common use of bibliotherapeutic approaches, however, is the group approach, which is best thought of as preventive (Warner, 1989). In this way, age is the determinant to pinpoint common developmental problems, which are then addressed through the use of selected novels or other literature, following generally agreed-upon bibliotherapeutic steps to process the material. From a psychological perspective, it is best to implement preventive bibliotherapeutic approaches prior to the age when students are likely to confront certain problems. The choice of an individual or group approach will be determined by the need and the goals teachers and counselors are trying to accomplish. The school librarian helps the special educator or counselor to select appropriate materials. In this way, he or she serves as an expert to discuss the merits of certain literature for a designated problem, incorporating such factors as ethnicity, socioeconomic status, gender, and disability into the selection decision. In group applications, the school librarian should feel quite comfortable in conducting group bibliotherapeutic applications from a preventive stance in concert with other school personnel.

CONDUCTING BIBLIOTHERAPY SESSIONS

Bibliotherapy is often referred to as the right book for the right student at the right time (Bodart, 1980). Once the school librarian has collaborated with colleagues and pinpointed a thematic area to pursue, the next step is to select an appropriate book to address the topic. A requirement inherent in this selection is that the librarian has read it in its entirety and evaluated its appropriateness for the individual or group. This point is vital to prevent problems of mismatch of topic, complexity of reading level, and students' ability and socioemotional needs. Additionally, the librarian must know the student or students for whom the material is selected.

Next, the librarian must decide on format—individual or group. Probably the task demands of the librarian preclude an individual approach to bibliotherapy. Typically, the low-risk intervention of the group approach is well suited for public school applications, for it obviates concerns regarding the "therapy" interpretation for an individual student. In addition, group applications offer the distinct advantage of high-yield payoff by allowing a large number of students to develop improved coping skills while at the same time enhancing reading satisfaction.

Group size varies depending on the age and maturity of the students, as well as the expressed goals of the bibliotherapy topic. Typically groups of three to five are recommended for younger children and groups of six to eight for adolescents. Overly shy children or those with poorly developed social skills might benefit from a buddy system pairing rather than a typical small group. Success with a friend is a sensible way to build a student's confidence while accomplishing goals of the bibliotherapy sessions. After a shy or socially unskilled student has success in a buddy pairing, the librarian should consider placement in a larger grouping.

Third, a decision must be made if the students will read the book themselves or have the book read to them. The developmental needs of the students primarily dictate the reading method. Once this is decided, the librarian will need to determine the number of sessions to accomplish this task. Each student in the group must have a copy of the book. Whether the book is read in its entirety initially or broken into many sessions over several weeks, time is a judgment call based on the age of the student(s), thematic content, reading difficulty, and length of the book. It is likely also that some students may have difficulty with the reading level of the book. In such a case, the librarian should provide steps to assist the student—that is, simplified vocabulary, structured outlines, and other remedial reading techniques. Collaboration with the exceptional educator or reading specialist will prove useful in this respect.

Fourth, and critical to the bibliotherapeutic process, are the feedback sessions. Here the student is provided the opportunity to explore feelings generated by identifying with the character(s) and outcomes of their actions. Critical in this exchange with the students is the determination of whether the student could relate the themes of the book with his or her real-life situation. Probing and thought-provoking questions by the bibliotherapist are used to draw out from the student his or her understanding of the material, if he or she can relate or identify with the struggles of the characters or the resolution of the story. If the librarian determines that the student is not understanding the relationships, other media and approaches can be used to facilitate the student's understanding. In conducting group processing sessions, the bibliotherapist should be sensitive to each student's emotional makeup and ask questions equally of all students in the group so that no one feels left out or overburdened. Pardeck and Pardeck (1990) suggest applying principles of cooperative learning to conduct group developmental literature sessions for promoting reading enhancement while facilitating the social-emotional development of children. (Information about cooperative learning is available in Chapter 11.)

Supplemental tasks to augment processing of the material could include group projects, such as a group collage, writing projects, such as a script followed by a short performance, or even a videotape interpretation of the book enacted through the students' point of view. Art, puppetry, and dramatic expression are potentially useful feedback supplements for elementary age children when conducting feedback sessions (Hendrickson, 1988). Supplemental activities are useful for promoting group cohesion while allowing for a nonthreatening forum for individual students to explore their feelings on potentially sensitive topics. Should the librarian determine at any time during the feedback sessions that a student has significant problems in need of professional intervention, he or she should contact the student's teacher or counselor to ensure a multidisciplinary approach to assist the student in resolving the conflict. It is possible that the bibliotherapeutic group might serve as a forum for a student to disclose a significant family or mental health problem. If that should happen, the utmost privacy to protect the student and his or her family and a timely disclosure with appropriate school personnel are required.

EVALUATION OF STUDENTS: AUTHENTIC ASSESSMENT

The primary purposes of bibliotherapy are to increase the student's satisfaction with reading, enhance his or her understanding of feelings through the shared reading experience, and prepare some students for further discussion with qualified therapists (Chatton, 1988). At the close of the sessions, the bibliotherapist assesses whether the specified goals were accomplished. The form in Figure 6.1 can be used to summarize student participation.

The bibliotherapist and student can use the form in Figure 6.2 to engage in a conference (Wesson & King, in press). The student has a chance to reflect on his or her enjoyment and effort, thereby promoting a greater sense of internal responsibility for his or her actions. The bibliotherapist compiles a permanent record of student growth while increasing the bonding between the student and himself or herself, as well as valuing the act of reading.

MATERIALS: LISTS TO GET STARTED

Librarians are well advised to use *The Book Finder* as a means to pinpoint a potential area to conduct a bibliotherapy session. *The Book Finder*, a compilation of children's literature that addresses the problems and developmental needs of children over the age of two, can be used as a selection

Figure 6.1
Sample Bibliotherapy Session Monitoring Form

Student: ______________________________

Date: ______________________________

Title: ______________________________

Page(s): ______________________________

Content	Comments
• prepared: student read material	
• asked questions	
• participated in group discussion	
• understood literal meaning of text	
• related to one or more characters: actions	
• related to one or more characters: feelings	
• related themes of selection to his/her own life experiences	
• enjoyed reading the text	

guide (Dreyer, 1989). To date, there has not been a uniformly agreed upon method by which to organize various childhood and adolescent topics (developmental needs, problems, etc.). For example, one recent catalog lists over sixty major topics suitable for bibliotherapy applications (Paperbacks for Educators, 1994). A sample from this listing includes topics on adoption, caring, cooperation, family illness, feelings and self-awareness, friendships, learning differences, school problems, self-esteem, social behavior, and teens' problems. Ouzts (1991) compiled an extensive list suitable for school applications inclusive of such topics as AIDS, absent fathers, death, disabilities, Down's syndrome, families, racial issues, and sibling rivalry (Ouzts, 1991, p. 203).

Other avenues exist as well by which to gather materials to begin a bibliotherapy application. Let us assume that the bibliotherapist has narrowed the topic to special education. Issues related to disabled children that are applicable for both disabled and nondisabled peers are often compiled

Figure 6.2
Sample Bibliotherapy Student Self-Reflection Form

Date: ______________________________

Student: ______________________________

Title: ______________________________

- Things I learned from reading this selection:

- The character(s) I related to best were:

- Things I am still not sure about or want more information about:

- I would rate my overall effort as:
- I would like to read another selection by the author: yes___ no___
- I would like to read another selection on this topic: yes___ no___

by national, state, and local organizations. One exciting development is the National Resource Library, recently described in the newsletter of the National Center for Youth with Disabilities: "The National Resource Library brings together comprehensive sources of information related to adolescents, disability, and transition. The easily accessible database contains four files: Bibliography, Programs, Training Materials, Technical Assistance" (*Connections*, 1993, p. 10). Many of the newly published materials use a combination of reading materials and optional video accompaniments.

An example of mining state resources comes from materials compiled by the Wisconsin Council on Developmental Disabilities. A list of books by Robert Perske (1992) that addresses various dimensions of exceptionality is provided; an example is embodied in the description of one of Perske's books, *Circles of Friends*: "This collection offers true stories and issues to ponder concerning friendships between people with disabilities and so-called normal people. These friendships cut across age groups, generations and races, enriching the hearts and world views of the friends" (Wisconsin Council on Developmental Disabilities). In a similar vein, Horning (1992) of Children's Services of the Madison Public Library has compiled an excellent list of books featuring fiction and nonfiction stories focusing on children and adults with exceptional needs. The list is divided into books suitable for children in grades K–3 and 4–6. By examining the area of exceptionality and disability, it is hoped that the reader will utilize resources from various outlets to gather appropriate materials for bibliotherapy applications. This listing is meant to demonstrate that excellent resources exist outside traditionally accessible avenues, but it in no way exhausts materials on this topic.

CONCLUSION

In using individually based bibliotherapeutic approaches, the school media specialist serves as a thematic expert in selecting appropriate material, working in concert with fellow school professionals, that is, the school counselor or special education teacher. This is not to say that the school library media specialist cannot do individually guided bibliotherapeutic interventions; rather, the problem is the competing task and time demands. As such, it is recommended that considerable attention be given to using group-based bibliotherapy applications that are best thought of as preventive in nature. The application of these procedures is important in that the school library media specialist can address the difficult stresses children and adolescents experience during the developmental years with pragmatic strategies. When they are properly and judiciously applied, students will likely experience psychological and emotional well-being in a trusting bond of humanistic caring that will better equip them for the challenges that lay before them.

REFERENCES

Adderholdt-Elliott, M., & Eller, S. H. (1989). Counseling students who are gifted through bibliotherapy. *Teaching Exceptional Children 22*(1): 26–31.

Barbe, W. B. (1964, April). Meeting the needs of exceptional children. *Education 84*:476–479.

Berry, F. M. (1978). Toward a research basis for the distinction between educational/humanistic and clinical modes of bibliotherapy. In M. Monroe (Ed.), *Seminar on bibliotherapy; proceedings of sessions* (pp. 1–23). Madison, WI: Library School, University of Wisconsin–Madison.

Bodart, J. (1980). Bibliotherapy: The right book for the right person at the right time—And more! *Top of the News, 36*(2): 183–188.

Brown, E. F. (1975). *Bibliotherapy and its widening applications*. Metuchen, NJ: Scarecrow Press.

Brown, L., & Alexander, J. (1991). *Self-esteem index*. Austin: PRO-ED.

Calhoun, G. (1987). Enhancing self-perception through bibliotherapy. *Adolescence, 22*(88): 939–943.

Chatton, B. (1988). Apply with caution: Bibliotherapy in the library. *Journal of Youth Services in Libraries 1*(3): 334–338.

Coleman, M., & Ganong, L. H. (1990). The uses of juvenile fiction and self-help books with stepfamilies. *Journal of Counseling and Development, 68*(3): 327–331.

Coopersmith, S. (1981). *Coopersmith self-esteem inventories*. Palo Alto, CA: Consulting Psychologists Press.

D'Alessandro, M. D. (1990). Accommodating emotionally handicapped children through a literature-based reading program. *Reading Teacher 44*(4): 288–293.

Dreyer, S. S. (1989). *The book finder*. Circle Pines, MN: American Guidance Service.

Gerber, P. J., & Harris, K. B. (1983). Using juvenile literature to develop social skills in learning disabled children. *Pointer 27*(4): 29–32.

Hendrickson, L. B. (1988). The "right" book for the child in distress. *School Library Journal 34*(8): 40–41.

Hinseth, L. (1978). Relation of bibliotherapy to psychiatric theory. In M. Monroe (Ed.), *Seminar on bibliotherapy; proceedings of sessions* (pp. 31–56). Madison, WI: Library School, University of Wisconsin–Madison.

Hopkins-Best, M., & Wiinamaki, M. (1985). Bibliotherapy for disabled students in school-to-work transition. *Techniques, 1*(6) 490–496:

Horning, K. T. (1992). *Bibliography: Recent books featuring children and some adults with disabilities*. Madison, WI: Children's Services, Madison Public Library.

Lenkowsky, R. S. (1987). Bibliotherapy: A review and analysis of the literature. *Journal of Special Education 21*: 123–130.

Lenkowsky, B., & Lenkowsky, R. S. (1978). Bibliotherapy for the learning disabled adolescent. *Academic Therapy* 14(2), 179–185.

Manning, D. T., & Manning, B. (1984). Bibliotherapy for children of alcoholics. *Journal of Reading 27*(8): 720–725.

Nickolai-Mays, S. (1987). Bibliotherapy and the socially isolated adolescent. *School Counselor*, 17–21.

Olsen, H. D. (1975). Bibliotherapy to help children solve problems. *Elementary School Journal 75*(7): 422–429.

Ouzts, D. T. (1991). The emergence of bibliotherapy as a discipline. *Reading Horizons 31*(3): 199–206.

Paperbacks for Educators. (1994). *Bibliotherapy for children and teens catalog*. Washington, MO: Author.

Pardeck, J. A., & Pardeck, J. T. (1984). *Young people with problems: A guide to bibliotherapy*. Westport, CT: Greenwood Press.

Pardeck, J. T. (1990). Children's literature and child abuse. *Child Welfare 69*(1): 83–88.

Pardeck, J. T., & Pardeck, J. A. (1987). Using bibliotherapy to help children cope with the changing family. *Social Work in Education 9*: 107–116.

———. (1990). Using developmental literature with collaborative groups. *Reading Improvement* 27(4): 226–237.

Perske, R. (1992). *Circles of friends*. Nashville: Abingdon Press.

Riordan, R. J., & Wilson, L. S. (1989). Bibliotherapy: Does it work? *Journal of Counseling and Development* 67: 506–508.

Roberts, A. (1984). Bibliotherapy: A technique for counseling blind people. *Journal of Visual Impairment and Blindness* 78(5): 197–199.

Rubin, R. J. (1978). *Bibliotherapy: A guide to theory and practice*. Phoenix: Oryx Press.

Russell, W. A., & Russell, A. E. (1979). Using bibliotherapy with emotionally disturbed children. *Teaching Exceptional Children* 11(4): 168–169.

Russell, W. A., & Shrodes, C. (1950). Contributions of research in bibliotherapy to the language arts program. *School Review* 58(3): 335–342, 411–420.

Schultheis, M. (1972). *A guidebook for bibliotherapy*. Glenview, IL: Psychotechnics.

Schultheis, M., & Pavlik, R. (1976). *Classroom teacher's manual for bibliotherapy*. Fort Wayne, IN: Benet Learning Center.

Sheridan, J. T., Baker, S. B., & de Lissovoy, V. (1984). Structured group counseling and explicit bibliotherapy as in-school strategies for preventing problems in youth of changing families. *School Counselor* 32(2): 134–141.

Staff. (1993). *Connections. The newsletter of the National Center for Youth with Disabilities* 4(2): 10.

Wallick, M. M. (1980). An autistic child and books. *Top of the News*, 37(1): 69–77.

Warner, M. (1989). Bibliotherapy: Two sides to the coin. *School Library Media Activities Monthly*, 6(3): 34–36.

Watson, J. (1980). Bibliotherapy for abused children. *School Counselor* 27(3), 294–298.

Wesson, C. L., & King, R. P. (in press). Portfolio assessment for the exceptional education classroom. *Teaching Exceptional Children*.

Winfield, E. T. (1983). Relevant reading for adolescents: Literature and divorce. *Journal of Reading*: 26(5): 408–411.

Zaccaria, J. S. (1978). *Bibliotherapy in rehabilitation, educational and mental health settings: Theory, research, and practice*. Champaign, IL: Stipes.

Zaccaria, J. S., & Moses, H. A. (1968). *Facilitating human development through reading: The use of bibliotherapy in teaching and counseling*. Champaign, IL: Stipes.

7 Accessibility of School Library Materials for Special Needs Students

William J. Murray

The built environment is one of many influences in the ongoing development of human behavior and is well reviewed in the environmental psychology literature (Gump, 1987; Moore, Tuttle & Howell, 1985; Sommer, 1969; Wohlwill & Weisman, 1981). Several common themes run through this literature and over time have taken on significance as emerging environment-behavior theories: transactional perspectives (Oxley, Haggard, Werner & Altman, 1986), phenomenological perspectives (Seamon, 1982), and interactional perspectives (Kaplan, 1983; Wicker, 1972). Transactionalists believe phenomena are made up of people and their psychological processes, the environment, and time, and thus should be studied as inseparable, holistic, and temporally related events. Phenomenologists attempt to separate themselves from all preconceptions, prejudices, and commonsense notions and to view the phenomenon as it is "in itself." Interactionalists look at a phenomenon in terms of its component parts, regardless of their function within the larger universal context. While much of this work justifiably seeks to point out the seeming indifference that has traditionally been paid to the built environment (Bednar & Haviland, 1969; Moore et al., 1985), an equally important but far less common cry is that which will be discussed in this chapter: the relative indifference given to the abilities of different types of users to function adequately in an environment designed for the fiftieth percentile man.

Social scientists have long been interested in the physical setting in which our lives transpire and have helped bring innovative solutions to difficult problems. Inaccessible, unequal, and poorly designed environments helped spur the advent of the independent living movement (Lifchez, 1987; Zola, 1982), which has brought new meaning to the cooperative efforts of social scientists and architects, with all society benefiting from an increasingly accessible world. Examples of the unforgiving demands of the fiftieth percentile run rampant in daily life and have often become the basis for action. Airplane seats that are too confining, restaurants that claim to be accessible (after the individual gets up one small stair), or shelves that are just out of reach are examples of the frustrations brought about by this world.

In the last twenty years, there has been a significant amount of literature looking at issues pertaining to the design of specialized settings for persons with a wide variety of disabilities. Perhaps one of the most thought provoking of these is the book *Rethinking Architecture* (Lifchez, 1987). Lifchez and the other authors challenge those in the design profession to extend their thinking from architecture as a source of aesthetic pleasure to that of architecture as a functional tool, usable by *all* people. Too often the design process is guided not by the needs or abilities of future consumers but by societal trends, personal interests, and a subjective sense of aesthetics.

The term *built environment* is often used interchangeably with the term *physical environment,* which can be defined as "that set consisting of those things (building materials, furniture, plumbing, elevators, etc.) and those conditions (the environmental variables—space, sound, temperature, color, texture, light and shape) which make up our spaces and buildings for human habitation" (Bednar & Haviland, 1972, p. 1). While humans are simultaneously part of a multitude of environments (the social environment, the psychological or emotional environment, and the cultural environment, to name a few), the influence of the physical environment is often neglected, for several reasons. One is that people adapt quite easily to new surroundings, and even the most uncomfortable of settings gradually "grow" on people. This adaptability may contribute to the design of inaccessible environments, since designers historically have not been required to think of the needs of those who fall outside the norm, and until recently, disabled persons have not strongly advocated for change (Shapiro, 1993). Another reason is that the sensation of environmental overload is often experienced (Milgram, 1970)—that is, an individual's inability to accept incoming environmental stimuli because they are either too numerous or come too rapidly. Finally, there exist so many environments in any situation that it is difficult to separate out the influence of the physical environment from the others (Bednar & Haviland, 1969).

This complex relationship between the built environment and human behavior has come to include disciplines beyond that of the design professionals and social scientists. Problems that face society require multidisciplinary approaches that ensure a comprehensive analysis; without such rigor, past failures will be recreated. An interdisciplinary approach helps ensure success.

INFORMATION ACCESSIBILITY

The school library media center is a central place where children partake in a quest for knowledge. Thomas (1986) argues that society must struggle to continue this quest for information and promote it as a viable resource that can help ensure children's success: "Our future, as a city, a state, a nation, and a society, depends on what we do to meet the challenge of providing a quality education for children and youth" (p. 77). The integration of special needs students into modern society—and many of them often fail to meet the standards of the fiftieth percentile—requires a commitment toward ensuring that information is accessible. Accessibility is achieved through research and the application of the findings. One research study presents a large collection of information pertaining to physically disabled people and their needs in libraries (Velleman, 1979). Much of the information is designed to enhance awareness on the part of society, to enable a greater understanding of the problems disabled people face. Consciousness raising is also dealt with by Sorenson (1988), who discusses methods by which librarians can begin to provide more sensitive services to users with disabilities. Strom (1977) looks at the role of the school library in the education of disabled children, not only from a needs perspective but also through the eyes of an individual who gives a personal story about the accessibility problems faced in libraries. Bennett (1974) describes a library environment where disabled people can go without being judged; personal choices can be made, and an individual can exert control over what happens. This type of setting can foster increased confidence and self-esteem and provide for a meeting and social setting where friendships can be made and interactions can take place.

While discussing the value of libraries as supplemental learning environments of segregated educational settings, Bennett (1974) describes two roles for the library: the library as an environment where integrated education occurs within a community context and a place where families are able to appreciate that which their children are learning and participate in the educational process. Although the author is discussing public libraries, both of these roles seem to be appropriate models for school libraries also. The school library can be a place where children are able to integrate, even within segregated school environments. It can be a place where children with and without special needs can come together and stereotypes can be broken. Nondisabled children, walking into the school library, see students with disabilities working with learning tools (a computer perhaps), and this creates a situation in which the two children may interact on an equal level, without the baggage that accompanies stereotypes. This emphasis on awareness will be carried through this chapter, for without increasing society's understanding of what disability entails, no significant change can be effected.

ARCHITECTURAL PLANNING

Architects must be willing to take the responsibility of including those who may be affected by change. Planning and design should be a participatory process during which broadly defined concepts begin to take on new forms, and the participants in the process learn about the needs of a setting's inhabitants beyond those of their own discipline. This helps facilitate increased awareness and allows the participants to move beyond their predispositions toward a more integrated solution. In reference to this practice in architecture, Thrun (1988) defines this as a "cooperative process of discovery," which "begins with qualitative information and progressively becomes more quantitative" (p. 67). This narrowing of information from the qualitative to the quantitative is an accurate description; however, the emphasis must lie in the cooperative nature of the discovery process. An interdisciplinary analysis of a problem exposes the needs and opinions of each discipline in an accurate, firsthand manner so that the resulting outcome is both quantitatively measurable and qualitatively pleasing.

Library planning should not be the sole province of the librarian, nor should it be the esoteric domain of the architect. Like other problems, an interdisciplinary approach must be taken so as to devise a plan that suits the needs of all involved. And in looking at the requirements of special needs children, it is imperative that persons who work within the educational system confer with those who are skilled in the planning of functionally and aesthetically pleasing spaces. The role of the architect in the design of accessible library materials goes beyond that of merely designing an aesthetically pleasing and barrier-free environment. A responsible architect will also offer to participate in the selection of appropriate furniture, color schemes, and other needs that the librarian notes during the planning stages.

INTERDISCIPLINARY PLANNING

To create a library for special needs students, the architect, the librarian or library staff, and students of diverse abilities should be participants in the planning process. The involvement of users in the design planning process is not new (Sanoff, 1988), but it is not consistently sought out by the architectural practitioner. Myller (1966) suggests that the close cooperation of the librarian and the architect may result in a more comprehensive understanding of the needs of the library, resulting in a successful setting.

Architects are problem solvers; they incorporate as many wishes and desires of the other participants as inexpensively as possible. A well-trained professional can help create an environment that is functional, meets the needs of the users, and is aesthetically pleasing. The selection of an architect is an important part of the design process, and Martin (1992) suggests several criteria to consider when selecting an architect: formal requests for information on previous work to assess the qualifications of the architectural firm, using a multidisciplinary selection team (these might include an experienced city building official and a representative from the city council, as well as representatives from the school board), and visiting at least one completed building that the firm was responsible for creating.

The role of the librarian or library staff is also well defined. The librarian must provide the architect with the information required to create a functional and pleasant environment. As Thrun (1988) notes, it is important that the librarian approach the planning process with a reasonable wish list that includes not only the essential items (space allocations for each department, furniture items needed, etc.) but also items that may help facilitate a creative learning center. The librarian must be prepared to discuss the needs of students in terms of specific abilities and disabilities and from an organizational and institutional perspective (e.g., what are the goals of the educational system for the school library?). The librarian and library staff know the children better than the professional architect does and may serve as mediator between these groups. Finally, librarians who have visited other libraries—both successful and unsuccessful—can more precisely state those features that are desirable, as well as those that are undesirable.

The special needs students' role in the planning process is much like that of the librarian, although they have the added informal responsibility of environmental consultant, for it is their educational, social, physical, and emotional needs and desires that must be accommodated above all others. Creative methods have been used to elicit information from children, and the architect is wise to survey this literature prior to sitting down to talk with the children. It is also important that the professional not view students as "token" participants in this process and then disregard their input and design whatever he or she feels is best. The role of the students is real and their ideas invaluable. For example, they can express their ideas of choice and control within the environment. Special needs students' lives are often filled with decisions that are made by others, and if given the opportunity to effect significant change in their own surroundings, a skill is taught that the student will carry through to adulthood. The architect should incorporate the valuable ideas of the special needs students into the design scheme.

The result of this participatory design process is the creation of a new environment with the best fit between the designers and the users. It is this fit toward which designers strive, for an accessible environment meets the needs of all children and users of the school library, not only special needs students. Accessible design provides an environment that allows greater interaction between all people who enter it and the environment itself. An excellent example, and one often cited, is the functional use of ramps. They provide physical access to a setting and are easy for all people to use; many nondisabled persons use the ramp when the choice exists (especially if pushing a cart or baby carriage). Within a school library, simple accessibility modifications may enhance the use of that environment for all persons.

THE DESIGN PROCESS

The creation of an architecturally accessible environment starts with several predesign stages. Architects refer to this process as programming, which involves the collection and subsequent processing of all information relevant to the facility type. "The facility designer and his or her client, confronted with the goal of producing a functional, durable, appealing and economical facility, must recognize the vast quantity and complexity of data required to achieve it" (Palmer, 1981, p. 3). The translation of these data into a form that designers can use to make decisions is the programming process. Preiser (1985) defines programming as "the process that elicits and systematically translates the mission and objectives of an organization, group or individual into integrated activity-personnel-equipment relationships, thereby resulting in an efficient, functional building or facility" (p. 1). Silverstein and Jacobson (1985) strongly advocate for the programmed environment; they state that programs can

> communicate rather complex issues by boiling them down to their consequences and showing possible environments that people can feel and understand. This means that architectural programs, if they are carefully drawn from deeply felt, real human problems, can of their own power help bring into being the very life they are designed to support: a good program not only defines a new building type, it fuels people's desire to build it. (p. 158)

Farbstein (1985) proposes a five-stage programming process:

1. *Literature review.* A survey of research findings and standard professional practices can help focus the direction of the programming process.
2. *User descriptions.* A thorough understanding of the potential users is the key to a user-oriented programming process. All potential users, the organizational goals, the cultural backgrounds of the users, and the projection of future needs are some of the pieces of information that may be required.
3. *Performance criteria.* The amount of space required for each user need should be calculated, along with projected circulation patterns, security considerations, and so forth.
4. *Program options and costs.* Options must be evaluated in terms of costs versus aesthetic requirements, functional needs, and other factors. Needs must be communicated to the designer at this time.
5. *Space specification.* A summary sheet helps the client evaluate the designer's recommendations by specifying the client's desired performance for the facility.

This process is a way to facilitate communication among designers, library managers or personnel, and the eventual users of the site—all students, including the special needs students. Information fuels this process, and many questions must be asked during the programming period. One way to come to the answers to these questions is by using the programming process. Programming is the first part of a cyclical design-evaluation process. After construction and occupation, the building is evaluated, and this information is fed back into the programming process, resulting in better design and construction that provides for the most appropriate fit between the users of the setting (library staff, children, parents, etc.) and the environment. The strength of evaluative research lies in the cooperation among designers, researchers, and the users of the setting. During the evaluation phase of the programming cycle, the designers' decisions and intentions are made explicit and can be translated into testable hypotheses. Perhaps the strongest result of this cooperation is that the people who work together to test these hypotheses gain new insights into the other participants' disciplines and learn new ways to attack problems. Each participant uses the other individuals to improve his or her own skills and in so doing enriches the design process. Farbstein's programming or planning process fits into the design-evaluation cycle (Figure 7.1).

DIFFERENT TYPES OF ACCESSIBILITY

Accessibility is a threefold concept that encompasses architectural accessibility, psychological accessibility, and programmatic accessibility. Architectural accessibility is rather simple if one views it conceptually: if one is able to gain access to a site, it is accessible. This image is challenged by Davis and Lifchez (1987), who argue that accessibility is not simply a matter of physical admittance to a site but a quality of experience: "How one feels about a place, how one interprets it, or even whether one can adequately interpret it—these are all less quantifiable, but crucially important, aspects of accessibility" (p. 40). Access has different meanings to different people; a physically disabled person might be able to gain access to a site, but a visually or mentally disabled person may have significant difficulty moving about that same location. The question then must be rephrased: "To whom is the environment accessible?" This leads to the second form of accessibility— psychological accessibility.

Lucas and Karrenbrock (1983) briefly discuss the notion of psychological accessibility when discussing materials access and the response of library staff to children with disabilities. An atmosphere of empathy and understanding is encouraged. The attitudes toward children with disabilities in the school library reflect society's feelings about their disabilities and their future potential. It is important that the library environment be designed in response to the special needs of the children using the setting, rather than

Figure 7.1
The Programming–Design–Evaluation Cycle

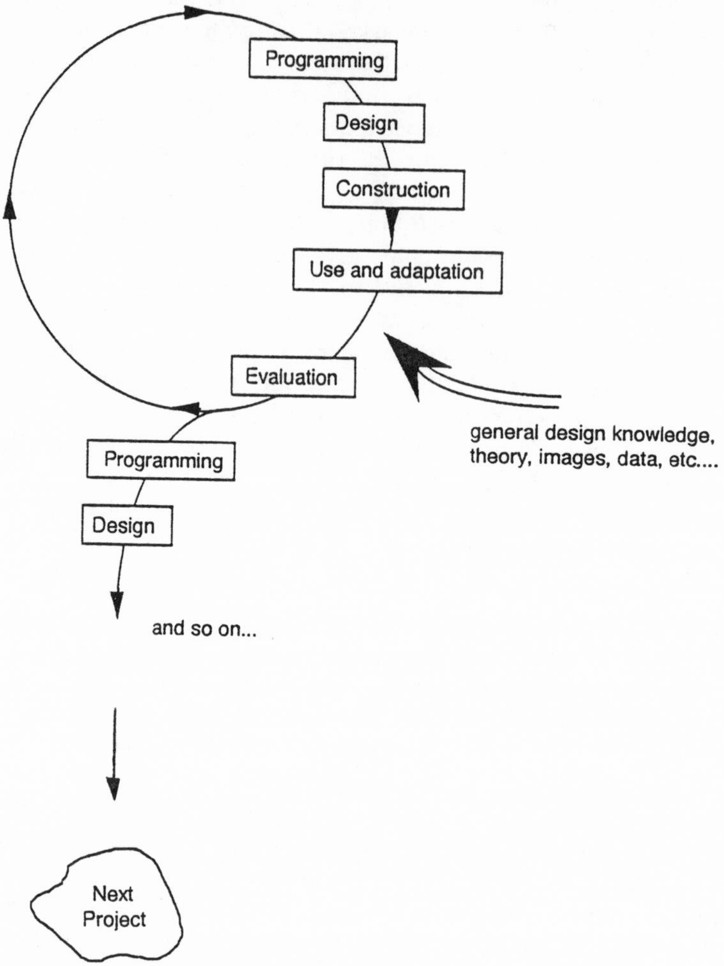

Source: Adapted From Zeisel, 1981, p. 36.

the requirements of the librarian or other school staff. One way to obtain this information is from the children themselves.

User participation is not a new method in architectural practice, although only a small percentage of architects feel that it is time well spent (Gordon & Stubbs, 1988). Due to the nature of the diverse disabilities present in a school that includes special needs students, it is likely that the opinions and needs of the students are often overlooked, for several reasons. Among these are the well-meaning but perhaps ill-placed intentions of the school staff and the feeling among some staff that "they know what's best" (Vanderburgh, 1983).

The third type of accessibility is programmatic accessibility. This term refers to legislative efforts targeting increased access to all environments (e.g., the Americans with Disabilities Act of 1990), as well as modifications that can occur within a setting to increase access to materials—for example, the use of computer technology and related modifications that encourage greater and easier access to information and the development of special programs that encourage integrated relationships among all users of the library system (Baskin & Harris, 1982; Lucas & Karrenbrock, 1983; Velleman, 1979; Wright, 1982). The impact of this type of access is significant and should be incorporated into all programming processes. Fortunately, with the standardization of many accessibility requirements and the proposed integration of educational needs (Stainback & Stainback, 1989), this type of accessibility should no longer be problematic. This leaves the former two, which again lead back to issues of environment-behavior cooperation.

These three categories may be linked to a larger categorical framework that provides guidance to the planning and design process for all settings that seek to provide users with an enhanced environmental "experience." This framework is provided by Ahrentzen (in press), who proposes an environment-behavior model with four environmental domains: the physical setting, the activities that occur in that setting, the social context, and the resulting environmental experience that culminates from a combination of these three domains (Figure 7.2).

EXPERIENTIAL QUALITIES OF THE ENVIRONMENT

The "experience" one has when entering a setting greatly determines the likelihood of recurrent visits to that site. This experience has been referred to as both the attributes of the environment (Weisman, 1981) and the experiential qualities of the setting (Ahrentzen, in press). Both terms refer to the "more enduring qualities of interdependence that can arise between people and places" (in Ahrentzen, in press). As Ahrentzen notes, "They are the social constructions of the intermingling of built forms and people; they are the product of the transaction between the setting's physical environment, activities, and the social context" (p. 3). People are often first struck by the characteristics of a setting—the crowd in a concert, the solace of a cathedral, or the energy of a sporting event, rather than the individual characteristics of the setting they have entered. These experiential qualities are the result of three interdependent areas: the physical characteristics of the setting, the individuals who make up the setting within a larger social context, and the activities that occur in that setting. For instance, in a school library that serves all children, including those with special needs, the "experience" that the setting may afford the users is composed of the built

Figure 7.2
Model Illustrating the Experiential Qualities of the Environment

Individual
Social
Organizational
Institutional

SOCIAL CONTEXT

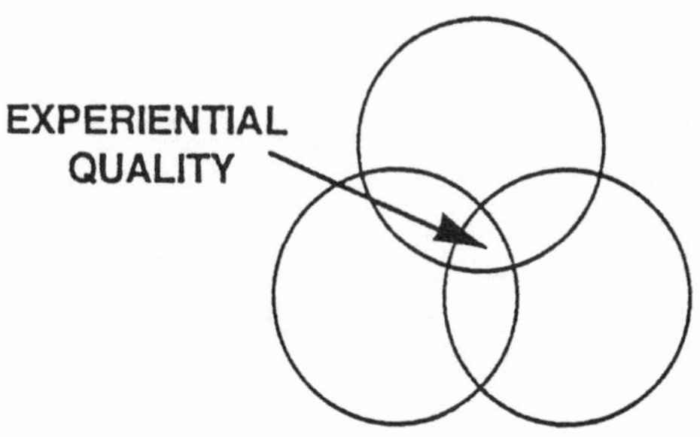

ACTIVITY
Type
Temporal, Procedural
Symbolic Characteristics

PHYSICAL CHARACTERISTICS
Spatial Organization
Communication Systems
Semifixed Feature Amenities
Ambient Properties
Architectonic Details

Source: Ahrentzen, in press.

environment (the physical structure housing the library), the social context (individual characteristics of the users as well as the larger organizational philosophies and institutional goals), and the activities of the users (children, teachers, library personnel, and parents, engaged in the everyday roles they play). In order to plan for this setting in the most effective manner, it is necessary to investigate and understand the relationships between these areas—how they interact with one another.

The model presented in Figure 7.2 serves to create several questions regarding the relationships of these three domains as related to the school library for all children, including those with special needs. Within each of the domains, the following are but a few of the numerous questions and research hypotheses that can be generated from this framework:

Physical Variables

- What are the architectonic features that aid in defining the most accessible environment?
- Which architectural features of the library seem to possess positive images for the students? Which seem negative? How do these relate to their behavior?
- How do physical manipulations of the environment affect library staff–student interactions? What about study patterns and ease of movement throughout the facility?

Social Context Variables

- How do opportunities for control and interaction within the library environment relate to students' satisfaction with that environment? How is library staff control related to student satisfaction or empowerment?
- Are materials easily accessed by those who want them? If not, are staff resources available to help?

Activity Variables

- How closely does staff and student behavior correlate with their verbal statements on use of the environment?
- Where do staff and students spend their time, and what are they doing?
- What role does student habit and routine within the library have in transforming "space" into "place"?

Experiential Qualities Variables

- How do staff and student interpretations of their environment differ? How does this relate to student independence and accessibility of materials?
- How do staff and student interpretations of their environment interact with one another to create a positive environment? Do they try? Do they believe it is necessary?
- How does one assess issues of meaning in students with a wide variety of special needs?

The development of questions of this sort during the programming phase helps to fill in several of the steps in the programming model detailed by Farbstein (1985). When the architect has devised a plan that meets the needs of the librarian and students, the planning phase is over, and it is time to begin the design and construction phases. The answers generated by the above questions (and others like them) provide a basic guideline by which to design. They are not inclusive, nor should they be viewed as the only way to solve a problem. There are a number of solutions to any single design problem, and for that reason it is difficult to prescribe a set of design guidelines to follow. However, understanding this limitation, there are several general principles that may be appropriate to the design process of school libraries for students with special needs.

DESIGN GUIDELINES

Goldsmith (1979) provides a comprehensive guidebook for the design of special schools for physically disabled children, and he looks at several areas, including the gymnasium, therapy rooms, bathrooms, and the school library. Design guidebooks appear often in the architectural and environmental psychology literature; another is Moore and Cohen's (1977) guidelines that provide behaviorally based design principles for the creation of outdoor environments for special needs students. Moss and Pace (1981) provide a guide for the renovation and construction of libraries serving visually impaired and physically disabled persons, and in a dated yet somewhat useful resource, Brown (1971) gives an overview that looks at various disability types and the importance of providing accessible and usable library services for all people. Myller (1966) also provides several excellent design recommendations for a library planning committee to consider. And, in a doctoral dissertation completed in 1979, Veatch discusses a comprehensive study that resulted in the compilation of a series of design guidelines to facilitate the design of public libraries for all people. Many of these recommendations are useful for the planning of school libraries, as well as for the goal of integrated education. Design should accommodate the needs of all persons, not just a specific group. The guidelines that follow are a culmination of information from references listed throughout this chapter, including many from the architectural research literature.

Image and Orientation

Many children who experience some type of disability are unable to comprehend a spatial "whole"—that is, their cognition of the environment as an interconnected set of spaces is difficult (Cruikshank, 1967). Children with special needs may also have difficulty navigating through an environment, not only because of physical limitations but because various parts of the environment may be remarkably alike. Bednar and Haviland (1969) state that each time a child with a disability enters a room, he or she may experience it as a completely new setting; thus, it is important to allow for maximum environmental marking to facilitate orientation and wayfinding. Differentiation of the environment facilitates an individual's ability to navigate throughout a setting.

The environment of the school library should possess clearly imaged orientation, facilitated through signage, differentiation of materials, and a simple floor plan.

Architectural Differentiation

Often an individual's capacity to navigate a setting is determined not by the placement of signage but rather through the location of other familiar objects in the setting. For instance, the location of the staircase, a picture window, posters of favorite cartoon characters, or plants can facilitate an increased awareness of where one is in a setting. These types of features help differentiate one space or area from another and can be a significant addition to a thorough signage system.

Color can also be an effective method of teaching discrimination skills to the special needs student (Fowler, Rowbury, Nordyke & Baer, 1976). The use of a consistent color pattern within distinct sections of the library aids the student in finding the section of the library for which he or she is looking. Also, within sections, another color coding system can be designed to break down the groups of materials. For instance, the biography section of the library may be designated as the blue section. Upon entering this section, the student can then make decisions about where to go from another set of visual cues: stripes, patterns, textures, and so forth. The range and type of coding system used is not as important as the function of the stimulus: to help differentiate library sections (although care should be taken to ensure that the children and staff are not overwhelmed by stimulus overload). The guideline becomes not so much dependent on color as it is stimulus oriented—variety can help facilitate differentiation.

Shapes and design images work much the same way as colors or textures and have an added advantage in that they signify certain meanings that may then be accentuated by color or texture. For instance, the layout of the shelves in the reference section of the library may be represented by a large question mark, or the section designed for adventure books might display a fantasy-type motif. Thus, shapes and images begin to take on larger forms, and multiple shapes combined help teach the child about the larger world.

Signage

Signage may be one of the most meticulously designed sections of the library, or it may be virtually overlooked. There exists no single answer to the issues surrounding signage, for the disabilities that fall within the term *special needs* are so vast that the signage requirements must also cover this same territory. Visual impairments dictate that braille be used to some extent, while auditory impairments, perceptual difficulties, learning deficits, and other situations all require specific types of sign usage. Some settings might require that signage be located at a lower level (or even on the floor) so that students might see it; other settings might require various type sizes or colors. Some settings might also require the strict use of pictorial images, whereas others may require simple words. The signage requirements for any one building must be thought out carefully and assigned according to the abilities of the children.

Simple Floor Plan

A simple floor plan can greatly assist an individual's ability to orient himself or herself in a setting. One can imagine a simple, I or T shaped floor plan and the ease of navigating inside the perimeters, versus floor plans that are oblique, such as an O or Z shaped plan. Simple plans help people navigate through a setting.

Barrier-Free Setting

Like other environments, the library can be a physical danger to disabled students because of tables located in awkward or unexpected places, doors that are difficult to open, and ramps installed at an improper angle or with a turning radius that is too tight. There are a host of other problems that are present in these settings, and many of them are peculiar to libraries. Shelving units may be too deep, too high, placed too close together, or made of flimsy materials. Tables are frequently too low for wheelchair users to get under them comfortably or have sharp edges that are dangerous to children who may fall (such as children who may be seizure prone).

Many of these issues are dealt with by project architects—things like proper ramp height and the use of electric doors—and should not be a concern for school personnel. But this is not always the case; all too often these issues are either neglected or thought of after the fact. Important issues to remember are keeping table edges rounded and providing tables at the proper height for wheelchair users (there is no single recommended height; what works well for one may not for another, so a variety of table heights and dimensions should be provided to allow use by all). Moss and Pace (1981) recommend that shelving units be kept at least forty inches apart, but a larger space is desirable to allow for maximum ability to turn. They also recommend doubled-faced shelving twenty-four inches deep, which accommodates most individuals' reaching abilities.

Diversity of Materials for Diverse Users

Often special needs students are unable to use a specific type of learning material (e.g., a visually impaired student cannot use regular books or a conventional computer program, but the provision of braille materials and a voice-interactive computer program opens up new worlds to that same student), and typically these students are inefficient learners (Baskin & Harris, 1982). If the materials available to a group of students do not meet their individualized needs, the materials may as well not be there in the first place. The solution to this problem pertains to the inclusion of a broad range of instructional materials, methods, and interior concepts to provide a diverse learning experience.

Adapted computers should be available for all users of school library services (Sorenson, 1988). The ability to control the learning environment can greatly influence individual satisfaction with that environment and might make the library setting a more positive place to be. Multiple sensory materials, which allow for a broad range of users, are preferable to materials that limit the type of individual who is able to use them. Sensory cues that provide information for all users should be included in the design phase.

Order and Definition

Many librarians, both school and public, want to maintain some semblance of orderliness and neatness in their setting. This may take the form of discouraging interaction with materials, and for the child with a disability who may have motor difficulties or difficulty comprehending defined social norms such as replacing things from where they are obtained, this may be highly discouraging.

Provision of an interactive play setting in the library should be provided. This may mean the duplication of some sources so that they can be available in both the ordered stacks and in the interactive section. This interactive section should be allowed to be messy; disorder should be tolerated because it might assist the student's desire to get involved with the materials. Velcro books with attachable pieces, ongoing storytelling times, or other interactive modes of communicating information will help include the student with special needs in the learning process. This area should be somewhat separated from the rest of the library because the noise and disruption may be irritating to others.

Range of Social Scales

Children with special needs are often more subject to the effects of crowding than the average child. They need places to work alone, to work on specific tasks, or to retreat for privacy (Gordon, 1972). Being alone and learning to accept oneself and others is also basic to the development of self-esteem and confidence. But group experiences are also important to the development of confidence in relations with others; not surprisingly, increased interest in interactions with others comes from greater social interaction (Moran & Kalakian, 1974).

A range of environmental spaces in relation to size, type, and enclosure provides greater opportunities for both individual and interpersonal/group experiences. Solitude and small groups may be experienced in small spaces, while large groups are organized in open spaces. Staff can work with children without interruption in small, out-of-the way spaces and use large, open spaces for group processes (e.g., films, plays, etc.). In large, open spaces, children are able to see into other spaces and determine if they want to become part of the activity.

Territorial Demarcation

All species, including humans, display behaviors indicative of a need to lay claim to a turf. Designers who do not provide for this need within a setting do an injustice to the inhabitants; users will find their own ways to create individual territories. The wise designer will provide for these spaces in the initial stages of development. Similarly, the placement of furniture, shelving units, and other relatively fixed items will require prudent forethought so as not to impinge on others' territory and maximize opportunities for quiet studying or reflection.

Gal, Benedict, and Supinski (1986) examined the influence of three different types of spatial markers on the territorial library behavior of college students. The purpose of this research was to look at issues regarding the design of comfortable and efficient workspace within libraries. The results of this study led to several design implications, among them the recommendation for the placement of four-person tables between bookshelves to minimize distractions and the use of carrel seating to facilitate serious studying. Myller (1966) pointed out that areas of high traffic should be designed to stay clear of seating and study areas so as not to intrude on others' learning.

Visual Access

Large spaces that are not visually accessible from one end to the other force students to design a cognitive map in their heads so that they can access other areas of the library from memory. Children with special needs may not have these cognitive skills, and to deny them the opportunity to explore the library freely is denying them the ability to develop skills of independence.

It is helpful to allow users of the library setting to see throughout the entire building (or as much as possible). A child who can see where it is that he or she wants to go can navigate through a group of shelves and find his or her way. This type of design negates the need for the individual to create cognitive maps of the setting and can be accomplished by the inclusion of large atriums or other open spaces. Another solution is to keep the shelving units low in the middle sections of the library so that most children can see through the space.

Outside Looking In—Inside Looking Out

Encouraging the use of the library and its materials by special needs students may require extra effort on the part of school officials; the students may have had difficulty in the past or done poorly and might be less inclined to visit the library.

The use of exterior and interior windows within the library aids in exposing the fascinating world that the library can bring to its users. An abundance of windows increases glare, causes book and furniture damage, makes reading difficult in uneven light, and will generally increase construction costs (Myller, 1966), although several carefully thought out and well-placed windows can create a pleasant environment and promote increased use of the library. Exterior windows allow people passing by to see what is occurring in the library (perhaps fostering an increased sense of security in the educational system), and the students can observe street activity and other outdoor events. Interior windows (between the interior library wall and the hallway) also allow schoolchildren to view the world inside and create a bright interior space.

Seating Arrangements

Library seating arrangements either facilitate interactions or discourage interactions. Many libraries seem to discourage interactions in informal areas (e.g., the "new books" or "periodicals" section), whereas these spaces could be used to facilitate quiet conversations about a new book or story that a child is reading.

Osmond (1966) coined the terms *sociopetal* and *sociofugal* seating to reflect individual preferences for specific seating arrangements, as well as the expected behavioral manifestations of these opposing arrangements. Sociopetal seating arrangements facilitate conversations (much like an executive meeting room where everyone is able to see and talk to one another), while sociofugal seating arrangements tend to discourage interactions between people (like airport seating or traditional classrooms with their "toward the front" alignment of chairs and desks). The design of seating arrangements and other areas of the school library may influence the degree to which the children will interact with one another. The wise architect and school librarian will use such a principle to encourage participation in some areas of the library (e.g., the story area) while discouraging interaction in other areas (e.g., the quiet study area).

CONCLUSION

Stainback and Stainback (1989) state that people are no longer satisfied providing separate-but-equal educational access to all children and have begun discussion on how educational personnel, programs, and resources can be merged to provide a unified, comprehensive educational system capable of meeting all children's needs. With this shift in emphasis, along with the change from an outward-directed teaching model to an individual learning model (Konya, 1986), the library will become the focal point of individual education. In terms of function and layout, the design of a library building depends on so many disparate factors that it would be unwise for a librarian or an architect to accept any one standard rule, applied in all situations. There are a multitude of solutions for any one design problem, and "since there is no one absolute formula for the best library, its conception, development, and execution becomes an art. The architect should therefore be free to use structure and materials as a poet uses words to create beautiful forms and spaces, not only to express and attractively house the library functions, but to achieve the environment which is most conducive to learning and to enjoying the wonderful world which the library has to offer" (Myller, 1966, p. 93).

REFERENCES

Ahrentzen, S. (in press). Socio-behavioral qualities of the built environment. In R. Dunlap & W. Michelson (Eds.), *Handbook of environmental sociology*. Westport, CT: Greenwood Press.

Baskin, B. H., & Harris, K. H. (1982). Selecting materials for the mainstreamed library. In M. Macon (Ed.), *School library media services to the handicapped* (pp. 75–88). Westport, CT: Greenwood Press.

Bednar, M. J., & Haviland, D. S. (1969). *Role of the physical environment in the education of children with learning disabilities*. Troy, NY: Rensselaer Polytechnic Institute, Center for Architectural Research.

Bennett, J. (1974). The library: The retarded person's alternative. *Catholic Library World 45*: 420–422.

Brown, E. F. (1971). *Library service to the disadvantaged*. Metuchen, NJ: Scarecrow Press.

Cruikshank, W. M. (1967). *The brain injured child in home, school, and community*. Syracuse: Syracuse University Press.

Davis, C., & Lifchez, R. (1987). An open letter to architects. In R. Lifchez (Ed.), *Rethinking architecture: Design students and physically disabled people* (pp. 35–50). Berkeley: University of California Press.

Farbstein, J. D. (1985). Using the program: Applications for design, occupancy, and evaluation. In W. F. E. Preiser (Ed.), *Programming the built environment* (pp. 13–29). New York: Van Nostrand Reinhold.

Fowler, S. A., Rowbury, T. G., Nordyke, N. S., & Baer, D. M. (1976). Color matching technique to train children in the correct use of stairs. *Physical Therapy 56*(8): 903–910.

Gal, C. A., Benedict, J. O, & Supinski, D. M. (1986). Territoriality and the use of library study tables. *Perceptual and Motor Skills 63*: 567–574.

Goldsmith, B. C. (1979). *Design data for wheelchair children*. London: Disabled Living Foundation.

Gordon, E. D., & Stubbs, M. S. (1988, May). Programming. *Architecture*, 203–210.

Gordon, R. (1972). *The design of a preschool therapeutic playground: An outdoor learning laboratory*. New York: New York University Medical Center, Institute of Rehabilitative Medicine, Rehabilitation Monograph 47.

Gump, P. (1987). School and classroom environment. In D. Stokels & I. Altman (Eds.), *The handbook of environmental psychology* (pp. 691–732). New York: Wiley.

Kaplan, S. (1983). A model of person-environment compatibility. *Environment and Behavior 15*: 311–332.

Konya, A. (1986). *Libraries: A briefing and design guide*. London: Architectural Press.

Lifchez, R. (1987). *Rethinking architecture*. Berkeley, CA: University of California Press.

Lucas, L. & Karrenbrock, M. H. (1983). *The disabled child in the library: Moving into the mainstream*. Littleton, CO: Libraries Unlimited.

Martin, R. G. (1992). *Libraries for the future: Planning buildings that work*. Chicago: American Library Association.

Milgram, S. (1970). The experience of living in cities. *Science 167*: 1461–1468.

Moore, G. T., Cohen, U&., & Team 699. (1977). *Outdoor environments for exceptional education: Behaviorally based programming and design*. Milwaukee: University of Wisconsin–Milwaukee, School of Architecture and Urban Planning.

Moore, G. T., Tuttle, D. P., & Howell, S. C. (1985). *Environmental design research directions: Process and prospects*. New York: Praeger.

Moran, J. M., & Kalakian, L. H. (1974). *Movement experiences for the mentally retarded or emotionally disturbed children*. Minneapolis: Burgess.

Moss, A., & Pace, M. M. (1981). *Planning barrier free libraries*. Washington, DC: National Library Service for the Blind and Physically Handicapped.

Myller, R. (1966). *The design of the small public library*. New York: R. R. Bowker.

Osmond, H. (1966). Some psychiatric aspects of design. In L. B. Holland (Ed.), *Who designs America?* (pp. 281–322). New York: Doubleday.

Oxley, D., Haggard, L. M., Werner, C. M., & Altman, I. (1986). Transactional qualities of neighborhood social networks: A case study of "Christmas Street." *Environment and Behavior 18*(5): 640–677.

Palmer, M. A. (1981). *The architect's guide to facility programming*. New York: American Institute of Architects.

Preiser, W. F. E. (Ed.). (1985). *Programming the built environment*. New York: Van Nostrand Reinhold.

Sanoff, H. (1988). Participatory design in focus. *Architecture and Comportement/Architecture and Behavior 4*(1): 27–42.

Seamon, D. (1982). The phenomenological contribution to environmental psychology. *Journal of Environmental Psychology 2*: 119–140.

Shapiro, J. (1993). *No pity*. New York: Random House.

Silverstein, M., & Jacobson, M. (1985). Restructuring the hidden program: Toward an architecture of social change. In W. F. E. Preiser (Ed.), *Programming the built environment* (pp. 149–164). New York: Van Nostrand Reinhold.

Sommer, R. (1969). *Personal space: The behavioral basis of design*. Englewood Cliffs, NJ: Prentice-Hall.

Sorenson, L. S. (1988). *Accessible library services: Taking action to enhance public library services for persons with disabilities*. Skokie, IL: Skokie Public Library.

Stainback, S., & Stainback, W. (1989). Integration of students with mild and moderate handicaps. In D. K. Lipsky & A. Gartner (Eds.), *Beyond separate education: Quality education for all* (pp. 41–52). Baltimore: Paul H. Brookes.

Stokols, D. (1986). Transformational perspectives on environment and behavior. In W. H. Ittelson, M. Asai, & M. Ker (Eds.), *Cross-cultural research in environment and behavior*. Tucson: University of Arizona.

Strom, M. G. (1977). *Library services to the blind and physically handicapped*. Metuchen, NJ: Scarecrow Press.

Thomas, L. C. (1986). Information poverty. School libraries: Then, today, and tomorrow. In J. P. Lang (Ed.), *Unequal access to information resources: Problems and needs of the world's information poor. Proceedings of the Congress for Librarians* (pp. 73–78). Ann Arbor: Pierian Press.

Thrun, R. R. (1988). The role of the architect in library planning. In E. Mount (Ed.), *Creative planning of special library facilities* (pp. 67–79). New York: Haworth Press.

Vanderburgh, L. (1983, February-March). A "plain talk" guide to the planning process. *Facilities Design and Management*, 82–87.

Veatch, J. L. (1979). *Library architecture and environmental design: The application of selected environmental design factors to the planning of public library facilities*. Unpublished doctoral dissertation, Florida State University.

Velleman, R. A. (1979). *Serving physically disabled people: An information handbook for all libraries*. New York: R. R. Bowker.

Weisman, G. D. (1981). Modeling environment-behavior systems. *Journal of Man-Environment Relations* 1(2): 32–41.

Wicker, A. W. (1972). Processes which mediate behavior-environment congruence. *Behavioral Science* 17: 265–277.

Wohlwill, J., & Weisman, G. D. (1981). *The physical environment and behavior: An annotated bibliography and guide to the literature*. New York: Plenum Press.

Wright, K. C. (1982). Federal legislation. In M. Macon (Ed.), *School library media services to the handicapped* (pp. 25–42). Westport, CT: Greenwood Press.

Zeisel, J. (1981). *Inquiry by design: Tools for environment-behavior research*. Cambridge: Cambridge University Press.

Zola, I. K. (1982). *Disincentives to independent living* (Monograph No. 1). Lawrence, KS: Research and Training Center on Independent Living.

Instructional Technology and Students with Special Needs in the School Library Media Center

8

Ann Higgins Hains and Dave L. Edyburn

The potential of instructional technology in education is widely discussed as a tool for improving educational outcomes for all students at all levels, from early childhood to college. Increasingly, information technology is viewed as a fundamental resource in educational reform efforts (Carnegie Foundation, 1988; Holmes Group, 1986; Mecklenburger, 1992; Newman, 1992). With the transformation of an industrial society to an information society (Naisbitt, 1982), educators suggest that students "must now learn something about computers in order to function effectively in society" (Kinzer, Sherwood & Bransford, 1986, p. 6). The intersection of information and technology occurs in the school library media center, and recent national guidelines challenge school library media specialists to expand their roles (American Association of School Librarians and the Association for Educational Communications and Technology, 1988).

The library has been the storehouse of knowledge and the book has been the information container of choice for centuries. Advances in digital technology, however, have resulted in a variety of electronic formats for storing information. While some library media centers have continued to acquire information through traditional purchases (Eisenberg, 1993), many libraries have expanded their services relative to nonprint information products: electronic encyclopedias, books on disk, full-text retrieval systems, CD-ROMs, and videodiscs. A vast number of reference tools have been developed to assist school library media specialists in identifying high-quality electronic instructional materials (a select list is provided at the end of the chapter). In addition to the developments in the marketplace, the knowledge base on the effective use of instructional technology has also grown (Kozma, 1991; Okolo, Bahr & Rieth, 1993).

Table 8.1
Major Legislation Influencing School Populations

Date	Public Law	Description of Populations Served
1975	PL 94-142	The Education of the Handicapped Act (EHA) established free and appropriate education for all students ages 5-18 (with state awards based on child count; 3- to 5-year-olds and 18- through 21-year-olds with disabilities could be included in the count).
1986	PL 99-457	Amended PL 94-142 by extending the full-services to preschoolers (3- to 5-years) and established a new program for infants and toddlers with disabilities and their families.
1990	PL 101-476	Changed the title of EHA to the Individuals with Disabilities Education Act (IDEA).
1991	PL 101-119	Amended IDEA so that all states now provide a free and appropriate public education to eligible 3- to 5-year-olds; states have options for applying for incentive grants to support the development of services for infants and toddlers with special needs and their families.

Given the dramatic changes in the marketplace and the high acquisition rates of technology by schools (Bruder, 1993), this chapter will focus on the role that instructional technologies can play in the school library media center for students with special needs. Advances in technology can radically change the use of instructional tools in education. Some of the issues to consider in planning for the use of technology in schools and library media centers include *whom* educators target for the use of technology, *what* instructional technologies are available, and *how* using technology facilitates educational goals.

WHO USES INSTRUCTIONAL TECHNOLOGIES IN SCHOOL MEDIA CENTERS?

The most obvious target populations for instructional technology in school library media centers are elementary and secondary students, and much of the literature on using computers in classrooms focuses on these populations (Lindsey, 1992; Lockard, Abrams & Many, 1987; Kinzer, Sherwood & Bransford, 1992). Students with diversity in ability and age range, however, are becoming part of school systems due to federal legislation (Table 8.1), and their use of technology poses some unique needs in school libraries.

First, the narrow definition of "student" is expanding. Tremendous progress occurred with the implementation of Public Law 99–457, reauthorized in 1990 as Public Law 102–119, which expanded services to infants and toddlers and extended the mandate for eligibility for special education and related services to begin at age three. This federal initiative supports preschool programs in public schools for three- to five-year-old children with special needs and early intervention (birth to age three) programs through state-defined lead agencies for supporting infants and toddlers with special needs and their families. All states must now provide public education services to preschoolers with special needs; in addition, some states serve infants and toddlers with special needs and their families through public school programs. Most school libraries do not include materials, much less instructional technologies, appropriate for this new student population.

Second, an increasing number of school districts serve students with severe disabilities in general education classrooms in their local, neighborhood schools (Snell, 1993). The Association for Persons with Severe Handicaps (TASH) defines individuals with severe disabilities as

> individuals of all ages who require extensive ongoing support in more than one major life activity in order to participate in integrated community settings and to enjoy a quality of life that is available to citizens with fewer or no disabilities. Support may be required for life activities such as mobility, communication, self-care, and learning as necessary for independent living, employment, and self-sufficiency. (TASH, 1989, p. 30)

With the move to full inclusion of these students into general education classrooms, resource management teams support them in the design and coordination of student-based services (Sailor, Gee & Karasoff, 1993). These teams often include general education teachers, special education teachers, therapists, parents, the school principal, and specialists from the school library media center, music, art, physical education, and other areas (McLaughlin & Warren, 1992). As part of the curricula, students learn vocational, daily living, and community skills (Browder & Snell, 1993; Moon & Inge, 1993). In the past, these students were not likely to be included in library media center activities; however, with assistive technology and computers, students requiring intensive support can participate in the media center.

Finally, schools are also serving families. Two initiatives are leading the expansion of the role schools play in family support and education: national emphasis on parent involvement in schools and family and professional collaboration through the Individuals with Disabilities Education Act (IDEA), which became law in 1975 as Public Law 94-142 and was reauthorized in 1990 as Public Law 101–476. This law guarantees certain rights to parents of students enrolled in special education programs. The national emphasis on expanding and coordinating prevention services for children from prenatal care to adolescence and on supporting parents as partners in the development of their children is found in a number of reports:

Educating America: State Strategies for Achieving the National Education Goals (National Governors' Association, 1990).

Right from the Start: NASBE Task Force Report on Early Childhood Education (National Association of State Boards of Education, 1991).

Caring Communities: Report of the National Task Force on School Readiness (National Association of State Boards of Education, 1991).

Profile of Preschool Children's Child Care and Early Education Program Participation (National Center for Education Statistics, 1993).

Increasingly, local communities are expanding public school systems to offer family support programs (Swan & Morgan, 1993). Model school programs provide an array of direct services to parents (e.g., on-site child care) as well as indirect support (e.g., information and referral services). This comprehensive focus for schools has a direct impact on the library media center and technology.

A second initiative for collaboration among parents and professionals has been established through special education and early intervention legislation. IDEA guarantees certain rights to parents in the education of children with disabilities from ages three through twenty-one (under Part B) and for infants and toddlers with disabilities and their families (under Part H). Participation by parents and professionals ensures that students receive appropriate education through the individualized education plan (IEP, defined in Part B). Moreover, services for infants and toddlers with disabilities and their families are included in the individualized family service plan (IFSP, defined in Part H). Thus, many schools are delivering family-centered services in addition to child-centered services (Edelman, Greenland & Mills, 1992).

The movement of schools to extend services to infants, toddlers, and preschoolers with special needs; address full inclusion, community living, and support employment for students with severe disabilities; and include family support and education challenges traditional assumptions about who uses instructional technology and educational resources in the media center.

INSTRUCTIONAL TECHNOLOGIES IN SCHOOLS

The traditional toolbox for instruction includes paper and pencil, textbooks, and a chalkboard. Within the past decade, technology has changed the way students work, play, and communicate. Advances in affordable technologies have enlarged the possibilities for equipping the instructional toolbox. In special education, the types of technology used by students and teachers are often divided into two areas: generic and assistive technologies (R. B. Lewis, 1993).

Generic Technologies

Generic technologies are designed for general use by the public; they are not adapted in any way (R. B. Lewis, 1993). Following are some common examples of generic technologies found in public and private schools:

Portable electronic tools: Calculators, spelling checkers, personal organizers, and instructional learning devices (e.g., Speak-N-Spell).

Microcomputers: Stand-alone computers, workstations connected to a local area network, and integrated learning systems.

Distance learning systems: Instructional programming delivered via satellite or cable.

Presentation systems: Overhead projectors, LCD panels, videocassette recorders, videodisc players, tape recorders, and televisions.

Video production tools: Camcorders and video editing facilities.

Communication systems: Telephones, message systems (e.g., homework hotlines), modems, and facsimile machines.

Information retrieval systems: Electronic card catalogs and CD-ROM-based reference products (e.g., electronic encyclopedias).

Educators often think of computers when they hear "technology," and indeed, computers are one of the common technologies in schools. Data from a recent survey show that more than 2.5 million computers are in K–12 schools, averaging one computer per nineteen students (Kinnaman, 1992). Other common technologies are calculators, tape recorders, and video equipment. Clearly instructional technology is increasingly diverse in size, shape, price, and function.

Assistive Technologies

Federal legislation has recognized the value of technology in special education and in the daily lives of persons with disabilities. Public Law 100–407, the Technology-Related Assistance for Individuals with Disabilities Act of 1988, addresses the need for technology by persons with disabilities and their families. This law defines an assistive technology device as "any item, piece of equipment, or product system, whether acquired commercially off the shelf, modified, or customized, that is used to increase, maintain, or improve functional capabilities of individuals with disabilities" (Technology Related Assistance for Individuals with Disabilities Act, 1988, Sta. 1046). Some assistive technologies are minor adaptations of generic devices and are referred to as low technologies (Church & Glennen, 1992; R. B. Lewis, 1993; Miller, 1993). For example, a preschooler presses a switch to activate a tape recorder during story time, an elementary student uses a keyboard overlay to write a story on the computer, or a high school student who has a visual impairment uses a calculator that "talks" to complete math problems. Other assistive technologies are sophisticated devices and are considered "high" technologies—for example, computers and electronic augmentative communication devices. (See the list of resources at the end of the chapter).

USING TECHNOLOGY FOR STUDENTS WITH DISABILITIES IN THE SCHOOL LIBRARY MEDIA CENTER

The school library media center serves as a depository of information stored in a variety of media. Common materials are books, maps, magazines, vertical files, audiotapes, videotapes, televisions, computers, computer text files, electronic networks, videocassette recorders, CD-ROM players, and interactive videodisc players. In addition, telecommunications and multimedia applications that integrate sound, text, graphics and video with computer programs are becoming more common in schools (Swisher, Spitzer, Spriestersbach, Markus & Burris, 1991; Troutner, 1991). Given that information is stored in a variety of media and that the student population is increasingly diverse, accessibility is a major concern.

A first goal is to ensure that students with disabilities have access to written materials. The Americans with Disabilities Act (ADA), enacted in 1990 by Public Law 101–336, states that individuals with hearing, vision, or speech impairments must be provided with appropriate auxiliary aids for effective communication by the public entity (such as educational institutions and libraries). Auxiliary aids include "such services or devices as qualified interpreters, assistive listening headsets, television captioning and decoders, telecommunications devices for deaf person (TDDs), videotext displays, readers, taped texts, brailled materials and large print materials". (U.S. Department of Justice, 1991, p. 4). These aids must be provided at no extra charge to the individual with a disability. Accessibility in the retrieval of information stored in typical media such as print, audiotape, or videotape can be accomplished easily with these aids.

ACCESSIBILITY AND TECHNOLOGY

A more challenging issue is electronic accessibility. Many resources in the electronic library require more than basic computer skills. The issue of computer literacy for typical students is addressed in a number of textbooks for teachers (Kinzer et al., 1992; R. B. Lewis, 1993; Lindsey, 1992; Lockard, Abrams & Many, 1987); however, for students with disabilities, little information exists on facilitating the retrieval of information when it involves technologies that are integrated or linked (e.g., multimedia, networks, and telecommunications). For example, high school students in creative writing classes write stories complete with soundtracks and illustrations from videodiscs or photographs scanned into the text. Elementary students use electronic encyclopedias through the network to browse through text, look at pictures or maps, and listen to audio recordings while working on science projects. In addition, each day a student sends an electronic mail message to a "pen pal" in another primary classroom in a neighboring state. In each of these situations, electronic accessibility becomes an issue for students with disabilities.

Common concerns about technology and electronic accessibility in the media center arise in terms of physical, sensory, and cognitive access for students with disabilities (Church & Glennen, 1992; Walling & Karrenbrock, 1993).

Physical Access

Physical access and environmental barriers in the library media center typically receive the most attention in schools (Walling, 1992). Wheelchair accessibility is commonly addressed first in making media facilities barrier-free. Other physical barriers such as space, architectural features, and furnishings are also readily apparent. Indeed, excellent resources are available for creating inclusive physical environments in school library media centers (Carson & Smith, 1993; Walling & Karrenbrock, 1993). (Chapter 7 of this book also addresses these issues.)

Clearly, a student's physical or motor abilities affect the use of technology. Motor impairments influence locomotion within the library media center and the ability to operate electronic equipment such as the standard computer keyboard. The degree of mild to severe motor impairment influences the accuracy and speed of motor movements, which, in turn, influences the type of adaptation and assistive technology options. Through an interdisciplinary team approach, the proper seating and positioning of the student along with the appropriate computer access method (e.g., keyguard, alternative or expanded keyboard, touch screen, touch tablet/pad) can be designed to meet the individual student's physical needs (a list of resources is provided at the end of the chapter).

Sensory Access

Sensory access to technology in school library media centers receives less attention than physical access. For students with sensory impairments, such as vision and hearing disabilities, not only are environmental features of concern (i.e., lighting and acoustics), but the reliance on print formats is a major barrier. This barrier is not exclusively related to technology or to sensory impairments; many children and adults need alternatives to print. From infancy through early childhood years, toys and books for promoting sensory stimulation and physical activity are appropriate. For students with severe disabilities and adults who are illiterate, nonprint displays of information (e.g., photographs or pictures) are useful. Specific assistive technology is available for making print materials accessible to children and adults with sensory impairments, but it is expensive and often dedicated to one purpose. For example, braille input-output devices are available for computers; however, they are limited to conversion of printed material, which means that pictures, maps, and diagrams found in texts are not communicated.

In addition, sensory problems affect a student's ability to use technology in the media center. For example, the operation of microcomputers relies on visual and auditory cues, and sensory difficulties impede a student's ability to discriminate those cues. A student who has a vision impairment may rely on speech as an information access strategy. The optimal strategy includes a speech recognition system that enables access by voice commands and the information on the computer screen is accompanied by speech. Some students may prefer to compose and review information in braille form or combinations of braille and speech; in this case, access occurs through a brailled keyboard overlay, a computer system that has talking features and uses braille (e.g., Braille N Speak Notetake), and a braille printer.

For a student with a hearing impairment, difficulties in technology can occur in determining the status of computer operations, auditory prompts from software, or auditory feedback from the keyboard or switch. Multimedia applications that include information by both sound (e.g., music, narration) and picture (art, maps, videoclips) and those that are interactive, so that the student chooses from multiple options, create unique access challenges to the interdisciplinary team working with students who have sensory impairments (Church and Glennen, 1992).

Cognitive Access

Little information on technology exists for assisting students with cognitive disabilities or delays in the school library media center. Two cognitive factors that create challenges in using computer technology effectively are attention (creating an inability to follow screen prompts and commands, difficulty with multistep procedures and "busy" screens, and difficulty with large amounts of computer speech or multimedia applications) and memory (creating difficulties with menus and recalling computer symbols or commands, inabilities in sequencing steps to complete commands, generalizing operations and procedures, and locating and recalling disk files).

These organizational and perceptual problems have an impact on the student's access to sophisticated operations based in technology. For instance, a student may be able to browse the shelves independently for books on animals but cannot conduct a search through the library's online catalog.

Likewise, the student can compose a letter at the typewriter to a pen pal but lacks the procedural and cognitive skills to use electronic mail successfully.

Interestingly, a study of sixth graders in New Zealand found that children (who did not have cognitive disabilities) encountered difficulties in using a traditional, nonautomated school library system (Moore & St. George, 1991). These children were unsuccessful in searching for card catalog information and in locating the books on the shelves. Thus, students with a wide range of cognitive abilities may need careful instruction in the general skills of information retrieval (Moore & St. George, 1991) before the introduction of technology.

The issues of technology and access become more complicated when students have multiple physical, sensory, and cognitive disabilities. The types and locations of computer equipment, adaptive peripherals, and other materials or devices will vary depending on the individual's needs and resources, space, and arrangement. For example, a high school student may need a computer keyboard overlay to press the keys accurately for conducting an electronic encyclopedia search, while a preschooler may need a switch to activate a story on the computer.

PLANNING SOLUTIONS

Designing optimal solutions to the complexities of technology for serving students with disabilities in the library media center means the determination of the student's abilities and specific needs, the formulation and implementation of a well-designed and integrated technology solution, and an evaluation of the plan. This process requires an interdisciplinary team approach with the participation of the professional staff, the family, and the student (when appropriate). Once the team assembles, their tasks include gathering information on the proposed technologies for use in the library media center, implementing the planning activities, and evaluating the success of the interventions.

Developing the Team

Given the diverse populations that school media centers are likely to encounter in terms of both the age and ability of the person seeking access, a planning team for specific technology services is imperative. In some cases, a team within the school building can reach solutions. For example, in order for Mary, a six year old who has cerebral palsy, to participate in the library media center, the teacher, parents, special education consultant, physical therapist, and library media specialist discuss how to position her on the floor so that she is comfortable, is appropriately supported with bolster, and can use the Muppet Keyboard with the computer to create her story.

Other situations require broader expertise from the school district staff who serve the larger school community (e.g., vision and hearing specialist, bilingual educator, school psychologist, nurse, computer support staff). For instance, children who require diverse types of technology devices that replace or augment bodily functions (e.g., mechanical ventilation, tube feeding, dialysis) often have a school nurse, who is part of their interdisciplinary team and can offer specialized expertise in adapting or arranging equipment for media experiences.

Finally, for some populations, an interagency or community team is necessary to plan solutions and offer financial support for them. Public libraries may already have an independent learning center, braille printer, toddler and preschooler storytime, and other community resources and activities. The early intervention program may house a Lekotek (play library) center for infants, which has a toy lending library, adaptive equipment for computer play, and family services (Trieschmann, 1988). Various service and civic organizations (Girl/Boy Scouts, JayCees, etc.), disability organizations (Association for Retarded Citizens, United Cerebral Palsy, etc.), social groups, senior citizens' associations, youth organizations, church groups, and local businesses may be sources for volunteer work, financial support, materials, and equipment donations.

In some situations, resource sharing may need to be statewide. In Pennsylvania, a statewide database is used to combine resources from over five hundred academic, public, special, and school libraries (Epler & Tuzinski, 1991).

The constellation of interdisciplinary or interagency teams for planning and supporting students and families in library media center activities will vary depending on individual needs. Clearly, a team approach expands accessibility to technology for students with disabilities.

Gathering Information

Once the team assembles, the first phase of planning for a student's participation with technology in the media center involves gathering information from a variety of sources. The library media specialist, in collaboration with parents, teachers, therapist, and other staff, may consider the student's needs by discussing the following questions:

- What instructional technology activities are important for the student to complete in the school library media center? Why? For example, does Susan need to learn to use the computerized catalog for college next year?
- Is it a goal or outcome that is included in the IEP? Should it be included? For example, does Carlo really need to learn how to perform a computer search, or are his social interaction goals a priority so that it is more important for him to play a computerized word game with a friend?

- Is there a low-technology solution that is more practical than a high-technology solution? For example, could a friend help Aziza access the file server for the program she wants instead of spending extensive hours teaching her the system? Similarly, would colored dots on the keyboard help Kim in the same way as an expensive overlay or alternative keyboard?
- If assistive technology is appropriate, can it be used in other environments (e.g., other classrooms, at home, in the community)? For example, will the voice recognition system used for informational retrieval in the school library be used anywhere else in the student's daily life?
- What resources are available to promote the use of technology interventions? For example, how will the school pay for a braille printer or an expanded keyboard?

Implementing and Evaluating the Plan

After the team develops a well-designed and integrated technology solution that contributes to the student's comfort, motivation, productivity, and independence in the library media center, implementation and evaluation occur. The team identifies each member's role in the process of implementation and evaluation. For example, Latisha is a fifth-grade student who has physical disabilities and significant cognitive and language delays. Her parents and teachers designed her educational goals to teach her many social and community living skills. Her parents are most concerned about her transition to middle school next year. They hope she will be able to communicate her needs with unfamiliar peers in her new school. Because numerous opportunities exist for such interaction in the library media center, the team decided to implement a plan whereby Latisha needs to ask a friend for help with loading her favorite social interaction game software on a computer in the library, then to generalize her request to an unfamiliar peer from another fifth-grade classroom. This plan extended the team's previous work on setting up her voice-output augmentative communication aids and teaching her to use it. The classroom teacher, special education consultant, and library media specialist decided that the special education consultant would initially work with Latisha in teaching her to ask her friend for help in loading the software in the library media center. Once she successfully and reliably asks for help from a friend, the classroom teacher and library specialist will arrange for Latisha to meet an unfamiliar peer in the computer area. Together they will facilitate the emergence of her request skills and monitor her progress in generalizing those skills.

Even a plan that has been carefully developed and implemented may encounter problems. Anticipating potential problems and planning possible solutions assists the team in overcoming barriers before they arise. Some questions for the team to consider at the point of implementation and evaluation include the following:

- Who will participate in teaching the student the initial skills needed to use the chosen technology (e.g., classroom peers, teachers, therapists, media specialists, parents, aides)?
- When, where, and how often will training occur?
- How will we monitor progress on an ongoing basis during the acquisition of the new skills?
- How will we know if our plan is successful? What evaluation procedures and criteria are important to employ? When and how often will we evaluate?
- What problems might occur in implementation? What are possible solutions?

CONCLUSION

The role of the school media specialist as information specialist, teacher, and instructional collaborator expands when it means assuming responsibilities and leadership throughout the school and community, not just the school library media center (Pickard, 1993). The current emphasis on interdisciplinary and interagency collaboration provides new opportunities for media specialists to work with many other professionals and community members and to share in decisions that affect the entire school population and their families (Keable, Williams & Inkster, 1993; C. G. Lewis, 1993). Through interdisciplinary collaboration, library media specialists, along with teachers and other professionals, create a shared vision of the instructional technology strategies, resources, and services that can improve the access to learning opportunities for all library users (Willeke & Peterson, 1993). As technological innovations continue, the collaborative team approach will be critical.

REFERENCES

American Association of School Librarians and the Association for Educational Communications and Technology. (1988). *Information power: Guidelines for school library media programs*. Chicago: American Library Association.

Browder, D. M., & Snell, M. E. (1993). Daily living and community skills. In M. E. Snell (Ed.), *Instruction of students with severe disabilities* (pp. 480–525). New York: Macmillan.

Bruder, I. (1993). Technology in the USA: An educational perspective. *Electronic Learning 13*(2): 20–28.

Carnegie Foundation for the Advancement of Teaching. (1988). *An imperiled generation: Saving urban schools*. Princeton, NJ: Carnegie Foundation.

Carson, B. B., & Smith, J. B. (Eds.). (1993). *Renewal at the schoolhouse. Management ideas for library media specialists and administrators*. Englewood, CO: Libraries Unlimited.

Church, G., & Glennen, S. (1992). *The handbook of assistive technology*. San Diego: Singular Publishing Group.

Edelman, L., Greenland, B., & Mills, B. L. (1992). *Building parent/professional collaboration*. St. Paul: Pathfinder Resource.

Eisenberg, M. B. (1993). Managing technology. In B. B. Carson & J. B. Smith (Eds.), *Renewal at the schoolhouse. Management ideas for library media specialists and administrators* (pp. 133–142). Englewood, CO: Libraries Unlimited.

Epler, D. M., & Tuzinski, J. H. (1991). A system for statewide sharing of resources: A case study of access in Pennsylvania. *School Library Media Quarterly 20*(1): 19–23.

Holmes Group. (1986). *Tomorrow's teachers: A report of the Holmes Group*. East Lansing, MI: Holmes Group.

Keable, D. M., Williams, S. Q., & Inkster, C. D. (1993). Facing the library media challenge of the nineties—Automation: A survey of Minnesota library media centers. *School Library Media Quarterly 21*(4): 227–236.

Kinnaman, D. E. (1992). 2.5 million strong—and growing. *Technology and Learning 13*(1): 67.

Kinzer, C. K., Sherwood, R. D., & Bransford, J. D. (1986). *Computer strategies for education: Foundations and content-area applications*. Columbus, OH: Merrill.

Kozma, R. B. (1991). Learning from media. *Review of Educational Research 61*: 179–211.

Lewis, C. G. (1993). Developing personnel. In B. B. Carson and J. B. Smith (Eds.), *Renewal at the schoolhouse: Management ideas for library media specialists and administrators* (pp. 49–60). Englewood, CO: Libraries Unlimited.

Lewis, R. B. (1993). *Special education technology: Classroom applications*. Pacific Grove, CA: Brooks/Coles Publishing Company.

Lindsey, J. D. (Ed.). (1992). *Computers and exceptional individuals* (2d ed.). Columbus, OH: Merrill.

Lockard, J., Abrams, P. D., & Many, W. A. (1987). *Microcomputers for educators*. Boston: Little, Brown.

McLaughlin, M. J., & Warren, S. H. (1992). *Issues and options in restructuring schools and special education programs*. Alexandria, VA: National Association of State Boards of Education.

Mecklenburger, J. A. (1992). The braking of the "break-the-mold" express. *Phi Delta Kappan 74*: 280–289.

Miller, J. (1993). Augmentative and alternative communication. In M. E. Snell (Ed.), *Instruction of students with severe disabilities* (pp. 319–346). New York: Macmillan.

Moon, M. S., & Inge, K. (1993). Vocational preparation and transition. In M. E. Snell (Ed.), *Instruction of students with severe disabilities* (pp. 556–587). New York: Macmillan.

Moore, P. A., & St. George, A. (1991). Children as information seekers. The cognitive demands of books and library systems. *School Library Media Quarterly 19*(2): 161–168.

Naisbitt, J. (1982). *Megatrends*. New York: Warner Communications.

National Association of State Boards of Education. (1991). *Winners all: A call for inclusive schools*. Alexandria, VA: Author.

National Center for Education Statistics. (1993). *Profile of preschool children's child care and early education program participation: National household education survey*. Washington, DC: U.S. Department of Education.

National Governors' Association Task Force on Education. (1990). *Educating America: State strategies for achieving the national education goals*. Washington, DC: National Governors' Association.

Newman, D. (1992). Technology as support for school structure and school restructuring. *Phi Delta Kappan, 74*: 308–315.

Okolo, C. M., Bahr, C. M., & Reith, H. J. (1993). A retrospective view of computer-based instruction. *Journal of Special Education Technology 12*(1): 1–27.

Pickard, P. W. (1993). Current research: The instructional consultant role of the school library media specialist. *School Library Media Quarterly 21*(2): 115–121.

Public Law 94–142, Sec. 3(a), Nov. 29, 1975, 89 Stat. 774.

Public Law 99–457, title IV, Sec. 406, Oct. 8, 1986, 100 Stat, 1174.

Public Law 101–476, title IX, Sec. 901(a)(1), (b)(1)-(9), Oct. 30, 1990, 104 Stat. 1141, 1142.

Public Law 101–119, Sec. 25(b), Oct. 7, 1991, 105 Stat. 607.

Sailor, W., Gee, K., & Karasoff, P. (1993). Full inclusion and school restructuring. In M. E. Snell (Ed.), *Instruction of students with severe disabilities* (pp. 1–30). New York: Macmillan.

Snell, M. E. (1993). *Instruction of Students with severe disabilities* (4th ed.). New York: Macmillan.

Swan, W. W., & Morgan, J. L. (1993). *Collaborating for comprehensive services for young children and their families: The local interagency coordinating council*. Baltimore: Brookes.

Swisher, R., Spitzer, K. L., Spriestersbach, B., Markus, T., & Burris, J. M. (1991). Telecommunications for school library media centers. *School Library Media Quarterly 19*(3): 153–160.

Technology Related Assistance for Individuals with Disabilities Act: 20 U.S. C., Chp. 24, Sec. 2202, Aug. 19, 1988, 102 Stat. 1046.

The Association for Persons with Severe Handicaps. (1989, May). *TASH resolutions and policy statements*. Seattle: TASH.

Trieschmann, M. (1988). *Innotek: Basic functions of microcomputers and adaptive equipment*. Evanston, IL: National Lekotek Center.

Troutner, J. (1991). Curriculum connections: Technology. *School Library Media Quarterly 19*(4): 239–240.

U.S. Department of Justice. (1991, September). *ADA highlights: Title II: State and local government services*. Washington, DC: Office on the Americans with Disabilities Act, Civil Rights Division, U.S. Department of Justice.

Walling, L. L. (1992). Granting each equal access. *School Library Media Quarterly 20*(4): 216–222.

Walling, L. L., & Karrenbrock, M. H. (1993). *Disabilities, children, and libraries: Mainstreaming services in public libraries and school library media centers*. Englewood, CO: Libraries Unlimited.

Willeke, M. J., & Peterson, D. L. (1993). Improving the library media program: A school district's successful experience with change. *School Library Media Quarterly 21*(2): 101–105.

RESOURCES FOR LOCATING INSTRUCTIONAL MEDIA FOR THE SCHOOL LIBRARY MEDIA CENTER

Buckleitner, W. (1993). *1993 Survey of early childhood software.* Ypsilanti, MI: High/Scope Press.

Educational Products Information Exchange (EPIE) Institute, (1991). *The educational software selector: The latest and best of TESS (91–92 edition).* Hampton Bays, NY: Author.

Emerging Technology Consultants. (1992). *Videodisc compendium for education and training (1993) edition). St. Paul: Author.*

Neill, S. B. & Neill, G. W. (1993). *Only the best. The annual guide to highest-rated educational software/multimedia from preschool–grade* 12. Alexandria, VA: Association for Supervision and Curriculum Development.

RESOURCES FOR FACILITATING ACCESS TO INSTRUCTIONAL TECHNOLOGY

Print Resources

Closing the Gap. (1993). *The 1993 Closing the Gap resource guide.* Henderson, MN: Author.

Trace Research and Development Center on Control and Computer Access for Disabled Individuals. (1993). *Trace resource book: Assistive technologies for communication, control, and computer access (1993–94 edition).* Madison, WI: Author.

Free Software Resources

IBM/compatible computers: AccessDOS and Easy Access are programs that enable users to make keyboard adjustments that turn off the repeat function or to activate multiple keys at the same time. Available free. IBM Special Needs Products, (800)426–7282 (order part number 84F9872).

Macintosh computers: CloseView is a file in the System Folder of all Macintosh computers to enable users to enlarge the size of the text on the screen. Easy Access is a file in the System Folder of all Macintosh computers to enable users to activate multiple buttons or keys at the same time, to turn off the repeat function, as well as to emulate the mouse, all using only one hand.

CD-ROM Resources

Hyper-ABLEDATA for Macintosh computers. (1993). (CDROM) $27.00. Trace R&D Center, University of Wisconsin–Madison, S-151 Waisman Center, 1500 Highland Avenue, Madison, WI 53705; (608)263–2309.

DOS-ABLEDATA for IBM/compatible computers. (1993). (CDROM) $27.00. Trace R&D Center, University of Wisconsin–Madison, S-151 Waisman Center, 1500 Highland Avenue, Madison, WI 53705; (608)263–2309.

ASSISTIVE TECHNOLOGIES COMMONLY FOUND IN SCHOOLS

Adaptations for Input

Keyguards

Apple lle, Apple llgs, IBM PS/2, Macintosh. (TASH Inc., Unit 1-91 Station Street, Ajax, Ontario, Canada L1S 3H2; (905)686-4129.

Alternative Keyboards

Intellikeys. IntelliTools, 5221 Central Avenue, Suite 205, Richmond, CA 94804; (800)899-6687.

Ke:nx On:Board. Don Johnston Developmental Equipment Inc., P.O. Box 639, 1000 North Rand Road, Building 115, Wauconda, IL 60084; (800)999–4660.

Key Largo. Don Johnston Developmental Equipment, Inc., P.O Box 639, 1000 North Rand Road, Building 115, Wauconda, IL 60084; (800)999–4660.

Muppet Learning Keys. Sunburst/Wings for Learning, 101 Castleton Street, P.O. Box 100, Pleasantville, NY 10570-0100; (800)321–7511.

TASH Mini Keyboard. TASH Inc., Unit 1-91 Station Street, Ajax, Ontario, Canada L1S 3H2; (905)686–4129.

Switch Interface Box

KENX. Don Johnston Developmental Equipment, Inc. P.O. Box 639, 1000 North Rand Road, Building 115, Wauconda, IL 60084; (800)999–4660.

Touch Screens

TouchWindow. Edmark Corporation, P.O. Box 3218, Redmond, WA 98073; (800)426–0856.

Adaptations for Output

Auditory

DecTalk. Digital Equipment Corporation, 30 Forbes Road, Northboro, MA 01532; (508)351–5205.

Echo Speech Synthesizers. Echo Speech Corporation, 6460 Via Real, Carpinteria, CA 93013; (805)684–4593.

Vert Pro. (TeleSensory, 455 North Bernardo Avenue, Mountain View, CA 94039–7455;(415)960–0920.

Visual

Kerzweil Personal Reader. Xerox Imaging Systems, Inc., 9 Cenenial Drive, Peabody, MA 01960; (800)343–0311.

Zoom Text Plus. Al Squared, P.O. Box 669, Manchester Center, VT 05255–0669; (802)362–3612.

School Library Media Specialist as Collaborator

III

An Active Role for School Library Media Specialists in the Identification and Placement Procedures for Special Needs Students

9

Deborah L. Voltz

School library media specialists play an integral role in helping students to develop to their fullest potential. Barron and Bergen see "the most important and critical role that the modern school library media specialist has to play [is] that of partner to the other members of the instructional team" (1992, p. 524). As a consequence of this partnership, school library media specialists share in the responsibility of identifying and serving students with special learning needs.

School library media specialists have unique skills and perspectives to contribute in the process of identifying students who have learning and/or behavior differences, which may indicate the presence of a disability. For example, the library media specialist has the opportunity to provide instruction to students in an environment other than the classroom and may establish a relationship with students that differs from that established with other teachers. Wehmeyer (1984) states,

> Librarians who are alert to the signs of poor vision, hearing loss, deficits in perceptual and linguistic processing, and other more subtle handicaps may have occasion to observe evidence of such needs as students relax in the relatively informal atmosphere of the library. Because they do not issue report card grades, media center staff may elicit students' acknowledgement of difficulties with school assignments, something pupils hesitate to share with a teacher. (p. 41)

Additionally, because of librarians' exposure to the spectrum of learners across the grade levels served by the school's library media center, the school librarian has greater opportunity than does the traditional classroom teacher to observe learners at various developmental levels. The school

Figure 9.1
Indentifying Students with Disabilities, from Prereferral to Placement

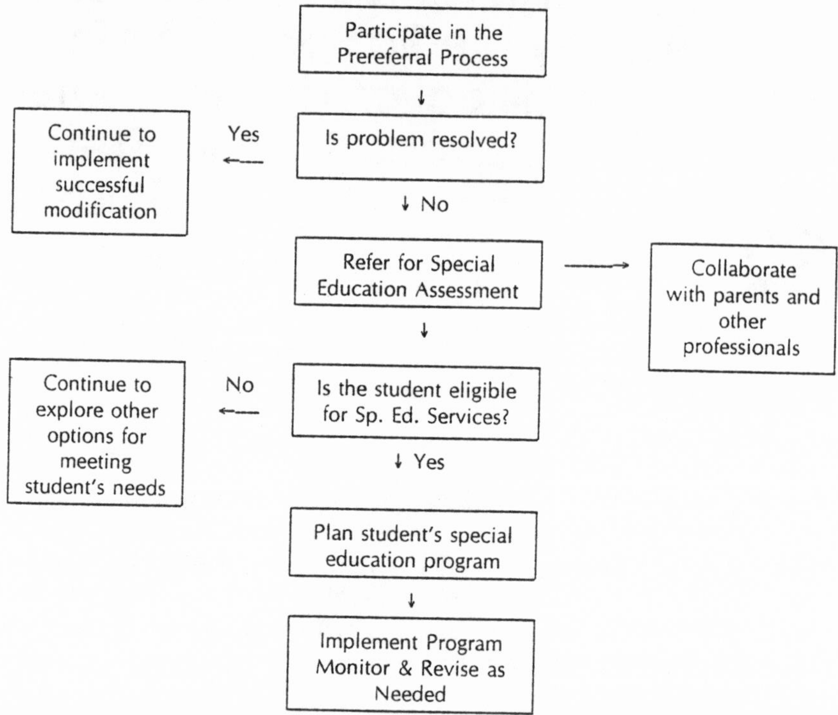

library media specialist also participates in instruction across the entire school curriculum. As stated by Coleman (1990), "Probably more than anyone else within the school, the librarian has a better view of the school's curriculum in action" (p. 46). Because of these unique perspectives, the school library media specialist can play an invaluable role in the identification of special needs students. The process of identifying students with disabilities and designing appropriate educational programs for them involves a number of steps: (1) prereferral, (2) referral, (3) data collection/eligibility determination, (4) program planning, and 5) implementation/ongoing monitoring (Figure 9.1).

PREREFERRAL

Before identification and placement procedures formally begin for a particular child, an effort generally is made to ameliorate learning difficulties within the context of general education. These efforts may take the form of informal problem solving between educators, or may involve more formalized procedures. For example, prereferral committees may be used as a means of promoting collaborative problem solving among professionals for the purpose of developing strategies to aid students experiencing difficulty in the mainstream. The prereferral committee may include special education teachers, general education teachers, specialty area teachers (e.g., librarian, art teacher, music teacher) building administrators, counselors, and others. The prereferral process can occur in several stages: initiation, problem delineation/intervention exploration, implementation, and progress sharing/decision making.

Initiation

Once a teacher notices a persistent learning or behavior problem and has made adaptations in the learning environment to ameliorate the observed problem, but to no avail, this teacher may wish to initiate a request to the prereferral committee for assistance. In initiating such a request, the teacher should be prepared to provide detailed information about the nature of the learning problem experienced by the student, the intervention strategies already tried, the period of time each was tried, and the impact of each strategy on the problem noted. Figure 9.2 presents a sample of a request for assistance form to submit to a prereferral committee in order to initiate the prereferral process. Once the request has been received by the committee, additional information may be requested, or a committee member may observe the student in the classroom in order to secure other helpful data.

Problem Delineation/Intervention Exploration

Once all needed information has been collected, the prereferral committee meets to discuss the problem and to brainstorm intervention strategies. The student's parents may be invited to participate in this process. Problems should be stated in an objective manner in order to facilitate problem solving. Compare the following problem statements:

Todd is very inattentive during library periods. He constantly disrupts lessons and provokes other students.

Todd engages in off-task behavior approximately 70 percent of the time during library periods. These behaviors include out-of-seat behaviors, poking and hitting other students, throwing books, and name calling.

The first statement provides a general idea of the nature of the problem; the second statement helps to clarify what is meant by "very inattentive," "disrupts," and "provokes." This added clarity can facilitate the problem-solving process.

After the problem has been clarified, factors that influence the problem can be discussed (e.g., time constraints, low skill levels). Here members of the prereferral committee may use questions such as, "Are there certain activities that seem to increase or decrease the occurrence of the problem behaviors?" These questions may refine the problem by eliciting responses

Figure 9.2
Request Form for Team Assistance

Student's Name______________________________ Grade Level__________

Referring Teacher ______________________________ Date____________

Describe the student's problem:

How often does this problem occur:

____ Several times a day Comments:
____ Daily
____ More than once a week
____ Weekly
____ Occasionally

Describe the modifications that have been attempted to solve this problem (e.g., assignments, instruction, curriculum, counsling, environment):

Have the parents been contacted about this problem? ___yes ___no ___don't know

Summary of consultation with parents:

Describe the student's learning strengths, special interests, or skills:

Additional information, other concerns about the student, general comments, and so forth:

Source: Wood (1989).

that can give insight into the factors within the instructional environment that influence the problem. This dialogue helps to provide a basis for brainstorming interventions that may be effective in ameliorating the problem. All members of the committee participate in generating a list of possible strategies to be tried in resolving the learning or behavior problem.

Once a list of potential strategies has been generated, those to be tried first can be identified by considering factors such as probability of effectiveness, difficulty of implementation, and impact on other students. A plan is then developed for the implementation of the selected strategy. Such a plan generally includes the following components: (1) the members of the prereferral committee who will be responsible for implementing various aspects of the selected intervention (e.g., the librarian will use bibliotherapy as a technique for teaching students socially appropriate ways to vent frustration; a special education teacher will provide consultation on the use of this technique), (2) the time frame for carrying out these activities, and (3) the target date for the committee to reconvene to discuss progress relative to the cited problem.

Implementation

After the plan has been developed, the strategy may be implemented. Throughout the implementation of the intervention, data should be collected regarding its effectiveness. The school personnel initiating the referral should be prepared to present these data to the prereferral committee when it reconvenes.

Progress Sharing/Decision Making

After the selected intervention has been implemented for the specified period of time, the prereferral committee reconvenes to discuss its outcome. The data that have been collected regarding the impact of the intervention are shared with members of the committee. If the intervention has resulted in the resolution of the problem, the process stops at this point. If not, the committee may again brainstorm other interventions. After all feasible interventions have been tried, but with no success, a referral for special education assessment may be initiated.

One purpose of the prereferral process is to eliminate inappropriate referrals to special education programs. A referral is considered inappropriate if the special needs of a student can be met entirely within the context of mainstream programs, thus rendering special education services unnecessary. By eliminating inappropriate referrals, the needless removal of students from the mainstream can be avoided. Prereferral procedures have been found to be effective in accomplishing this goal (Graden, Casey & Bonstrom, 1985; Hayek, 1987).

The potential role of the school librarian in the prereferral process is twofold: (1) to assume the role of the referring teacher, and thus initiate the prereferral process for a student suspected of having a disability, and (2) to serve on the prereferral committee. Because of the unique skills and perspectives of the school library media specialist, his or her input in the prereferral process is very important.

REFERRAL

If the prereferral process does not result in satisfactory amelioration of the learning problem, a formal referral for special education evaluation is submitted. Information generally requested on a referral form focuses on the nature of the problem, strategies already tried, and the impact of these strategies on the learning problem. Information obtained during the prereferral process is useful in submitting a referral form. If the school library media specialist is initiating the referral, he or she is responsible for completing and submitting the form. Ideally, parents of this student would have been involved from the time that the problem was recognized and would have participated in the decision to make the referral. If this is not the case, however, parents must be notified when a referral for special education assessment takes place.

DATA COLLECTION

After the submission of the referral form and parental consent is obtained, the process of gathering more formal data about the student can begin. A multidisciplinary team of professionals conducts a number of assessment procedures in order to obtain more information about the student to determine whether a disabling condition exists. For example, school psychologists administer individual intelligence tests to ascertain the student's general level of cognitive functioning and individual academic achievement tests designed to compare the student's performance with that of his age and/or grade peers. Special education teachers may be responsible for administering diagnostic or criterion-referenced tests, which pinpoint areas of strength and weakness relative to specific skills. Behavior rating scales or adaptive behavior measures, or both, may be completed by school personnel (e.g., classroom teachers, librarian) as well as by parents. These measures are designed to solicit the perceptions of persons who regularly interact with the student regarding the student's behavior in a variety of settings. Observational data may be gathered by school counselors, special education teachers, or others in order to note pertinent student behaviors that occur in various settings within the school environment. For example, a member of the multidisciplinary team may observe a student in the classroom, in the library, and during recess. Hearing and vision assessments may be completed by the school nurse or by hearing and vision specialists. Speech-language clinicians may evaluate the student's oral communication skills.

Figure 9.3
Teacher Checklist for Measuring Problems in Social and Emotional Development

Teacher Checklist: This measure was designed to be used by teachers in any classroom to make them more aware of their students' behavior. This list might help identify behavior that otherwise might be overlooked or misunderstood. From here the teacher might want to take frequency counts of identified behavior, or in some other way further analyze the situation.

	Frequently	*Not Frequently*
1. Self-Image		
A. Makes I can't statements		
B. Reacts negatively to correction		
C. Gets frustrated easily		
D. Makes self-critical statements		
E. Integrity:		
cheats		
tattles		
steals		
destroys property		
F. Makes excessive physical complaints		
G. Takes responsibility for actions		
H. Reacts appropriately to praise		
2. Social Interaction		
A. Seeks attention by acting immaturely: thumbsucking, babytalking, etc.		
B. Interacts negatively		
C. Fails to interact		
D. Initiates positive interaction		
E. Initiates negative interaction		
F. Reacts with anger, verbally		
G. Reacts with anger, physically		
3. Adult/Teacher Relationships		
A. Seeks attention by acting immaturely		
B. Excessively demands attention		
C. Reacts appropriately to teacher requests		
D. Inappropriately reacts to authority figures		
4. School-Related Activities		
A. Attends to task		
B. Exhibits offtask behavior		
C. Interferes with the other students' learning		
D. Shows flexibility to routine changes		

Date the checklist and complete one for each child. Once the checklist has been completed and reviewed, a narrative report can be written with explanations and suggestions for the future. For the list to be effective, the teacher must use the results to actually make changes in the classroom.

Source: Hammill & Bartel (1990).

After the members of the multidisciplinary team have completed their evaluations, the information they have collected, along with that collected during the prereferral and referral process, is considered in determining whether the target student is eligible for special education services. As part of this process, the members of the team meet and share their findings, then collaboratively decide whether the student is eligible for special education services and if such services would be appropriate. Again, parents are encouraged to be present at this meeting and to participate in decision-making.

The role of the library media specialist in the data collection and decision-making process can be quite varied. For example, the librarian may be asked to complete a behavior rating scale. Figure 9.3 illustrates such a device. As is shown, the librarian would be asked to indicate how frequently the student demonstrates the given behaviors while in the library setting. The perspective of the librarian is valuable in the decision-making process, because he or she provides information gleaned from working with the student in an environment other than the general education classroom. This information could be used in analyzing the impact of setting and setting demands on student behavior and performance.

The librarian also may serve as host for observational procedures conducted by other members of the multidisciplinary committee. This may be the case particularly if the librarian initiated the referral process. The observer generally will consider factors such as physical properties of the setting (e.g., noise, temperature, lighting, arrangement of furniture); instructional arrangements used (e.g., large group, small group, one-to-one, cooperative learning); instructional techniques used; the nature of student interaction with the teacher and other students; student on-task behavior; and student success with the learning tasks presented. As host for an observation, the librarian provides a time when the observation may best be completed and conducts the library period in the usual manner.

A third role of the library media specialist in data collection and decision-making is to serve as an active participant in the multidisciplinary team meeting. In order to be successful in this role, the library media specialist should complete requested data collection prior to the meeting, prepare a written summary of data collected, attend the meeting of the multidisciplinary team, and participate in the problem-solving process.

Complete Requested Data Collection

Several examples of the kinds of data a librarian may be asked to provide have been described previously. In addition, the librarian may be asked to provide information about the student's ability to use reference materials, read for pleasure, and use other resource-based learning skills. Since the referral to placement process must occur within a certain time frame (generally ninety days), it is imperative that all members of the committee conduct assigned data collection procedures in a timely fashion.

Prepare Written Summary

Depending on the practices of local school districts, each participant on the multidisciplinary team may be asked to provide a written summary of the data he or she collected. It also may be required that this written summary be made available to all team members prior to the group meeting. This practice may facilitate the decision-making process.

Attend the Meeting and Actively Participate

Each member of the multidisciplinary team may be required to be present at the team meeting. In order to maximize the effectiveness of the team, all members must actively participate in the process of determining how best to meet the needs of the student in question. Determining whether accomplishing this goal requires placing the student in a special education program is the charge of the multidisciplinary team. The needs of the student, however, should remain the primary concern of the team. Eligibility for special education should be considered only as it relates to meeting student needs. Eligibility in most states is determined on a categorical basis. That is, students in need of special education services are identified as having a specific disability (e.g., learning disabled, emotionally disturbed). Individual programs designed to meet these students' needs are then developed.

PROGRAM PLANNING

Parental participation is encouraged in the process of program planning, and prior to the placement of any student in special education programs, parental consent must be obtained. If the multidisciplinary team has determined that a student is in need of special education services, a plan to deliver those services must be developed. This plan involves the designation of an appropriate service delivery model and the development of an individualized education plan (IEP).

Selecting a Service Delivery Model

One of the guiding principles of selecting an appropriate service delivery model is the concept of the least restrictive environment, which has been defined as the "appropriate placement closest to the mainstream of education" (Lewis & Doorlag, 1991, p. 14). This means that the student must be integrated into general education classes to the maximum extent possible while still meeting his or her educational needs. Among the commonly used service delivery options are general education classes with consultation, collaboration, and/or team teaching; resource rooms; part-day special classes; self-contained special classes; special schools; and residential facilities.

Placement in general education classes with consultation, collaboration, and/or team teaching is the service delivery option that provides the student with disabilities greatest interaction in the mainstream while still providing special education support. The student spends the entire school day in general education classes and receives special education services indirectly. The special education teacher provides consultation to the general education teacher regarding modifications that the student needs.

Students served through the resource room approach remain in the mainstream for the majority of their school day but attend special classes for specified periods. These special classes, often referred to as resource rooms, typically provide remedial instruction designed to address identified areas of weakness. Resource room teachers also provide consultation to mainstream teachers.

Part-day classes provide special education services to students with disabilities for the majority of their school day. Students are mainstreamed, however, for portions of the day. For example, students may be integrated with their nondisabled peers for art, music, physical education, or library periods in addition to noninstructional periods, such as lunch and recess.

Self-contained classes provide only limited opportunities for students with disabilities to interact with nondisabled peers. In the self-contained model, all instruction occurs in the special setting. In some cases, however, students with disabilities may eat lunch or go out to recess with their nondisabled peers.

Special school settings are placements in which the entire school is designed to serve special needs students. Through this model, intensive, highly specialized services may be provided; however, opportunities for interaction with nondisabled students are severely limited since all students attending the school are special needs students.

Residential settings provide, in addition to instructional services, living facilities for special needs students. Obviously, this approach severely limits, or completely eliminates, opportunities for students with disabilities to interact with their nondisabled peers—during both school hours and other times when students with and without disabilities may interact with each other in the community.

There are other approaches to service delivery as well. Sometimes referred to as "pull-in" approaches, special education personnel deliver services within the context of the mainstream rather than pulling students out of the mainstream. Co-teaching is an example of a pull-in approach in which special education teachers team teach with mainstream teachers. Under a co-teaching model, special education teachers may team teach with school library media specialists during library periods attended by students with special needs.

In making decisions about which service delivery model is appropriate for a given student, the multidisciplinary team considers the severity of the learning problem, as well as the need to provide for interaction with nondisabled peers. Once these considerations are discussed, more specific plans are developed regarding the student's educational program.

Developing an IEP

Using the data previously collected about the student, an IEP is developed. It contains a summary of the student's level of performance, the nature of the special education services to be delivered, the extent of participation in the mainstream, goals and objectives that target desired learning outcomes, the procedures and timetables to be used in determining whether objectives have been met, dates indicating when services are to be initiated and completed, and related services to be provided (services needed in order for the student to benefit from the prescribed educational program, such as physical or occupational therapy, speech-language therapy, counseling, transportation, or health services).

The library media specialist can play a significant role in the development of IEPs. He or she can assist in determining goals and objectives to be set for a student in terms of academic and social skills. The librarian also can assist in determining the need for various related services. Additionally, some specific IEP objectives may be addressed in the library setting. Because of the unique learning atmosphere of the library, the perspectives of the librarian add a different—and needed—dimension to the problem-solving process.

IMPLEMENTATION AND MONITORING

Once an educational program for a special needs student has been developed, the implementation process begins. Typically, this process involves the coordinated efforts of a range of professionals. For example, in the case of a student served through a resource program, the special education resource teacher, general education teacher(s), and other specialty area teachers (e.g., librarians, art, music, physical education teachers) are jointly responsible for providing the educational program detailed in the IEP. In many cases, modifications in the general education environment are required to support the special needs student in the mainstream. In this event, an important role of the librarian would be to make the required adaptations needed for library periods. Additionally, librarians may assist in locating and purchasing special materials needed to implement IEPs.

Communication among the professionals involved in implementing a student's educational program is critical. Each person should carefully monitor the student's progress in the educational program and share this progress with other professionals who are jointly responsible for the education of the student. If warranted, changes in the educational program designed for a student may be made based on feedback provided by the various professionals working with the student.

Figure 9.4
The Role of the Library Media Specialist in the Identification and Placement Process

Step	Purpose/Procedures	Potential Role of Library Media Specialists
Prereferral	• prevent inappropriate referrals • meet student needs within context of general ed.	• request team assistance • participate in function of prereferral committees • implement or assist in implementing interventions • collect data about effectiveness of intervention
Referral	• alert appropriate personnel that special education assessment is needed for a given student	• complete and submit referral form • make sure parents are aware of the referral
Data Collection	• determine eligibility for special education	• serve as member of the multidisciplinary team • complete informal assessment • serve as host for observations
Program Planning	• develop program to meet student's needs	• participate in determining service delivery model • participate in developing goals and objectives
Implementation	• deliver instructional program • monitor effectiveness of instructional program	• make needed modifications in instruction, materials, or physical setting • team teach with special education professionals • monitor effectiveness of ed. program • participate in on-going collaboration with other professionals

The role of the school library media specialist in the identification and placement process can be significant. Figure 9.4 highlights this role. At each stage of the process, the input of the school librarian is important. As Wehmeyer (1984) stated:

> To work closely with individual students over a period of years, to have time and opportunity to lead them step-by-step to increased competence and greater maturity, is one of the most noteworthy advantages of the profession of school media librarianship. These ongoing relationships are particularly significant to the gifted and talented, the handicapped, and others with special needs. (p. 45)

The unique perspectives of the school library media specialist make his or her input vital in the identification and placement, as the following case example shows.

CASE EXAMPLE

Alice is a third-grade student. Ms. Jennings, the school library media specialist, was concerned about Alice because of her extremely withdrawn behavior during library periods. When given cooperative learning assignments, Alice never joined a group on her own accord, she always had to be assigned to one. And even when assigned to a group, Alice would not work with the other children; she merely sat and looked. Alice appeared to be an isolate; none of the other children wanted to interact with her, and she appeared not to want to interact with any of them. During storytime, when books were read aloud to the students, Alice never showed any signs of affect, no matter how humorous, happy, or sad the stories were.

Ms. Jennings talked with other teachers who worked with Alice and found that they also had similar concerns, as did Alice's parents. At that point, Ms. Jennings decided to submit a request for assistance to the school-based prereferral committee. The committee was formed, and the prereferral process was initiated. As a committee member, Ms. Jennings worked collaboratively with the others to develop strategies that might reduce Alice's withdrawn behavior. Alice's mother was present during the committee meeting and shared in the problem-solving process.

Through the prereferral process, a number of strategies were developed. Ms. Jennings, in consultation with Mr. Clark, the emotional disturbance (ED) teacher, implemented the strategies developed by the committee. Student progress was recorded and reported when the prereferral committee was reassembled. Unfortunately, the strategies failed to have a positive effect. Consequently, the committee felt that a referral for special education assessment was needed. At that point, Ms. Jennings completed the referral form and submitted it to the appropriate personnel.

After parental consent was obtained, the special education assessment process began. A number of individuals were involved in the process, including a school psychologist, a counselor, a social worker, the teacher, and, of course, Ms. Jennings. Ms. Jennings's role as a team member of this multidisciplinary team was to complete a behavior rating scale and to permit an observation of Alice during a library period.

When all the necessary data had been collected, the team met to discuss Alice's eligibility for special education services. It was determined that Alice's needs would best be met through programming for students with emotional disturbances. Her parents agreed. The committee then developed a plan to provide the services to Alice. One of the provisions of Alice's educational plan was for Mr. Clark to team teach with Ms. Jennings during selected library periods. This would allow Mr. Clark to help structure interaction between Alice and her classmates and to model the use of bibliotherapy in working with her. Through these services, as well as others provided to Alice in the general education classroom, many of her withdrawn behaviors were reduced. By taking the initiative to start the identification to placement process and by working collaboratively with Alice's parents and other professionals, Ms. Jennings was able to make a positive change in Alice's academic life.

REFERENCES

Barron, D., & Bergen, T. J. (1992). Information power: The restructured school library for the nineties. *Phi Delta Kappan 73*: 521–525.

Coleman, J. G. (1990). Characteristics of at-risk youth and the library's role in dropout prevention. *Tech Trends 35*(4): 46–47.

Graden, J. L., Casey, A., & Bonstrom, O. (1985). Implementing a prereferral intervention system: Part II. The data. *Exceptional Children 51*: 487–496.

Hammill, D. D., & Bartel, N. R. (1990). *Teaching students with learning and behavior problems*. Boston: Allyn & Bacon.

Hayek, R. A. (1987). The teacher assistance team: A prereferral support system. *Focus on Exceptional Children 20*(1): 1–7.

Lewis, R. B., & Doorlag, D. H. (1991). *Teaching special students in the mainstream*. New York: Merrill.

Wehmeyer, L. B. (1984). *The school librarian as educator*. Littleton, CO: Libraries Unlimited.

Wood, J. W. (1989). *Mainstreaming: A practical approach for teachers*. Columbus: Merrill.

Wood, J. W. (1992). *Adapting instruction for mainstreamed and at-risk students*. New York: Merrill.

10 School Library Media Specialists as Partners with Classroom Teachers in Generalizing the Skills of Students with Special Needs

M. Lewis Putnam

Why can a student spell a word correctly on a test only to misspell the same word in a composition for an English class? Why can students compute problems in their mathematics book but seem unable to compute the average rainfall in a geography lesson? These are some of the many questions that perplex special education teachers when students appear to have mastered a skill for one set of circumstances but fail to apply the same skill to other situations that require them.

The ability to learn in one situation and to use such learning in other appropriate situations is known as transfer of learning, or *generalization*. Generalization of newly learned skills is important for all students, and particularly for students with special needs. As these students are increasingly integrated into all facets of society, many professionals believe that often the main stumbling block to success is their difficulty with skill generalization.

The problem of generalization has thus become a central issue in special education (Deshler, Schumaker & Lenz, 1984; Ellis, Lenz & Sabornie, 1987a, 1987b; Keogh & Glover, 1980; Moleskey, Reith & Polsgrove, 1980) as the demands of various settings are often above the skill level of students with special needs (Putnam, 1992a, 1992b; Putnam, Deshler & Schumaker, 1992). Indeed, it is one of the most difficult challenges for teachers of students with special needs. After having demonstrated an appropriate level of mastery of a specific skill in the special education classroom, many students with special needs do not automatically use the newly acquired skill across settings, time, conditions, materials, or persons (Lenz & Bulgren, in press). The purpose of this chapter is to address the concept of generalization of skills, especially for students with special needs.

GENERALIZATION: A DEFINITION

Generalization has been defined as the "occurrence of relevant behavior under different non-training conditions (i.e., across subjects, settings, people, behaviors, and/or time) without the scheduling of the same events in those conditions as had been scheduled in the training condition" (Stokes & Baer, 1977, p. 350). In other words, generalization refers to the extent to which a student successfully and effectively applies a skill outside the setting in which it was learned. Skills learned in the classroom need to be transferred to a new setting, such as the school library media center.

Generalization is often also defined in terms of the dimensions under which the special education teacher expects that generalization will be required to occur. These dimensions allow special education teachers to determine the nature of the differences between the instructional situation (e.g., the special education classroom) and the target generalization situation (e.g., locating a book in the school library media center) so that they can understand why generalization is not occurring and can plan instruction to enhance and facilitate it. The most common dimensions are across persons, stimuli, natural consequences, settings, and time (Haring & Liberty, 1990). Although these are single dimensions, often generalization may occur across more than one dimension, such as across settings and persons.

Generalization across Persons

Generalization across persons refers to the ability to use a newly acquired skill with someone other than the person who provided the instruction. The only difference between the instructional situation (the special education classroom) and the generalization situation is the individual(s) whom the student interacts with while performing the skill. Failure to use the newly acquired skill consistently within this dimension may explain why individual students display different skills for different teachers. For example, a student may demonstrate the skill of alphabetizing for the special education teacher but be unable to do so for the school library media center specialist when attempting to locate a book in the card catalog.

Generalization across Stimuli

This dimension includes a variety of descriptors, such as the ability to generalize newly acquired skills across different types of materials, directions, and tasks. For example, a student with special needs might locate in his or her content-area textbook a topic, like hurricanes, but have difficulty locating the same topic in an encyclopedia.

Generalization to Natural Consequences

The goal here is for the student to generalize the newly acquired skill using only the consequences or reinforcers available within a setting (like the school library media center) instead of the consequences provided during the instruction in the special education classroom. This dimension is important because reinforcement and feedback are not always provided consistently (e.g., verbal versus nonverbal, specific versus general) across instructional settings. For example, in the special education classroom a student may earn points for displaying appropriate classroom behavior; however, in the school library media center, the student may not receive any reinforcement for displaying the same appropriate behavior because it is expected of all students.

Generalization across Settings

Generalization across settings refers to the student's ability to demonstrate the newly acquired skill in a different setting. For example, a student may have acquired the skill of locating a card in an alphabetical set of cards in the special education classroom but have difficulty demonstrating the same skill in the school library media center.

Generalization across Time

This dimension refers to the student's ability to transfer a newly learned skill across various spans of time—one week, one month, one grading period, and so on. For example, once a student has demonstrated the ability to locate information in an encyclopedia in the school library media center, he or she would be expected to demonstrate the same skill later in the school year.

INEFFICIENT SKILL GENERALIZATION

Skill generalization across these five dimensions does not occur automatically or spontaneously. Often it fails to occur because special education teachers do not pay adequate attention to the transition from the acquisition of skills to the generalization of those skills when planning an instructional sequence. Another dilemma is locating a colleague who can act as a collaborator to facilitate generalization across the five dimensions.

Many professionals contend that the lack of a systematic plan to facilitate the generalization of newly learned skills is a major reason that many students with special needs do not retain skills they have mastered previously or fail to apply them across the various generalization dimensions (Ellis & Friend, 1991; Gable, Hendrickson & Shellady, 1992; Vaughn, Bos &

Lund, 1986). Research has shown that not all teachers routinely plan for instruction beyond the acquisition stage of learning (Deshler, Alley, Warner & Schumaker, 1981; Haring, Lovitt, Eaton & Hansen, 1978; Smith, 1981). Thus, most planning and instructional time in special education classrooms is spent on the acquisition of new skills, leaving little time for systematically promoting generalization of these skills.

While most teachers hope that the skills they teach will carry over to other persons, materials, consequences, settings, and time, this "train and hope" approach to generalization (Stokes & Baer, 1977) often does not yield positive results. Instead, teachers must adopt an instructional philosophy (Ellis & Friend, 1991, p. 539) in which the success of instruction is defined by the degree to which students with special needs apply the skills they have learned in the special education classroom to solve problems, adapt to new setting demands, and cope successfully in other settings (e.g., home or community) (Haring & Liberty, 1990).

If students are expected to use their newly acquired skills in circumstances other than those in which the instruction was delivered, they need to be taught both how to perform the skill and how to generalize it. Teachers must develop ways to teach so that students can use their learning to solve new and different problems next week, in other settings, under different conditions, and so forth. Generalization is guaranteed only if students are specifically taught how to generalize. In many instances, therefore, generalization must be taught systematically as skills in and of themselves. Gable et al. (1992) went as far as stating, "If students do not apply knowledge or are unable to perform skills learned in the classroom when they are in noninstructional situations, then the functional worth of the instruction is in doubt" (p. 35).

GENERALIZATION MODEL

In order for students with special needs to maintain and generalize newly acquired skills, teachers should view generalization not as an instructional phase that follows the initial acquisition of the skill but as "a framework in which all instruction is couched, rather than being considered a phase of instruction through which the student merely passes" (Deshler et al., 1984, p. 110) (Figure 10.1).

Ellis et al. (1987a, 1987b) viewed generalization as a phenomenon that is affected by variables *prior to* (e.g., attitudes, relevancy), *during* (e.g., teacher effectiveness, student learning characteristics), and *after* (e.g., self-management skills) the instructional process. Consequently, their model addresses generalization from this perspective, classifying activities into four levels: (1) antecedent generalization (prior to), (2) concurrent generalization (during), (3) subsequent generalization (after), and (4) independent generalization (after).

Antecedent Generalization

Antecedent generalization consists of four tasks that the special education teacher must accomplish: (1) the identification of the skills to be taught to students, (2) the determination as to whether students can demonstrate mastery of those skills, (3) the development of generalization objectives in the student's individualized education plan (IEP) for those skills not mastered, and (4) the planning of his or her instruction of the target skills.

The first task is for the special education teacher to identify the skills to be learned and eventually generalized by the students. According to Haring and Liberty (1990), the skills that students are most likely to generalize are those they perceive as useful in other situations. Teachers can utilize curriculum guides, scope and sequences, and other instructional aids to determine which skills to teach. For example, learning an organizer to write a theme in the special education classroom would also be useful in other situations, like the science class.

The second task requires the special education teacher to determine students' present level of performance and their prior knowledge of the target skill across the five dimensions of generalization before the actual instruction begins. Often teachers select for instruction skills that students have previously acquired and have already generalized (Billingsley, Thompson, Matlock & Work, 1984). This wastes the teacher's time that could be devoted to instruction in and the generalization of skills not previously mastered.

Accurate selection of appropriate goals and objectives requires a thorough analysis of a student's strengths and weaknesses in all areas. A variety of techniques is available to the special education teacher for this purpose. Included are norm-referenced measures (see Hammill, 1987, and Taylor, 1993, for a discussion of the advantages and disadvantages of using these instruments with students with special needs), criterion-referenced measures, curriculum-based measurement (Shapiro & Ager, 1992), interviews, observations, and teacher-made assessment procedures.

It is also important to determine the student's level of prior knowledge of the target skill. Prior knowledge includes everything a student has ever thought of or experienced, any prior exposure to the new skill, and the background information the teacher would like him or her to bring to the class (Marshall, 1989) that may affect the student's willingness to participate in learning the target skill. Numerous techniques are available to determine a student's prior knowledge (Putnam & Wesson, 1990).

Based on this information, teachers may need to change the target skill to make it more relevant to the students, thereby increasing the likelihood of acquiring the skill and, more important, future generalization (Putnam & Wesson, 1990). By satisfying the prior-knowledge requirements, a teacher can quickly check a student's knowledge base and decide how to augment

Figure 10.1
Generalization Model

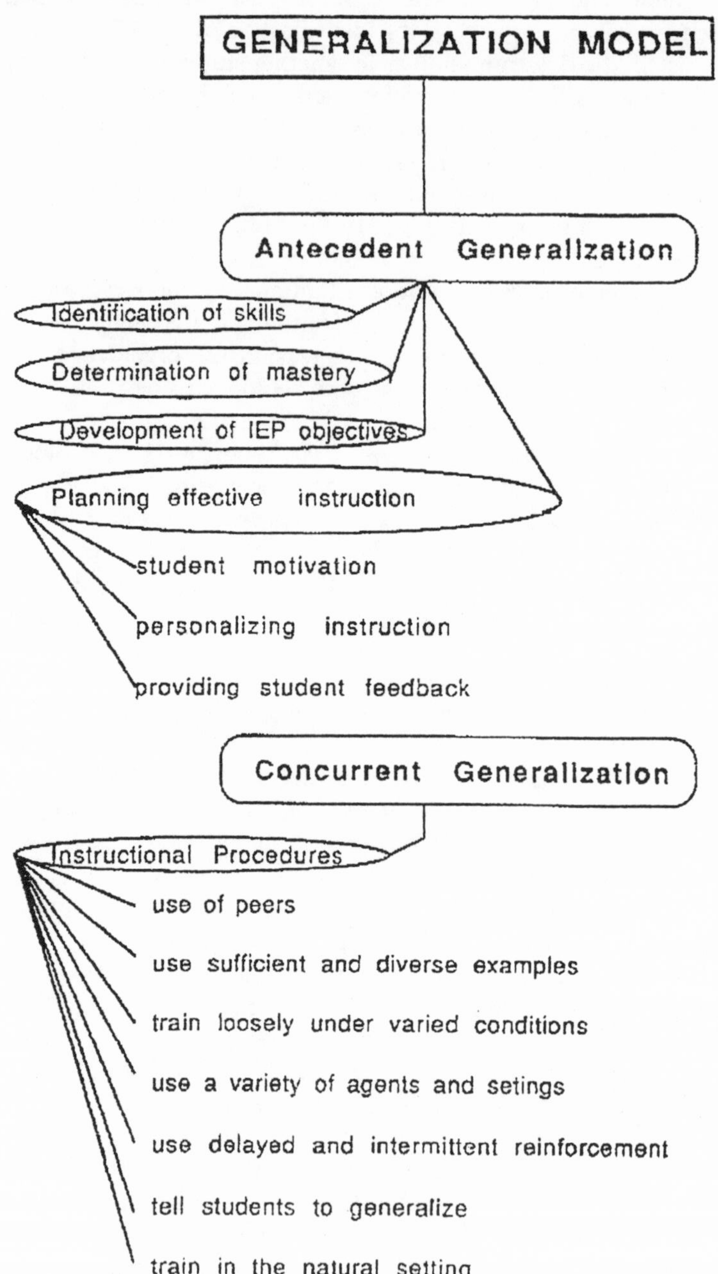

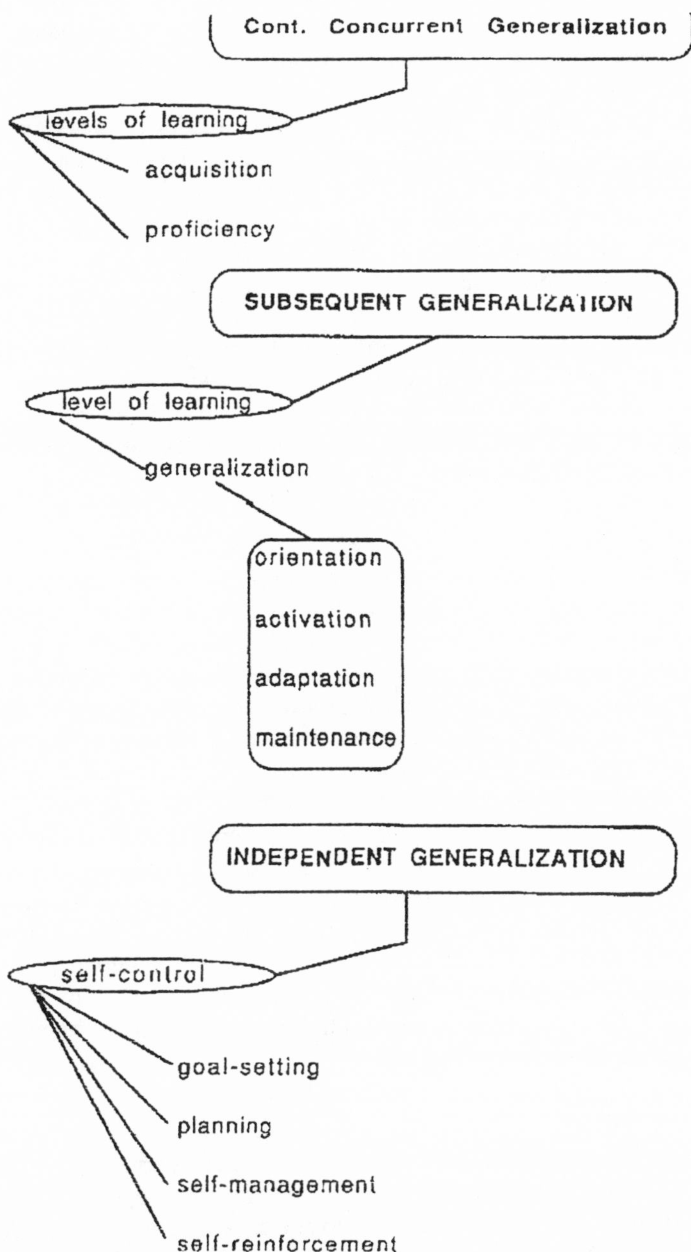

Adapted from Deshler, D. D., Schumaker, J. B., & Lenz, B. K. (1984), Academic and cognitive interventions for LD adolescents; Part 1. *Journal of Learning Disabilities*, *17*, 108–117. Copyright 1984 by PRO-ED, Inc. Adapted with permission.

his or her background knowledge. Such assessment "will identify the type of instructional approach most appropriate: instruction for acquisition and mastery, instruction for maintenance, or instruction for generalization" (Haring & Liberty, 1990, p. 8).

The third task, based on the student's degree of prior knowledge about the target skill, is for the special education teacher to develop objectives for generalization into a student's IEP. These objectives include the same basic components as any other well-written behavioral objective—for example, "The student will demonstrate mastery of the use of guide words to locate a topic in reference materials in the school library media center with 100 percent accuracy."

In the fourth task, as part of antecedent generalization, the special education teacher plans effective instruction based on procedures that research has shown increases a student's acquisition and generalization of newly acquired skills: the student's motivational level, personalizing the instruction, and providing effective feedback.

Student Motivation

Many students with special needs experience difficulty making a commitment to learn or perform (Ellis & Friend, 1991). Results of research directed at understanding motivation in educational settings suggest that this one factor may be a major reason for the failure of students with learning disabilities to show generalization and maintenance of newly acquired skills (Adelman & Taylor, 1982; Switzky & Schultz, 1988). In that motivation is defined "as a state of need or desire that activates the person to do something that will satisfy that need or desire" (Hunter, 1984a, p. 5), special education teachers must identify a student's needs or desires to learn the new skill. Variables known to be related to the amount of motivation are the degree of interest in learning, the level of previous success, the difficulty of learning the new skill, a student's knowledge of past effort in learning, and the relation of the activity to an internalized goal. Thus, for example, a special education teacher could motivate a student by relating the target skill (computing the average) to his or her interest (the average score of a professional football team).

Personalizing Instruction

Much of what students learn in school is forgotten soon after they have demonstrated mastery. What they remember largely depends on how personally useful and meaningful it is to them. Therefore, a key part of planning effective instruction is to personalize the skill to be learned by allowing and encouraging options in the completion of assignments related to the new skill, prompting generalization of the skill to student experiences, and encouraging a student to discuss how, when, and where he or she might be able to use the skill (Lenz & Bulgren, in press).

The first method of personalizing skill acquisition allows for options in the completion of assignments. Such options should enable a student to complete assignments in a manner that allows him or her to express personal interests and utilize strengths by completing alternate but equivalent assignment formats. For example, a student may be encouraged to complete a project, such as a pictorial collection of architectural styles, instead of a written report.

Another method of personalizing skill acquisition is to ask the student to apply the new skill to his or her experiences and background. For example, a student could relate the causes of the Civil War to recent events, such as racial unrest in the United States, or use the card catalog when doing a research project on endangered species for a science class.

The third method of personalizing instruction is to discuss with the student how, when, and where to use the new skill. For example, as a student is learning the skill of writing complete sentences, the teacher could lead a discussion related to the application of that skill in writing a composition in English class or writing a laboratory report in science class. In addition, relating the skill to out-of-school activities and to the future as an adult greatly personalizes the instruction. To continue with the previous example of writing complete sentences, the special education teacher could share the need to complete personal statements on job applications or writing letters of complaint about products purchased.

Student Feedback

Feedback is discussed as part of antecedent generalization; however, it is important that effective feedback be provided throughout the four levels of generalization. Recent studies have demonstrated that several teacher behaviors can enhance the effectiveness of feedback. Ellis and Friend (1991) have provided the following suggestions:

1. Feedback should focus on types of correct behavior as well as error types.
2. Feedback on performance should be relative to established mastery criteria.
3. Effective feedback involves the students' elaboration on the feedback.
4. Effective feedback includes establishing goals for improving specific behaviors.
5. Effective feedback is provided just before a practice attempt.
6. Feedback should be directive during the initial stages of practicing a skill.
7. Feedback should be mediative when students are building fluency.
8. Feedback should be structured so that an awareness of where students have been and where they are going is facilitated. (p. 540)

In summary, a special education teacher should accomplish four tasks as part of antecedent generalization: the identification of skills to teach, the level of mastery of those skills by individual students, the incorporation of generalization objectives into the IEP, and planning effective instruction to enhance the acquisition and generalization of newly acquired skills.

Concurrent Generalization

Once antecedent generalization has been addressed, instruction in the skill can begin. Concurrent generalization encompasses the special education teacher's use of a variety of instructional procedures that promote generalization and adherence to the four levels of learning to be discussed later (acquisition, proficiency, generalization, and adaptation).

Instructional Procedures

Numerous professionals have described techniques and methods for promoting generalization across the five dimensions (Gable et al., 1992; Stokes & Baer, 1977; Vaughn et al., 1986). These procedures are important to the success of any educational program designed to teach skills to be applied outside the special education classroom. Used in combination, the procedures are sufficiently powerful to enable students to acquire a new skill quickly and efficiently. Thus, it is important that as many as possible of the following procedures be incorporated into the instruction of skills.

1. Use peers. The use of peers in the acquisition of skills across the various dimensions is an important instructional principle. Research on the effects of students' working together (e.g., peer tutoring, student learning teams, cooperative learning groups) indicates that learning can be greatly facilitated (Beals, 1984; Cooke, Heron & Heward, 1983; Johnson, Johnson, Warring & Maruyama, 1986). In such arrangements, the goal is to transfer the responsibility of learning from the teacher to a student's peer or peer group, with the student's assuming the responsibility for participating in the group activity (Lenz & Bulgren, in press).

In order to create settings that facilitate peer-assisted instruction, the teacher must be familiar with certain principles associated with cooperative learning. Johnson, Johnson, Holubec and Roy (1984) note that certain cognitive prerequisites appear to be necessary in order for a student to respond appropriately to any type of cooperative arrangement. First, students must recognize that they are members of a group and that each member has a specific role. Second, students must be able to identify and respond to the actions and performance of others. And third, students must be aware of the nature of the goals of cooperation and interdependence and how attainment of these goals can affect the performance of all the members of the group.

Students may learn as much from their peers as they do from teachers about how a skill is performed. Therefore, it is important to provide opportunities for students to interact when practicing the skill as well as to discuss among themselves how the skill is perceived and used (Lenz & Ellis,

1987). As an example, in cooperative learning groups, students could discuss the difference between guide words in a dictionary and in the card catalog, then demonstrate to another group the differences.

2. *Use sufficient and diverse exemplars.* A powerful principle for increasing generalization is to incorporate many different examples while providing instruction in the target skill. For example, as part of a lesson on reference skills, the special education teacher and the school library media specialist could have students locate a topic (e.g., rodeos) in different sources (e.g., dictionary, encyclopedia).

3. *"Train loosely" under varied conditions.* Special education teachers should plan to incorporate a variety of characteristics or conditions of a lesson in their teaching of a new skill. If a special education teacher teaches a skill under only one condition (e.g., time or setting), the students will associate the use of or generalization of that skill only under that one condition. The conditions that could be varied are endless: wording of directions, presentation mode, response format, modality, time, question type, performance criteria, and many others. In addition, the teacher could incorporate general education curriculum, school library media center resources, audiovisual presentations, computer applications, and so on. Varying these and other conditions while teaching can increase the generalizability of a newly acquired skill because the skill will be associated with many conditions instead of only a specific few.

4. *Use a variety of agents and settings.* Generalization can be facilitated by varying the individuals (agents) who provide the instruction and the settings in which the instruction occurs. This instructional principle suggests that it is not in a student's best interest if the special education teacher is the only one who delivers instruction or evaluates a student's learning or if the special education classroom is the only setting in which such instruction takes place.

The importance of varying instructional agents was underscored by Dyer (1978), who discussed the danger of students with learning disabilities becoming so dependent on the special education teacher that they are unable to make satisfactory instructional progress with other teachers. One way to break such dependence is to involve more than one teacher, for example, the school library media specialist, in the instructional effort. This encourages the student to concentrate on the skill rather than the instructional agent.

As an example, instruction in a social skill might include the use of role playing. In order to approximate the real world, the role plays might feature many different combinations of partners (peer-adult, peer-peer, same sex–opposite sex, older-younger, mixed race, stranger-friend, etc.). Such arrangements increase generalization beyond what would be obtained if the student role-played only with the special education teacher, for example.

This instructional principle is one of the most difficult to operationalize because it requires scheduling arrangements and coordination with other school personnel and students. It can be more easily accomplished if the special education teacher involves other individuals, like the school library media specialist, in cooperative planning.

5. *Use delayed and intermittent reinforcement.* This instructional principle draws on a well-established learning principle: intermittent reinforcement schedules are particularly resistant to extinction. Therefore, generalization is promoted by gradually moving from continuous reinforcement to intermittent schedules or delayed reinforcement (Kazdin & Polster, 1973).

Although recent research emphasizes the importance of immediate and frequent reinforcement for the acquisition of new skills (Kline, Deshler & Schumaker, 1991), the opposite—fading of reinforcement—is critical to the generalization of newly acquired skills. As reinforcements are faded, the student cannot easily discriminate between the instruction and another situation but begins to perform the skill consistently across each situation. The key feature "of using intermittent schedules for student reinforcement is their expectancy coupled with their unpredictability" (Deshler et al., 1981, p. 420). Special education teachers should schedule reinforcers so that students expect that reinforcement will take place without being able to predict when the reinforcement will occur.

6. *Tell students to generalize.* The least expensive and certainly the most straightforward instructional principle for promoting the generalization of newly acquired skills is to tell students to generalize what they have learned. Special education teachers often assume, incorrectly, that a student will see the connection between the skills taught in the classroom and what is expected of him or her in other settings, like the school library media center. Frequent reminders to try out and practice the skills learned in the special education classroom across the five dimensions can be very effective (Deshler et al., 1981). As an example, the special education teacher might say, "Remember to use your test-taking strategy today on Mr. Hoffman's test!"

7. *Train in the natural setting.* This instructional principle is one of the most dependable. Instruction in the target skill is provided directly in at least one other setting to which the skill should be generalized, like the school library media center. Such instruction ensures that the new skill is supported and maintained by the natural contingencies in the other setting.

As special education teachers plan for each day's lesson, they must consider the instructional principles that facilitate generalization. "No one of these principles is the most powerful; the potency of each . . . changes in relation to a particular learning situation so teachers must constantly be aware of the presence or absence of all of them" (Hunter, 1984b, p. 7).

Levels of Learning

Haring et al. (1978) contend that the effectiveness of the instructional principles just discussed depends on the entry level of the student. Some of the principles facilitate more automatic performance of a newly acquired skill, and others encourage generalization, maintenance, or adaptation of a given skill. Therefore, teachers must also consider the levels of learning (Haring & Eaton, 1978) that ultimately result in successful generalization of newly acquired skills. These levels are not isolated. They are interactive and should be considered neither as "individual entities nor as developmentally hierarchical, though instruction becomes more complex at each successive level" (Hudson, Colson & Braxdale, 1984, p. 6).

At the first level of learning, *acquisition,* the student enters the learning process with little or no knowledge of how to perform the skill accurately. After a period of instruction, the student learns the skill so that he or she can perform it accurately at a 90 to 100 percent accuracy level. The second level of learning, *proficiency,* aims to enable the student to perform the skill with both accuracy and sufficient speed or to meet a predetermined level of mastery. To require student mastery of instructional objectives is an important concept underlying effective instruction for a student with special needs. Unfortunately, this is often the most frustrating stage of learning for both the teacher and the student because frequently the newly acquired skills are not retained at as high a level as in the previous stage and plateaus at about a 70 to 80 percent accuracy rate. However, research has shown that unless students can proficiently perform the skill at the specified mastery levels, generalization is not likely to occur (Schmidt, Deshler, Schumaker & Alley, 1988).

Subsequent Generalization

The third level of learning, *generalization,* moves the student with special needs into the third phase of generalization, subsequent generalization. Activities during this phase use other individuals, like the school library media specialist, to facilitate generalization of the newly mastered skills across the five dimensions.

The need to program systematically for instructional generalization requires that the special education teacher, the student, and the school library media specialist engage in a process of cooperative planning that results in a closer link between instruction in the special education classroom and generalization of skills in other settings, like the school library media center. In addition, a student needs to generalize library skills learned within the general and special education classroom outside the school, such as the public library. As part of this process, the special education teacher is responsible for teaching the student how to generalize the newly acquired skill, the student is responsible for engaging in the actual generalization process, and other personnel are responsible for facilitating the generalization of the newly acquired skill.

Cooperative Planning

Cooperative planning is "an ongoing process by which two or more professionals work together to develop, implement, monitor, and/or revise a plan of instruction for a student or a group of students" (Lenz & Keming, 1981, p. 1). Schmidt (1983) found that cooperative planning was an effective approach to increase generalization for students with special needs who fail to generalize after instruction in the special education classroom. The cooperative planning procedure requires that the special education teacher confer with other school personnel with whom the student with special needs has frequent contact.

The goal for these "brief and business-like" (Schmidt, 1983, p. 10) cooperative planning sessions is to ensure that students are applying the newly acquired skill across the five generalization dimensions. For example, one objective of a cooperative planning session might be to explain to the school library media specialist what skills the student with special needs has mastered that could also be demonstrated in the school library media center (generalization across setting and agent). In addition, situations within the library media center in which the student could use the new skill could be identified (generalization across conditions). Finally, some of the instructional principles that promote generalization could be shared, like the use of multiple examples of a new skill. As a means of facilitating cooperative planning, this generalization stage can be divided into four tasks: orientation, activation, adaptation, and maintenance (Ellis, Deshler, Lenz, Schumaker & Clark, 1991).

Orientation

The purpose of this task is to make the student aware of the need for applying the skill to meet relevant setting demands and to help prepare the student for the actual generalization of the newly acquired skill. For example, the student with special needs may need to be told that the same behaviors expected from him or her in the special education classroom are also expected in the school library media center. Ellis et al. (1991) suggested that as part of this task, the special education teacher should complete some of the following activities with students:

1. Identify rationales for using the skill across dimensions.
2. Explain why specific attention to skill generalization is necessary.
3. Identify which settings are most likely to require the use of the skill.
4. Discuss how students might remind themselves to use the skill in different settings.

5. List the steps of the skill on 3" x 5" cards, and place the cards in textbooks, notebooks, and other materials used in settings in which the skill might be applied.
6. Specify verbal and written cues that exist in other settings that could signal use of the skill.
7. Review different types of materials the student might encounter across the dimensions, and discuss how the skill might or might not be applied.
8. Deliberately evaluate materials where the skill should not be applied, and discuss reasons why the skill is not appropriate.
9. Discuss which aspects of the skill seem to be most helpful and least helpful.
10. Generate ways to improve or adjust the skill to make the skill more responsive to setting demands.
11. Identify other skills that might be combined with the new skill to make the skill more effective and improve the student's overall performance.
12. Make cards on which the student writes positive affirmations that connect use of the skill with success in meeting a specific setting demand and reviewed on a daily basis.

Activation

The purpose of this task as part of subsequent generalization is to encourage students to use the newly acquired skill, to monitor the application of the skill across dimensions, and to prompt effective and efficient generalization when it does not occur (Ellis & Friend, 1991). To accomplish this, the responsibility for promoting generalization, which up to this point in the process generally had been left to the special education teacher and the student, must be shared by other individuals, such as the school library media specialist. The following activities focus on a variety of interactions that could take place among these individuals (Ellis et al., 1991):

1. Apply the skill to a specific assignment related to another class and, afterwards, demonstrate and describe how the skill was used to complete the assignment.
2. Apply the skill to a variety of assignments that must be done at home or in another setting, and demonstrate and describe how the skill was used to complete these assignments.
3. Set daily and weekly goals related to increasing the use of the skill across the dimensions and to improving performance.
4. Develop a plan related to how to increase application of the skill to meet these goals.
5. Monitor implementation of the plan and effects of using the skill across the dimension.
6. Request feedback from others, like the school media specialist, on application of the skill.
7. Develop a chart and record progress related to applying the skill and its results on related measures of performance.

8. Reinforce progress and success in the form of self-congratulatory statements and, if necessary, extrinsic rewards.

Although part of the responsibility for ensuring skill generalization rests with the special education teacher, the school library media specialist also must assume responsibility for facilitating generalization. He or she can help the student recognize the relationship between the demands of the school library media center and appropriate skill use and guide the student to identify and apply the skill automatically and independently to meet those setting demands (Lenz & Bulgren, in press). For example, the school library media specialist should be encouraged to:

1. Obtain from the special education teacher a short description of the skills that the student has been taught, the conditions or criteria for correct and successful application, and what the student has been taught with regard to applying the skill across the dimensions.
2. Determine if the student has been taught to identify specific cues to indicate when a skill or part of the skill is to be used.
3. Evaluate teaching materials, presentation routines, and activities to ensure that sufficient opportunities are available in the school library media center for the student to use a specific skill.
4. Determine which situations and activities in the school library media center best lend themselves to direct monitoring of skill generalization (Ellis et al., 1991, p. 22).

Adaptation

The third task of subsequent generalization, adaptation, provides opportunities for the student to begin to change the skill to become his or her own skill as a means of meeting new and different setting demands. For example, a student may have learned the steps required to access the school library media center's holdings through the computer. During this task, the student may begin to realize that all of the steps are not necessary and that several can be combined or eliminated. Thus, the student has adapted the newly learned skill to meet his or her individual needs. Here the special education teacher and the school library media specialist should encourage students to:

1. Identify how the skill can be modified to meet additional setting demands.
2. Write down the skill modifications and how they can be used.
3. Repeat the orientation and activation activities that might be necessary to learn to apply these modifications (Ellis et al., 1991, p. 21)

Maintenance

The purpose of the last task of subsequent generalization, maintenance, is to ensure that a student continues to use the skill across the various dimensions. Thus, the special education teacher, school library media specialist, and a student jointly develop a plan for promoting long-term use of the newly acquired skill. For example, through cooperative planning, it may be determined that a student will maintain a personal log of his or her trips to the school library media center and the various methods by which he or she located a book. The student and teacher should be encouraged to attempt some of the following tasks:

1. Discuss rationales related to long-term use of the skill.
2. Identify habits and barriers that might prevent the student from continuing to use the skill.
3. Determine how the student might monitor long-term application of the skill.
4. Discuss ways in which the teacher can help to monitor long-term application and successful use of the skill.
5. Set goals related to monitoring long-term application of the skill.
6. Determine how many times a week the teacher should check the use of the skill.
7. Determine how this check will be conducted and if others, like the school media specialist, will be involved.
8. Specify the criteria for successful performance of the skill.
9. Plan the procedures that will be used to improve the student's performance if he or she is not applying the skill effectively or efficiently.
10. Review the student's positive affirmation cards on a daily basis.
11. Determine the duration for weekly maintenance checks.
12. Discuss and identify when the skill can be considered permanent and when maintenance checks will no longer be needed.
13. Develop a chart and record the results of efforts to maintain use of the skill.
14. Indentify self-reinforcers or self-rewards that can be used in conjunction with successful maintenance of the skill.

Independent Generalization

The last of the four phases of generalization, independent generalization, transfers the responsibility for generalization to the student. This shift toward more student responsibility is a critical component of generalization; however, even in this phase, the special education teacher continues to play a vital role. A number of self-regulation factors can affect the degree to which students with special needs generalize newly acquired skills (Ellis, 1986). For example, these students tend to think that they are not in control of their learning (Bryan, 1986; Licht & Kistner, 1986), often set few personal goals (e.g., to generalize the newly acquired skill), and put forth little personal effort to generalize those skills (Pearl, Bryan & Donahue, 1980). Therefore, as a means of increasing independent generalization, students with special needs often require explicit instruction in self-regulation techniques, such as accepting responsibility for their personal effort, goal setting, self-monitoring their progress, and self-reinforcing their effort.

Self-control

Given the repeated educational failures of many students with special needs, it is not surprising that they often give up in their efforts to learn new skills. Although they may have tried to succeed, the cycle of failure these students have usually experienced has taught them that there is little relationship between their effort and success. Perceiving their efforts and skills as incapable of leading to success, students with special needs often believe that success is out of their control. Consequently, they have been described as having "learned helplessness" (Morgan, 1986). Often as a result of this learned helplessness, they depend heavily on their special education teachers to mediate the few successes they have (Ellis, 1986). As a result, many "perceive themselves as passive recipients of whatever life dishes out and have little control over their own destinies" (Lenz & Ellis, 1987, p. 1).

To counteract this tendency, both special education teachers and school library media specialists must strive to promote these students' feelings of control and power over their own future by helping them to develop skills in decision making and providing opportunities to make decisions, recognize the causes of success and failure so that instead of always blaming themselves they come to feel that their efforts will influence the outcome, and develop coping mechanisms and strategies for responding constructively to failure (Lerner, 1988). For example, the school library media specialist can allow a student to decide whether to use the computer or the card catalog to locate a book.

Factors such as effort may outweigh student awareness of an appropriate skill to be used in a given situation, thus negatively affecting generalization of the newly acquired skill. Because many students with special needs seem to believe that their successes are largely due to factors beyond their personal control (e.g., "I did well on the test because the test was easy"), the role of personal effort is a key factor to consider when teaching these students. "Successful generalization, in the simplest form, is related to a student's ability to choose a skill that can effectively address the demand of the setting and then try as hard as possible to use the skill in the correct way" (Ellis & Friend, 1991, p. 546).

Ellis et al. (1987b) suggested a sequence of instructional steps for capitalizing on the association between attribution and generalization. First, special education teachers should teach a student to make statements that reflect his or her own effort ("Wow, I really studied hard for this test, and I made a good grade!"). Second, they should teach them to attribute their difficulties to ineffective skill use ("Gee, I guess underlining every line in the chapter was not a good study skill to use!"). Finally, special education teachers should arrange for a student with special needs to experience a fair amount of success with the newly acquired skill.

Goal Setting

Research has demonstrated that instruction in goal-setting techniques can promote higher rates of generalization (Ellis, 1985; Schunk, 1985; Seabaugh & Schumaker, 1983; Tollefson, Tracy, Johnsen & Chatman, 1986). In Lenz, Ehren, and Smiley's (1991) goal attainment system, for example, a student sets academic goals, develops a plan to reach those goals, implements the plan, and monitors his or her progress toward achieving the goals.

During the first part of this goal attainment system, a student, with guidance from the special education teacher, sets individual goals for meeting the demands of various settings. Lenz, Ehren, and Smiley (1991) contend that the purpose of goal setting is for the student to identify exactly what needs to be done (e.g., generalize the newly acquired skill) and across what dimensions (e.g., agent and setting). There are three distinct types of goal-setting activities: (a) evaluating task expectations (e.g., What are the criteria for completing the task?), (b) generating alternatives or options (e.g., Which newly acquired skills can I use to complete the tasks?), and (c) clarifying and selecting goals (e.g., Which specific goal will help me reach criteria for the task?). For example, the school library media center specialist may work with the special education teacher in setting goals for each student, such as reading one book each week.

The next part of the system, goal actualization, requires the student to develop a plan for reaching the goal (What steps are required to complete the task successfully?), embellish or expand the plan (Can the task be completed by following these steps?), and evaluate the plan (What constraints are there on completing the task?). Following along with the same example, the student may plan to check out a new book each Friday and attempt to read as much as possible over the weekend. Then the plan may include having the student share with the special education teacher or school library media specialist on Monday how much he or she has read. Finally, on Wednesday, the special education teacher may check with the student to determine if he or she will meet the goal of reading a book per week.

The third part of the goal attainment system has a student learn how to self-manage his or her progress toward achieving the established goal. This includes self-recording, self-monitoring, and self-evaluation. An abundance of research has demonstrated that students with special needs can be taught these self-management techniques (Hallahan, Lloyd, Kosiewicz, Kauffman & Graves, 1979; Hallahan & Sapona, 1983; Rooney, Hallahan & Lloyd, 1983).

Lenz and Ellis (1987) report that self-management involves determining when a skill should be used (Should I use skill A or skill B?), applying the various steps of the skill (What step of skill A do I do next?), and monitoring the process to ensure themselves that things are going as they should (Am I on course using skill A to achieve my goal?). For example, the student may maintain a chart to record the number of pages read each day in order to reach the goal of reading one book a week.

Alley and Deshler (1979) outlined several techniques for special education teachers for helping students with special needs monitor their work:

1. Teach students specific procedures for monitoring their work.
2. Provide time at the end of each lesson for students to check their work.
3. Incorporate a point system to encourage students to check their work.

The last part of the goal attainment system is the ultimate challenge for students with special needs: to demonstrate their use of a newly acquired skill across the various dimensions without the support, reinforcement, or encouragement of others. Students determine how they will reinforce themselves for the progress they make toward achieving their stated goals (How will I evaluate my progress? How will I motivate myself to complete the task?) (Lenz, Ehren, & Smiley, 1991).

Research has demonstrated that students with special needs who make self-affirmation statements (a positive statement to themselves to affirm their belief in their ability to complete the tasks) can greatly increase their application and generalization of a newly acquired skill (Hughes & Schumaker, 1991). For example, a student might say to himself or herself, "I can find this book in the school library media center because I know how to use the card catalog."

CONCLUSION

Students with special needs experience difficulties in the generalization of newly acquired skills. Teachers cannot assume that generalization will happen automatically; therefore, it must be taught systematically as a skill in and of itself. Significant and efficient generalization occurs only when special education teachers teach to achieve it. As students with special needs are increasingly required to cope with the demands of all facets of society, the ability to generalize skills is a particularly critical survival skill. The ultimate purpose of teaching skills that generalize is "to provide the individual with the means for adapting to new situations, solving problems, and living in a changing world" (Haring & Liberty, 1990, p. 2).

Successful generalization involves four levels: antecedent, concurrent, subsequent, and independent. Although a great deal of generalization instruction and training involves primarily the special education teacher and the student, the various levels also require the cooperation of other school personnel, such as the school library media specialist. These individuals play a significant role by providing opportunities for application and generalization of newly acquired skills across five dimensions—persons, stimuli, time, setting, and natural consequences—by utilizing various research-based instructional principles that promote skill generalization.

REFERENCES

Adelman, H. S., & Taylor, L. (1982). Enhancing the motivation and skill needed to overcome interpersonal problems. *Journal of Learning Disabilities, 5*: 438–446.

Alley, G. R., & Deshler, D. D. (1979). *Teaching the learning disabled adolescent: Strategies and methods*. Denver: Love.

Beals, V. R. (1984). *The effects of large group instruction on the acquisition of specific learning strategies by learning disabled adolescents*. Unpublished doctoral dissertation, University of Kansas, Lawrence.

Billingsly, F. F., Thompson, M., Matlock, B., & Work, J. (1984). Generalization and the educational ecology of severely handicapped learners. In N. G. Haring, *Institute for education of severely handicapped children: Washington Research Organization: Annual report FY 83–84*. Seattle: University of Washington, College of Education.

Bryan, T. (1986). Self-concept and attributions of the learning disabled. *Learning Disabilities Focus* 1: 82–89.

Cooke, N. L., Heron, T. E., & Heward, W. L. (1983). *Peer-tutoring: Implementing classwide programs in the primary grades*. Columbus, OH: Special Press.

Deshler, D. D., Alley, G. R., Warner, M. M., & Schumaker, J. B. (1981). Instructional practices for promoting skill acquisition and generalization in severely learning disabled adolescents. *Learning Disability Quarterly* 4: 415–421.

Deshler, D. D., Schumaker, J. B., & Lenz, B. K. (1984). Academic and cognitive interventions for LD adolescents: Part 1. *Journal of Learning Disabilities* 17: 108–117.

Dyer, W. G. (1978). Implications of the helping relationship between learning disabled students and their teachers. *Learning Disability Quarterly* 2: 55–61.

Ellis, E. S. (1985). *The effects of teaching learning disabled adolescents an executive problem solving strategy*. Unpublished doctoral dissertation, University of Kansas, Lawrence.

Ellis, E. S. (1986). The role of motivation and pedagogy on the generalization of cognitive strategy training. *Journal of Learning Disabilities 19:* 66–70.

Ellis, E. S., Deshler, D. D., Lenz, B. K., Schumaker, J. B., & Clark, F. L. (1991). An instructional model for teaching learning strategies. *Focus on Exceptional Children* 23: 1–24.

Ellis, E. S., & Friend, P. (1991). Adolescents with learning disabilities. In B. Y. L. Wong (Ed.), *Learning about learning disabilities* (pp. 505–561). San Diego: Academic Press.

Ellis, E. S., Lenz, B. K., & Sabornie, E. J. (1987a). Generalization and adaptation of learning strategies to natural environments: Part 1: Critical agents. *Remedial and Special Education* 8: 6–20.

Ellis, E. S., Lenz, B. K., & Sabornie, E. J. (1987b). Generalization and adaptation of learning strategies to natural environments: Part 2: Research into practice. *Remedial and Special Education* 8: 6–23.

Gable, R. A., Hendrickson, J. M., & Shellady, S. (1992). Strategies for improving maintenance and generalization of academic skill—so students "don't leave class without it." *Preventing School Failure* 37: 35–41.

Hallahan, D. P., Lloyd, J., Kosiewicz, M. M., Kauffman, J. M., & Graves, A. W. (1979). Self-monitoring of attention as a treatment for a learning disabled boy's off-task behavior. *Learning Disability Quarterly* 2: 24–32.

Hallahan, D. P., & Sapona, R. (1983). Self-monitoring of attention with learning-disabled children: Past research and current issues. *Journal of Learning Disabilities 16:* 616–620.

Hammill, D. D. (1987). *Assessing the abilities and instructional needs of students.* Austin: PRO-ED.

Haring, N. G., & Eaton, M. D. (1978). Systematic instructional procedures: An instruction hierarchy. In N. G. Haring, T. C. Lovitt, M. D. Eaton & C. L. Hansen (Eds.), *The fourth R: Research in the classroom* (pp. 23–48). Columbus, OH: Merrill.

Haring, N. G., & Liberty, K. A. (1990). Matching strategies with performance in facilitating generalization. *Focus on Exceptional Children* 22: 1–16.

Haring, N. G., Lovitt, T. C., Eaton, C. L., & Hansen, C. L. (Eds.). (1978). *The fourth R: Research in the classroom*. Columbus, OH: Merrill.

Hudson, F. L., Colson, S. E., & Braxdale, C. T. (1984). Instructional planning for dysfunctional learners: Levels of presentation. *Focus on Exceptional Children 17:* 1–12.

Hughes, C. A., & Schumaker, J. B. (1991). Test-taking strategy instruction for adolescents with learning disabilities. *Exceptionality* 2: 205–221.

Hunter, M. (1984a). *Motivation*. El Segundo, CA: TIP Publications.

Hunter, M. (1984b). *Teach for transfer*. El Segundo, CA: TIP Publications.

Johnson, D. W., Johnson, R. T., Holubec, E. J., & Roy, P. (1984). *Circles of learning: Cooperation in the classroom*. Alexandria, VA: Association for Supervision and Curriculum Development.

Johnson, D. W., Johnson, R. T., Warring, D., & Maruyama, G. (1986). Different cooperative learning procedures and cross-handicap relationships. *Exceptional Children* 53: 247–252.

Kazdin, A. E., & Polster, R. (1973). Intermittent token reinforcement and response maintenance in extinction. *Behavior Therapy* 4: 386–391.

Keogh, B. K., & Glover, A. T. (1980). The generality and durability of cognitive training effects. *Exceptional Education Quarterly* 1: 75–82.

Kline, F. M., Deshler, D. D., & Schumaker, J. B. (1991). Development and validation of feedback routines for instructing students with learning disabilities. *Learning Disability Quarterly* 14: 191–206.

Lenz, B. K., & Bulgren, J. A. (in press). Promoting learning in the content areas. In P. T. Cegelka & W. H. Berdine (Eds.), *Effective instruction for students with learning problems*. Needham Heights, MA: Allyn & Bacon.

Lenz, B. K., Ehren, B. J., & Smiley, L. R. (1991). A goal attainment approach to improve completion of project-type assignments by adolescents with learning disabilities. *Learning Disabilities Research and Practice* 6: 166–176.

Lenz, B. K., & Ellis, E. S. (1986). *Learning strategies for learning to live.* Paper presented at the Florida Strategies Intervention Model Conference, Tampa.

Lenz, B. K., & Kemig, J. (1981). *Promoting generalization through a cooperative planning model.* Unpublished manuscript.

Lerner, J. (1988). *Learning disabilities* (3d ed.). Boston: Houghton Mifflin.

Licht, B. G., & Kistner, J. A. (1986). Motivational problems of learning-disabled children: Individual differences and their implications for treatment. In J. K. Torgeson & B. Y. L. Wong (Eds.), *Psychological and educational perspectives on learning disabilities* (pp. 225–255). New York: Academic Press.

Marshall, N. (1989). The students: Who are they and how do I reach them? In D. Lapp, J. Flood & N. Farnan (Eds.), *Content area reading and learning* (pp. 59–69). Englewood Cliffs, NJ: Prentice-Hall.

Moleskey, J., Rieth, H. J., & Polsgrove, L. (1980). The implications of response generalization for improving the effectiveness of programs for learning disabled children. *Journal of Learning Disabilities* 13: 287–290.

Morgan, S. R. (1986). Locus of control in children labeled as learning disabled, behaviorally disordered, and learning disabled/behaviorally disordered. *Learning Disabilities Research* 2: 10–13.

Pearl, R., Bryan, T., & Donahue, M. (1980). Learning disabled children's attributions for success and failure. *Learning Disability Quarterly 3:* 3–9.

Putnam, M. L. (1992a). Testing practices of mainstream secondary classroom teachers. *Remedial and Special Education* 13: 11–21.

Putnam, M. L. (1992b). Characteristics of questions on tests administered by mainstream secondary classroom teachers. *Learning Disabilities: Research and Practice* 7: 129–136.

Putnam, M. L., Deshler, D. D., & Schumaker, J. B. (1992). The investigation of setting demands: A missing link in learning strategy instruction. In L. Meltzer (Ed.), *Strategy assessment and instruction for students with learning disabilities: From theory to practice* (pp. 325–354). Austin, TX: PRO-ED.

Putnam, M. L., & Wesson, C. L. (1990). The teacher's role in teaching content-area information. *LD Forum* 16: 55–60.

Rooney, K. J., Hallahan, D. P., & Lloyd, J. W. (1983). Self-recording of attention by learning disabled students in the regular classroom. *Journal of Learning Disabilities 17:* 360–364.

Schmidt, J. L. (1983). Suggestions to increase the transfer of skills learned in the resource room to the regular classroom. *Pointer* 27: 8–10.

Schmidt, J. L., Deshler, D. D., Schumaker, J. B., & Alley, G. R. (1988). Effects of generalization instruction on the written language performance of adolescents with learning disabilities in the mainstream classroom. *Reading, Writing, and Learning Disabilities* 4: 291–309.

Schunk, D. H. (1985). Participation in goal-setting: Effects on self-efficacy and skills in learning-disabled children. *Journal of Special Education* 19: 307–317.

Seabaugh, G. O., & Schumaker, J. B. (1983). *The effects of self-regulation training on the academic productivity of LD and NLD adolescents.* Research Report 37. Lawrence: University of Kansas Institute for Research in Learning Disabilities.

Shapiro, E. S., & Ager, C. (1992). Assessment of special education students in regular education programs: Linking assessment to instruction. *Elementary School Journal* 92: 283–296.

Smith, D. D. (1981). *Teaching the learning disabled.* Englewood Cliffs, NJ: Prentice-Hall.

Stokes, T. F., & Baer, D. B. (1977). An implicit technology of generalization. *Journal of Applied Behavior Analysis* 10: 349–367.

Switzky, H. N., & Schultz, G. F. (1988). Intrinsic motivation and learning performance: Implications for individual educational programming for learners with mild handicaps. *Remedial and Special Education* 9: 7–14.

Taylor, R. L. (1993). *Assessment of exceptional students* (3d ed.). Needham Heights, MA: Allyn & Bacon.

Tollefson, N., Tracy, D. B., Johnsen, E. P., & Chatman, J. (1986). Generalization and maintenance of appropriate behavior through self-control. *Journal of Consulting and Clinical Psychology* 43: 577–583.

Vaughn, S., Bos, C. S., & Lund, K. A. (1986). But they can do it in my room: Strategies for promoting generalization. *Teaching Exceptional Children 18:* 176–181.

11

Fostering Relationships among Special and General Education Students in the School Library Media Center

Caren L. Wesson, Mary Ann Fitzgerald, and Jane Glodoski

Students of all ability levels find enjoyment and learning through participation in a school library program. However, research has shown students with special needs often face rejection and isolation from "regular education peers" (Gottlieb & Leyser, 1981). Even when schools embrace an inclusive education philosophy and integrated classrooms are the norm, mere proximity to special needs peers does not foster understanding, respect, or friendship. Providing library experiences that focus on increasing the development of positive social interactions among all students may prove to be one valuable opportunity for students to learn about and enjoy one another. At the same time, students should be able to increase their library skills and find enjoyment in the school library.

The school librarian, in collaboration with classroom teachers, may guide students toward recognizing and appreciating students' differences as well as similarities. In the comfortable and inviting atmosphere of the library, students may find the common ground that leads to the development of friendships. Through specific strategies, the rejection and isolation students have traditionally faced may be replaced with more appropriate social interactions.

This chapter explores and suggests strategies that the school librarian, in collaboration with the classroom teacher, may employ to enhance the informal peer support and friendships for students who may not initially appear to have much in common. The school library provides the setting for such interactions to occur while still fostering students' achievement of their own academic goals. Clearly, students who feel a sense of belonging and acceptance will have a better chance of success in all their educational pursuits.

SENSITIZATION ACTIVITIES

A prerequisite for the development of friendships is the ability of students to understand and respect each other. Activities designed to help students recognize and celebrate individual differences, often referred to as sensitization activities, have two main goals: to provide knowledge of various disabling conditions and to demonstrate ways in which people may be different, but, more important, the same. Sensitization activities are designed to involve students through reading, films, projects, discussions, and simulations.

The school librarian and the classroom teachers may collaborate to plan sensitization activities that may be introduced in the library and followed up in the classroom. The following sensitization activities are organized by three basic themes:

Awareness of Disabling Conditions

- Explore available media kits relating to specific disabling conditions such as learning disabilities, cognitive disabilities, physical and other health impairments, emotional disturbance, visual impairments, speech/language, and deaf/hard of hearing. Kits provide filmstrips/movies, tapes, and activities designed to provide information about specific disabilities.
- Identify famous individuals with disabilities, particularly those who have been assigned a special education label. Use encyclopedias, biographies, and the newspaper for current stories. Have students read and share information about these people and prepare a matching worksheet of famous people and their disabilities. Discuss the feelings shared by people in the books and articles, and let students relate these to feelings and experiences they too may have had.
- While discussing and sharing information about disabilities, provide simulation activities within the library setting. For example, students could be grouped according to an arbitrarily designated disability. The student assigned a visual impairment could wear a blindfold and attempt to locate places within the setting by memory or touch. (A guide will be necessary to ensure safety.) The "learning disabled students" could write their assignments with their nondominant hand to simulate visual-motor difficulties. All student groups could then share the most challenging aspect of this simulated activity (Wesson & Mandell, 1989).
- Students could identify adaptations available for people with disabilities within the library setting (for example, wheelchair access and braille or large-print books).
- When students enter the library, assign them a specific disabling condition and give them a list of activities they would normally be expected to do during a typical day. Students then work in groups according to assigned labels and make a list of adaptations they would need to complete these tasks.
- Place students in cooperative learning groups and have them design an adaptation for individuals with disabilities to use. This could range from adaptive

devices for persons with physical disabilities to developing techniques for working with the emotionally disturbed. Remind students that adaptations may not always be tangible or visible.

Respect for Individual Differences

- Students could devise a talent survey that lists a variety of talents and teachers, staff, and other students could complete this survey. The compiled surveys could be cross-referenced, and an all-school directory could be developed, to be kept in the library as a resource for staff and students.
- Have students use graphing skills to indicate their preferences for various foods, music, games, books, and school subjects.
- Read books that help students understand the concept that we are all the same, yet we are all different. Follow up these readings by having students chart ways they are the same and the ways they are different. Stress the concept that similarities are more important than differences, but differences make us interesting.
- Have people with disabilities visit the library and share their talents; for example, a deaf person could teach the students sign language, or a person with visual impairments could demonstrate how to read braille.
- For students in intermediate grades, a bibliography of literature (across grade levels) pertaining to disabilities could be developed. Students could also write their reactions to the various materials available in the library relating to the topic.
- Students could use the library's dictionary and/or thesaurus to make a list of character traits. They could then draw self-portraits and label them "people packages." These pictures would include the character trait vocabulary that best represents themselves.

Celebrating Diversity

- Discuss book banning and book burning. Create a list of banned books. Form debate panels to debate pros and cons of censorship in the library.
- Have students learn about family differences and make posters about people in their families.
- Approach learning about cultural differences from the perspective that everyone has a culture and that all cultures are valuable and deserve respect. Diversity enriches the classroom. In the classroom have students prepare and share information about heritage (food, clothing, language).
- Have students look up the origin and meaning of their name and then use maps and atlases to look up the country of origin of their family. Then they prepare reports, choosing the format: oral, visual, individual, group, or some other alternative.
- Students read and research fables from various countries.
- Students research and write an autobiography.
- Students read about famous women in history and then prepare a report on the discrimination women have faced.

- Students read, discuss, and share ideas about racism in society. In cooperative groups students may choose a topic pertinent to racism to cover and share with the large group. Topics may include (but are not exclusive to) reasons for racism, effects of racism, and ways to overcome racism and bias.

By providing sensitization activities for students through the collaborative efforts of the school librarian and classroom teacher, students may be more prepared to develop and accept friendships. However, teachers and librarians must also pay attention to the development of each class as a community of learners.

CREATING A CLIMATE OF COMMUNITY IN THE LIBRARY

The majority of activities related to turning a class into a community will be done in the classroom; however, some carryover activities may help the feeling of community transcend to other settings. (Possibly, the librarian may be teaching a class in which special needs students are included for only "specials," such as gym, music, art, and library. If this is the case, the librarian cannot be expected to convert a class into a cohesive community of caring, sharing students who accept and assist each other within a short time span.)

Specific Activities

When introducing the concept of community, the librarian may have the students generate a definition. A discussion of various communities—church, school, families, work, and neighborhood—will also be helpful, along with the African proverb, "It takes a whole village to raise a child." The librarian may have the class talk about their birth communities and look them up on maps. Making a mural of different communities of people may also be an early-in-the-year activity. Using newspapers to discover contributions individuals have made to the local communities is a way to tie in a library skill with the community discussion. Regularly held class discussions that focus on class-related issues, questions, and concerns will help extend the concept of community, the sense of belonging, and friendship.

A "Community" Mind-set

Language used by the librarian and all staff members is very important. The use of labels such as *students with disabilities* is preferred to using *MR students* or *LD students*. Using terms of ownership such as "our" students as opposed to "yours" generally tells everyone that the entire school is a community. All staff members should feel some responsibility for all students in the building, which means that teachers correct hallway or assembly misbehavior even if they do not know the students involved personally and teachers participate in schoolwide decision making whenever the opportunities arise. Responding to student comments by pointing out similarities among people as opposed to differences is also a habit to develop. School personnel can make positive statements about all students, especially ones who appear to be uninvolved with others, and be advocates for students as well as encouraging them to advocate for themselves. This may mean teaching them to ask questions when they are confused about directions for a task or saying positive things about themselves and feeling proud of their accomplishments and behavior. This also means that feedback is given in a positive way as opposed to a punishing, derogatory way. Effort as well as achievement receive attention from the librarian. Special needs students may need more of this attention than their general education peers. What is said and how it is said will have great influence over how successfully the concept of community will be established. As students see the staff accept and value individuals, they imitate that language and behavior and hopefully grow into adults who value community and individual differences as well.

Making a Class a Community

Some educators in Massachusetts have identified five components of community: safety, affirmation of self, responsibility, relevance, and cooperation (Boston Area Educators for Social Responsibility, 1984). *Safety* needs to be established both physically and psychologically. Students need to feel safe from threats to personal property or physical harm so that they are free to take risks, and some risk taking is necessary for learning to occur—"Try it again." All learners must feel comfortable making mistakes and view mistakes as learning opportunities. Staff members may model this concept by pointing out the mistakes they make themselves and how they laugh at themselves and learn from their errors. When a student uses energy protecting his or her self-image, valuable learning time is wasted. Some means by which safety may be established in the library include setting up rules of conduct using student input and then posting and implementing these rules. Rules should be stated in a positive manner (avoid use of the word *no*) and be simple and few in number. Occasional reference to the rules will help the students remember that they are in effect and that they may need updating from time to time. The rules might include:

1. Respect others.
2. Keep aisles clear.
3. Respect others' property.
4. Do not put down others.
5. Listen to each other.

The feeling of community in the library may be a concluding discussion the librarian initiates so that the students have the opportunity to analyze and evaluate how well they are working together. The librarian may ask each of them to write a brief note to him or her about how well students worked together. Another aspect of safety is the organization of the library's physical resources. If the library is messy and shelves are cluttered, students may not feel comfortable in moving through the room. Students with disabilities may feel especially threatened or unwelcome if they must negotiate around obstacles.

The second component of a community mind-set employs the concept of *affirmation of self*, meaning that the librarian takes advantage of opportunities to celebrate the differences and similarities among the students. Using bulletin boards to display work with positive comments written by both librarian and fellow students is one commonly used means of self-affirmation. Students may be given the chance to talk about their own interests, abilities, talents, and skills, as many of their choices for book selection may relate to these areas. Infusing language and literature that fosters appreciation of differences in culture, race, religion, ethnicity, gender, age, learning style, ability levels, family makeup, and so forth will also allow all individuals to feel valued. Multicultural education and unbiased language are areas in which many educators may improve, but improvement will take place only with an awareness of what should be done or said. Developing a different mind-set is not easy and will require effort and reflection. Sometimes it is helpful to have a signal that reminds oneself about the language or behavior one is attempting to alter. For example, if a librarian is trying to use praise more often, a black dot on the back of the hand may serve to signal a "look-see" around the class for an opportunity to praise.

The third component of community, *relevance*, means that students perceive their work as important to their lives. In other words, they are not assigned meaningless tasks but rather participate in developing the parameters of the thematic unit. Student input into a number of instructional decisions will help facilitate their interest and capitalize on intrinsic motivation. As a unit is beginning, the librarian and teacher may conduct a brainstorming session with the students to determine what they already know about the topic and to help the students understand the breadth of the topic as well as how it relates to past learning. Students may identify subtopics from this brainstorming that are especially interesting to them and may be the focus of their group or individual project. They may be able to choose from a number of project options, such as writing a script for a play, a poem, or a rap song to demonstrate what they have learned about a topic. Another means of keeping instruction relevant is to get ongoing feedback from the students, both verbal and written comments. Journal writing is particularly effective as a means of finding out what the students are thinking because it is a private form of communication. Often a special

Figure 11.1
Contract

"I __________ (student's name) agree to read three novels by October 1, 1994. The specific novels are _______, _______, and ______. I will demonstrate that I have read these books by discussing them with the librarian to his or her satisfaction.
I __________ (librarian's name) agree that if __________ (student's name) reads the books listed above, he or she will be asked to participate in the special activity group in October which will focus on writing a Halloween booklet.

Date __________
Student's signature______________________
Librarian's signature______________________

notebook is used to record information, impressions, and reflections on a frequent basis. Both the librarian and teacher may review these journal entries and make comments to the students. When students have this kind of communication with the educators, it is more likely that instruction will maintain relevance as educators may remain more responsive.

Responsibility is the fourth component of community building. Independent citizenship is one of the goals of education for all students; however, there is seldom direct instruction or even explicit acknowledgment that this is an aim of education. Helping students take responsibility for themselves within the school and library is one way responsibility and independence may be fostered. Responsible behavior needs to be evident in school work and classroom interpersonal behavior. Again, student input into decision making fosters this element of a community-oriented perspective. Suggestion boxes may be useful; they allow students to give advice on how the library should be run. Having students perform jobs within the library is also important. They may be responsible for cleaning up after lessons, handing out work, or setting up audiovisual materials. The librarian may want to introduce the idea of contracts into the library because when students sign a contract, they are indeed taking responsibility. A contract could follow this form shown in Figure 11.1.

Students may also keep records on their own progress. Several kinds of records may be kept in regard to the library, such as a list of books read, books and authors the student wants to read, and library information skills mastered. (See Chapter 2 for more information on this topic.) Self-recording helps students develop an internal locus of control, which directly relates to fostering responsibility.

Cooperation is the fifth component of developing a sense of community. Clearly, if independent work is the only type of learning structure students are exposed to, there is little opportunity for developing a sense of community. In contrast, when students help each other by working together, sharing ideas, and comparing work, they develop an appreciation of each other and of the notion that "we are all in this together."

The physical layout of the library lends itself to cooperation because usually there are tables at which students sit in groups. The librarian may assign students to tables or allow them to choose their own team. The groups may be used to review what was learned in the library during their last visit, to set the agenda for the time in the library for that day, to discuss the book being read by each student, or to review appropriate library behavior. A partner system may be used instead of a group constellation. With younger students and those inexperienced with cooperative activities, a smaller group of two may work better in the beginning.

Given these five components of community, the librarian will make the library a place in which all children feel welcomed and cared for.

DIRECT INSTRUCTION OF SOCIAL SKILLS

Another means by which inclusion may be fostered is by directly teaching special needs students the social skills they need to be more like their typical peers. Most children learn the subtleties of human interaction through simple observation of scenarios repeated over and over. They watch their parents greet guests, introduce people to each other, extend compliments to many people, and use polite words, such as *please* and *thank you*. Parents and teachers often follow these experiences with some general directions about how to do these behaviors and praise of appropriate behavior that their children demonstrate. Most social skills are taught on an informal basis, and seldom do typical peers require direct instruction of social skills. However, some students, often those with special needs, do require a more direct instruction approach as they learn to interact with their peers and adults in an acceptable manner. They do not seem to learn social graces through osmosis, but rather seem oblivious to some social cues most people spot immediately. For example, most people understand that if the person one is conversing with begins to look at his or her watch every thirty seconds or so, that person is saying nonverbally that he or she has to leave or the guest should leave because the person has something else to do. Some students need direct instruction concerning these types of social behaviors.

Goldstein and colleagues (Goldstein, Sprafkin, Gershan & Klein, 1980; McGinnis & Goldstein, 1984) have provided a framework for direct instruction of social skills as well as a taxonomy of social skills ranging from the very basic, such as saying *thank you*, to the more complex, such as conflict resolution. Their basic framework for instruction has five steps: introducing the skill, demonstrating the skill, role playing with the students, providing feedback, and generalizing or practicing the skill in other settings and conditions.

An example of a social skill that might be taught in the library is how to ask for assistance. Before the librarian introduces this skill, he or she must clearly delineate what this behavior would look like and what variations would be acceptable. For this skill, the librarian might conduct a task analysis (see Chapter 1) of asking for assistance and determine that this is a four-step process. The steps the student should use are:

1. Ask yourself, "Do I need help?"
2. Ask yourself, "Who should I ask for help?"
3. Ask yourself, "How should I ask for help?"
4. Ask the question and take note of the answer.

Introducing the Skill

As the librarian introduces this skill, he or she explains when the skill might be used and asks students for some ideas as to how to ask and whom to ask for help. Students should give examples of when they themselves have asked for help, as well as provide examples outside their own lives, such as someone with a fire in their house calls the fire department for help. In other words, the librarian should help the students see the need for this particular skill in all sorts of settings and situations and then direct the conversation to a particular use of this skill in the library. For this skill used within the library, the most important question is when to ask for help because the librarian does not want students to be overly dependent on assistance when they could find the answers themselves. During this first step, the librarian stresses the importance of learning the skill.

Demonstrating the Skill

The next step is demonstrating the skill for the students to observe while pointing out each step. First, the librarian should list the four steps for this skill on the board or hand out a sheet with the information. These steps should be read aloud and then the demonstration should begin. For this skill, only the last step is an overt behavior; the rest are cognitive, covert behaviors. Thus, the librarian will pretend his or her brain is talking aloud. In other words, the librarian will think aloud to demonstrate the first three steps for the students and then do the actual asking in the fourth step. The conversation for the first three steps may sound like this:

OK, now, I think I am stuck. I am supposed to make a map of Argentina, and I don't know how. Well, wait a minute; I do know how. You trace over a map or copy it as best you can. But first you have to find a map of what you want to copy. That's what I don't know—how to find a map of Argentina. Let me think about this. Do I know where I could find maps? Sometimes maps are in the encyclopedias, but those aren't very detailed, and what I need is a map with lots of details because this is for a major report, and I have to include lots of details. Now, I know there is some other kind of reference material that has maps, but I can't remember the name of it. It would be easy to ask the librarian, but first I think I will go over to the reference section and see if anything jogs my memory about the kind of reference material that has maps. I don't want to waste the librarian's time if I can figure out the answer for myself. [At this point the librarian should wander around the reference section briefly.] No, I don't remember which type of book has the maps. I really am stuck and do need to ask for help. Who should I ask? Let me see; there are no other kids here from my class, or I could ask one of them. There are only younger kids in here now, so I guess I need to ask the librarian. So now let me think about how I will ask this question. I know I'll say, "Ms. Harrison, I know there are reference materials that are filled with maps. I need to find a map of Argentina. Could you tell me the name of the reference material that contains maps so I could find the material for myself?" OK, now I am ready to get help. I know I need it, I know who to ask, and I know how to ask the question. Here I go.

Then the librarian would pretend to ask the librarian the question and the librarian would answer. The students may then be asked if they have any questions.

Role Play

Next, students role-play this social skill by imitating the librarian. The librarian would help them generate ideas about what may require help in the library, and one student would run through a mental dialogue. Perhaps the student cannot remember the name of an author and needs to look it up in the card or automated catalog. The librarian may use verbal or visual prompts at this time to help the student with the spoken-aloud mental dialogue. Other students may also chime in. Many students should have a part in the discussion before the role plays are over. About three sample questions should be posed and discussed. The librarian should try to provide fewer and fewer prompts as the students get the gist of the social skill.

Feedback

After each mental dialogue/discussion, the students are given feedback from the librarian, both compliments for what was done well and suggestions for what could be done more effectively. Students may give each other feedback at this time as well. Giving feedback could be one of the social skills they are taught in the beginning of social skills training. Some general principles for giving feedback include the following:

1. Make it as positive as possible. Use phrases such as, "Do say . . . " as opposed to "Do not say . . . "
2. Make sure the tone of voice is friendly and constructive.
3. Give an appropriate amount of feedback so that the students do not feel overwhelmed and get the impression that they could never learn this skill.
4. Have students repeat in their own words how to improve their use of the social skill being taught.

Feedback is a very important step in the direct instruction of social skills; however, that does not mean that it should take a lot of time. The feedback exchange may only take a few minutes, or it could last ten to fifteen minutes. The skill might be taught in one session, or the students may require more instructional time, more role plays, or rehearsals of the skill. As the teacher and librarian collaborate, decisions about the pace and content of instruction will be made.

Generalization

It is one thing to use a social skill in an artificial atmosphere during direct instruction and another to use it in situations that occur naturally. Generalizing to another setting, situation, person, and content area is often very difficult for special needs students (see Chapter 10). Opportunities for practicing the skill need to be planned.

After the social skill has been taught in a structured setting, the librarian needs to see the skill in a natural setting. He or she should plan for activities during which the recently taught social skill will come up or observe the class and look for naturally occurring situations in which the social skills should be used. Many of the social skills may be taught directly by the special education teacher, and the librarian's role may lie solely in helping the student to generalize the skill to another instructor in a different setting.

Direct instruction of social skills is not necessary for all students; most of them learn the subtleties of human interaction by simple observation. Direct instruction is necessary only for students who have not learned the skill on their own. Before intensive instruction, the student should be asked to demonstrate the skill to determine whether he or she knows it, but does not know when to use it versus not knowing how to perform the skill. The librarian and the special education teacher will likely collaborate not only on which students need to be taught social skills but also which skills should be taught, in what sequence, and at what pace. Social skills instruction is very effective when these steps are used. These skills are every bit as important as the academic skills to which educators devote so much time and energy.

FRIENDSHIP-BUILDING ACTIVITIES

Friendships and peer supports are often noted as keys to the success of inclusive education. Some professionals have gone so far as to state that peer supports and friendships are not luxuries but necessities (Grenot-Scheyer, Coots & Falvey, 1989; Stainback & Stainback, 1987; Stocking, Arezzo & Leavitt, 1980). Friends are essential to all social beings, and they are critical to the social and emotional well-being of students. Through friendships, students can develop a sense of acceptance and belonging. Peers provide the support, encouragement, and understanding that is needed to reach individual potential. Self-esteem and self-confidence are enhanced when students have friends. For students with disabilities, the feelings of isolation and rejection that may be initially present upon entering a typical classroom can be replaced with more positive interactions. Mere proximity to typical students will not guarantee the development of friendships, and friendships cannot be forced but they may be facilitated in order for all students to know, respect, and appreciate each other as individuals.

Facilitation is a process in which students with disabilities are viewed in terms of their strengths and the contributions they will make in relationships (Schaffner & Buswell, 1992). The message that facilitators convey is that all students are givers and receivers and can develop mutual friendships. The classroom teacher and the school librarian can collaborate and share this role of facilitator. Through this sharing, students can view them as models of mutual respect. Together, they can communicate that every student is an important and worthwhile member of the class.

Specific skills that the facilitators hope to develop between friends may include the following:

initiation of communication
kindness and thoughtful actions
fairness
nonjudmental behaviors
positive interaction style
praise and reinforcement
attentive listening skills
sharing belongings and feelings
development of areas of mutual compatibility
taking the perspective of a friend
loyalty and trustworthiness
confidentiality
cooperative working behaviors

With the common belief that through the development of friendships and peer supports, school can be a caring community, friendship facilitators can use a number of resources designed to promote these relationships, and develop a variety of activities.

- When a new student is expected in the library class, the librarian can engage the other students in a brainstorming session regarding what can be done to make the new person feel welcome.
- Arrange for peer buddies within the library. Students can interview each other to discover areas of common interest. Peer buddies can share assignments and work on special projects, typically for a minimum of four weeks so that a relationship can develop. Peer buddies can then be reassigned so each student has a chance to work with a variety of students.
- The school librarian and classroom teacher can collaborate on a friendship unit. Students can read books about friendship, watch videos about special relationships, interview teachers in the building about their best friends, design want ads for new friends, and complete art activities with friendship as a theme.
- Have students select areas of interest to explore using the library media center. Pair students according to common areas of interest. Engage the whole class in discussion regarding how they can participate in the selection and completion of a project related to their area of interest. Discuss ways in which students of varying ability levels can contribute (e.g., a student with learning disabilities may choose to do an oral presentation while his partner may do the written portion).
- Develop a "circle of friends" (created by Marsha Forest; refer to videotape *With a Little Help From My Friends*, Forest & Flynn, 1988) around a student who displays a need to be included in both school and nonschool activities. This is a voluntary support system for students who are willing to be an important part of another person's life.
- Engage in a brainstorming session in the library regarding the characteristics of a good friend. Have students employ dictionary skills to define these terms and use them in a story about a friend.
- After listing the qualities of friends and the skills needed to be a friend, teachers should reinforce those skills regularly. In both the library and the classroom, students should be acknowledged for their kindness and thoughtfulness.
- The school could have a "Friendship Week" and students could earn a special ticket each time they were observed to display a specific friendship skill. Tickets could be accumulated and exchanged for prizes.
- The development of peer mediation and conflict resolution committees can be an asset in the development of appropriate social relationships. The librarian could become a trainer for mediators and demonstrate the resolution of conflict in the library setting.

- Assist classmates in understanding a student's communication by modeling and encouraging them to communicate with him or her directly. If a student signs or uses assistive technology, demonstrate these techniques for the other classmates.
- Value the existing friendships that are present in the classroom or library settings, and remember to structure daily opportunities to broaden that circle.
- Involve parents in efforts to facilitate friendships. Invite them to participate in class and share information about their child. Keep them informed regarding emerging friendships.

As the school librarian and the classroom teacher facilitate the development of friendships and peer supports in an inclusive environment, it will be important to keep in mind that the goal is to have every member of the class feel accepted and valued. This does not mean that it is necessary for every student to have many friends, but it does mean every student should be made aware of the ways in which people show others they are respected and accepted. Perhaps the most important way to get this important message across is for teachers to be good role models. As the classroom teacher and the school librarian share the role of facilitator of friendships, they have an opportunity to assist in the development of a caring school community.

COOPERATIVE LEARNING

Cooperative learning is a systematic structuring of student interactions. There are several different models of cooperative learning (Slavin, 1993), but the model described here was devised by Roger and David Johnson at the University of Minnesota. Johnson and Johnson characterize the structure of instruction as competitive, individualistic, or cooperative. Prior to the recent emergence of cooperative learning, the primary structures used in public schools have been the former two. Interest in cooperative learning has been growing rapidly.

Rationale for Cooperative Learning

One of the fundamental principles underlying cooperative learning is that the more students talk, the more they understand. Individuals learn more when they attempt to teach someone else than they do by reading the textbook or by listening to a lecture. Active involvement is very important. Research shows that cooperative learning is superior to competitive and individualistic structures in terms of academic achievement and affective outcomes, including social skills and self-esteem. Of particular importance is the notion that cooperative learning teaches interpersonal skills at the same time it teaches academic content. Interpersonal skills are a crucial component of instruction; individuals who lose their jobs are not likely fired because they were not capable of performing the tasks but because they did not get along with their co-workers. When done correctly, cooperative learning can serve to accomplish many goals in one fell swoop. This is not to say that the only goal structure that should be used in schools is cooperative learning. Competitive and individualistic goal structures are necessary and more efficient for learning certain kinds of skills. For example, trying to improve one's own score (individualistic) is an effective way to structure mastery of multiplication facts.

Elements of Cooperative Learning

Cooperative learning has five elements (Johnson & Johnson, 1989) that characterize the nature of the interactions among the students and the librarian and students. First, cooperative learning requires face-to-face oral interaction. Students must have time to talk to each other. They cannot be so bogged down with the assignment that they do not have time to share their ideas with their peers. Second, cooperative learning is structured so that the group has positive interdependence; either all group members succeed, or they all fail. No member of a group can succeed and the others fail or, conversely, no one member can fail while the other group members succeed. The third element is individual accountability. Despite the fact that the work is occurring in a group structure, the librarian must still plan for a way to make each individual accountable for learning the material. Librarians may, for example, have students do an activity designed to help them learn particular content. After the project is completed, the librarian may ask the students to take a test on the material or randomly select one group member to take an oral quiz on the content. In some way, the librarians must structure the activity so that there are no "wallflowers," students who sit back and let others do the work without learning the information themselves. The fourth element is that as the groups are working on their activity, the librarian takes an active role in monitoring their interactions, answering questions, clarifying directions, and teaching the social skills necessary for high-functioning group interaction. The final element is the processing of the group interactions following the completion of the activity. Either individually, in groups, or as a whole class, all students must have an opportunity to think and talk about the interactions of their group. They should focus on a variety of interpersonal communication skills, which can be as basic as using first names and making eye contact, to sophisticated skills such as resolving group conflict, paraphrasing for understanding, and extending the ideas of other group members.

Three Types of Groups

Several different kinds of groups may be formed for different purposes. Informal groups can be formed instantly and for short-term activities. For example, the librarian may direct the students," Turn to the person sitting on your right, and discuss the last two points I just made." Formal work groups are formed for the purpose of completing a long-term multifaceted project. For example, pairs of students may be writing a research report on a country of their choice. They will be expected to write a paragraph on eight different aspects of the country. Each member of the pair needs to learn all the information about each aspect. A third type of group is called a base group; it is a long-term group whose role is to provide support and accountability for the group members. Base groups may last for an entire semester or year, meeting weekly to help each other keep up on assignments and deadlines, share resources, and provide moral support. This kind of group can be particularly helpful to students who are new to the class.

Use of cooperative learning will help students learn how to work together and get beyond merely being present in the same class. No student can be ignored or left out when cooperative activities are implemented. Cooperative learning definitely will enhance the integration of special needs students.

A CASE EXAMPLE: THE COMMUNITY QUILT PROJECT

The project related in this example has been used several times in a large, midwestern school district with great success. It has helped students view their class as a cohesive unit with every individual a part of the whole. The concept of community may be taught through a thematic unit—a patchwork quilt. Within the structure of the library, numerous projects can be used to reinforce the use, image, and creation of a community quilt in both people and cloth form. A patchwork quilt used for demonstration and left at school for display is important to this unit. If one is not available, photos can be used, though with diminished effect, as can a teacher-made paper quilt of shapes glued on a large piece of paper. The first step in using the quilt is to let the students examine it closely.

The first structured use of the quilt should be a sensitization activity covering individual differences and similarities. The type of quilt used in this unit may be a "Scrap-aholic" quilt, constructed of three-inch squares laid in a pattern of concentric circles (Hughes, 1987) (Figure 11.2). The pattern is important in that it lends itself not only to a discussion of same and different but also to one of community and friendship circles.

In the beginning of a discussion with the students, have them first select a square or patch that they most like. Enter into a discussion as to how their

Figure 11.2
The Scrap-aholic Quilt by Trudie Hughes (1987)

individual patches are different from the rest and then how they are the same. Move to a discussion of same and different, using two or more people in the room (this is often easiest using two adults). Be sure to highlight throughout the activity that we are all more alike than different but that our differences make us interesting. This activity is also conducive to exploring the arena of feelings. All people have feelings and want friends, so the conversation naturally moves in this direction. Wrap up the sensitization activity with a summary of community, indicating that the group of students in the room appear as a quilt. Asking for reflections of that belief, discuss the need for community and supports. If the quilt has concentric circles, it can again be used as an image of community—family, close friends, peripheral friends, acquaintances, and so on.

The use of the quilt can be a one-time lesson, but optimally it would be a catalyst for a thematic unit on community that moves over a range of library activities:

- Find articles and books in the library to research people who have been accepted and included despite their differences (e.g., Stevie Wonder, Wilma Rudolph, Franklin Roosevelt).
- Research the structures of community—what comprises a community—and then develop a model community in which everyone is accepted and honored.
- Investigate the variety of quilts across cultures. Determine the use of quilts and how they differ depending on climate and culture.
- Discover how quilts have been used as storytelling maps. Move into a storytelling unit.
- Create a collage of the many types of quilts and their uses. Books in the library offer a huge assortment of styles.
- Within the realm of social studies in the library, find out how methods of quilt making reflect periods of history (western settlement in the United States, slavery, Victorian period, etc.).
- Incorporate math activities on measurement and geometric patterning. If a quilt is made as a long-term project, purchasing and budget lessons could be developed.
- Identify several pieces of literature (from picture books to adult novels) that incorporate the image of quilts and would be appropriate for supplemental reading activities and discussions.
- Incorporate art projects in the library on the use of color, design, and textures. Numerous books are available on fiber arts. Dying fabrics for art quilts has become very popular, and students could research and create their own fabrics.
- Construct a quilt using the various resources in the library that explain history, styles, techniques, color, and design.

The construction of a community quilt in an inclusive classroom has been successful. Working as a team, the teachers and librarian provide hands-on activities (creation of the quilt) along with various supplemental projects and lessons. The quilt has interlocking fabric pieces that ultimately create individual pattern blocks with space for each student to sign his or her name with fabric pens.

When a quilt was completed at one elementary school, the students named their piece of art, "All the Pieces Fit." Throughout the remainder of the school year, every time a student in the inclusive program (sixth graders and students with emotional disabilities) was observed by a teacher to commit an act of kindness and community to a classmate, that child's name was put on a slip of paper and dropped into the jar. On the last day of school, a name was drawn, and that student kept the quilt.

CONCLUSION

One of the greatest marks educators can make on a child is helping to boost his or her self-esteem. Fostering positive relationships among students is one way to address issues of self-worth directly. School librarians can be central figures in the efforts to link special needs and general education students. With effort and patience and armed with the techniques set out in this chapter, school librarians are bound to make a real difference in the lives of all children as everyone benefits from expanding their friendship circles.

REFERENCES

Boston Area Educators for Social Responsibility. (1984). *Taking part: An elementary guide in the participation series*. Cambridge, MA: Author.

Forest, M., & Flynn, G. (Directors). (1988). *With a little help from my friends*. Toronto: Center for Integrated Education.

Goldstein, A. P., Sprafkin, R. P., Gershaw, N. J., & Klein, P. (1980). *Skillstreaming the adolescent*. Champaign, IL: Research Press Company.

Gottlieb, J., & Leyser, N. (1981). Friendships between mentally retarded and non-retarded children. In S. Asher & J. Gottman (Eds.), *The development of children's friendships* (pp. 150–181). Cambridge: Cambridge University Press.

Grenot-Scheyer, M., Coots, J., & Falvey, M. (1989). Developing and fostering friendships. In M. Falvey (Ed.), *Community-based curriculum: Instructional strategies for students with severe handicaps* (pp. 345–358). Baltimore: Paul H. Brookes Publishing Co.

Hughes, T. (1987). *More template-free quiltmaking*. Bothwell, WA: Patchwork Place.

Johnson, D. W., & Johnson, R. T. (1989). *Learning together and alone: Cooperative, competitive, and individualistic learning* (2d ed.). Englewood Cliffs, NJ: Prentice-Hall.

McGinnis, E., & Goldstein, A. P. (1984). *Skillstreaming the elementary school child*. Champaign, IL: Research Press Company.

Schaffner, C. B., & Buswell, B. E. (1992). *Breaking ground: Ten families building opportunities for integration*. Colorado Springs, CO: Peak Parent Center.

Slavin, R. E. (1983). *Cooperative learning*. New York: Longman.

Slavin, R. E. (1990). *Cooperative learning: Theory, research, and practice*. Englewood Cliffs, NJ: Prentice-Hall.

Stainback, W., & Stainback, S. (1987). Facilitating friendships. *Education and Training of the Mentally Retarded* 22: 18–25.

Stocking, S., Arezzo, D., & Leavitt, S. (1980). *Helping kids make friends*. Alan, TX: Vargus Communications.

Wesson, C., & Mandell, C. (1989). Using extended simulations to promote understanding of adapting to a handicap. *Teaching Exceptional Children* 22(1): 32–35.

12

The Special Needs of Gifted and Talented Students in the School Library Media Center

Caren L. Wesson and Margaret J. Keefe

Gifted and talented students also have special needs. Educators are obligated to provide an environment for instruction that will enable all students to feel challenged and successful. In most school districts, instruction for the gifted and talented students occurs primarily in the regular classroom. Although some districts have segregated programs or schools for this group, most use pull-out programs in which students are enrolled in a special gifted and talented class for only a portion of their school day or week. In the latter situation, it becomes imperative that the library media center provide extension opportunities for these students that enable them to use enrichment resources and activities. In fact, students who are gifted need access to the library sooner and more frequently than their typical peers (Greenlaw & McIntosh, 1988). Clark (1992) goes as far as to say that children who are gifted need "unlimited access to the library" (p. 290). In order for the time in the library to be used effectively, it is important that the school librarian and the student's teachers collaborate to determine the curriculum for the student and the specific activities that should be pursued in the library.

DEFINITIONS OF GIFTED AND TALENTED STUDENTS

There is no universally accepted definition of gifted and talented students. The government, through Public Law 97–35 passed in 1981, uses the following:

> Gifted and talented children are now referred to as children who give evidence of high performance capability in areas such as intellectual, creative, artistic, leader-

ship capacity, or specific academic fields, and who require services or activities not ordinarily provided by the school in order to fully develop such capabilities.

Renzulli (1978), a well-known researcher in the area of gifted and talented, defines giftedness as the interaction of three traits: above-average intellectual ability, high levels of task commitment, and high levels of creativity. Gardner (1993), on the other hand, defines the gifted and talented as those with superior abilities in one of the following kinds of intelligences: body-kinesthetic, interpersonal, intrapersonal, linguistic, logical-math, spatial, or musical. Regardless of which definition is applied, the need for instruction beyond that which is traditionally used is evident.

Many schools do not identify children who are gifted and talented until they are in third grade (Bryant, 1989). The general rule of thumb that applies to other special needs children should be used with this population as well; the earlier the identification and specialized instructional programming begins, the better off the student will be with respect to attaining his or her full potential. One of the primary factors involved in defining the population is the budget related to these services. If there is little money available for such programs, few children will be enrolled in the programs— and typically little money is dedicated to the education of gifted and talented students. This is a very shortsighted policy, which may hurt the nation as the brightest students are not encouraged to use all their skills and knowledge. The instruction they receive in the general education classes tends to be the same as that provided to all other children; for gifted and talented children, this is an unmotivating environment.

MOTIVATING ENVIRONMENT

Special needs students, like all others, need to be challenged and motivated. Concentrating on providing a motivating environment may prove to be more beneficial than focusing on motivating individual children. When the atmosphere is exciting and stimulating, the child will be motivated; this generalization applies to all children. Educators talk about the unmotivated student rather than the unmotivating environment, sentiment that blames the child rather than the adult in the situation.

The library may be made a motivating environment by providing a physically stimulating setting, as well as a responsive learning atmosphere. The physical space might, in part, resemble a laboratory setting with multiple stations set up based on student interests; students themselves may construct learning centers. An idea for learning centers in the library might be directions for using an atlas that includes an explanation of how to use the atlas, two or more atlases, and questions to answer. Perhaps a gifted student's tape-recorded message tells the center user how to use the atlas. The physical setting should be colorful and filled with sound and texture. Students may help establish the atmosphere by contributing to the physical space. Large-group discussion time should be allowed and facilitated by a generous open area. Space for small-group work should also be evident in a responsive learning environment. Also, the library needs to be open to these students during all school hours because these students do not need to be in the general classroom receiving instruction on a task they already know how to do or on content they already have mastered. Redundant instruction makes the environment unmotivating.

Kessig and Zsiray (1989) suggest that the most important areas of the library for gifted students are current events, biographies, and literature. Current event information is critical because it provides students with "an understanding of world news, its interpretation and its impact on our global society" (p. 27). The materials in a current events area include periodicals, newspapers, radio and television news programs, and online computer sources. The biography section should contain information on local heroes and biographies of world-famous individuals. Classical and young adult literature will assist the gifted student in stimulating creative, analytical thoughts.

The responsive learning environment is flexible and complex, encouraging students to synthesize information across disciplines. A new wave of contemporary theory is changing the focus of instruction from fact learning to the construction of meaning. Mere memorization of facts acquired by reception and rehearsal is no longer an acceptable goal for learners. The constructivist theory posits that new knowledge must have meaning and be attached to prior learning and experiences (Ganapole, 1989). Characteristics of gifted students, including an accelerated pace of thought processes, high retention of information, ability to understand complex concepts, heightened capacity for seeing relationships among disparate data, advanced verbal ability, and ability to generate original ideas and solutions (Ganapole, 1989), make use of the constructivist theory extremely important for these students.

In order for a school librarian to base instruction for gifted students on constructivist theory, several characteristics of the environment should be in place (Greenlaw & McIntosh, 1988). The emphasis should be on student-centered instruction as opposed to teacher centered. In other words, topics for research and projects should be based on student interest rather than selected by the teacher. Similarly, choices with respect to the products produced through projects should be acceptable. Second, students should work independently as much as possible; indeed, they need little direct instruction. If there is a resource they need to learn how to use, the librarian may quickly explain it to them and walk them through the process of using that source. Elaborate lessons useful for general education students are probably not necessary for these bright students. Third, the activities should be open-ended rather than closed. These students have no need for pat answers and simple solutions. Rather, the ideas and content should be multifaceted and complex, necessitating inquiring minds. Given the environment described here, information about the content of instruction is the next piece of the puzzle for constructing library instruction for gifted students.

MODIFYING THE CURRENT ENVIRONMENT

Gifted students need a change of curriculum from that which is typically provided; otherwise, they are likely to be bored. The term for determining content currently being used by educators of gifted students is *differentiated curriculum* (Greenlaw & McIntosh, 1988). It requires not only that the curriculum be different from that of general education peers but qualitatively different. Dimensions along which the curriculum may be differentiated include levels of abstractness and complexity, subject variety, and increased study of people and methods of research. Two primary means of modifying curriculum for the needs of gifted students are an accelerated curriculum and an enriched curriculum.

Accelerated Curriculum

An accelerated curriculum means that the student is allowed to work ahead of general education peers. The student may enroll in school before the typical age or be placed in a higher grade for all or some content areas. Some students are "double-promoted" and skip a grade. An accelerated curriculum may be used within the student's age-appropriate grade as well. Acceleration is an effective and positive approach (Kulik & Kulik, 1984) with a number of benefits. This system may be used in any school, and it generates less boredom and dissatisfaction. Studies show that the gifted student in an accelerated program interacts well with older peers, and social and emotional adjustment is generally high (Clark, 1992).

Curriculum compacting is a useful tool if acceleration is used for gifted students. Curriculum compacting refers to an assessment system that allows the student to be tested and the mastery of various skills to be documented. Through pre- and posttesting, every skill already known to the student may be identified, so no time is taken to teach him or her something already known. The three major objectives of this system are to create a more challenging learning environment, guarantee proficiency in the curriculum, and allow time for enrichment activities (Clark, 1992). The Informal Library and Information Skills Inventory (found in Chapter 2) facilitates the librarian's use of this concept.

The school librarian may find that gifted and talented students are ready to learn library and information skills at a much earlier age than the regular education students and thus can be accelerated. Teaching first and second graders how to use the card catalog to find information for an accelerated project they have been assigned is an example of accelerated curriculum. By collaborating with the classroom teacher, these skills can be taught as the need arises, successfully compacting the curriculum for these students.

Enrichment

Enrichment refers to using more complicated or sophisticated content that requires complex thought and synthesis of material across content areas. Generally, the higher levels of Bloom's Taxonomy—with levels progressing from knowledge, comprehension, application, analysis, and creative thinking (synthesis) to critical thinking (evaluation)—are addressed. As a student's curriculum is planned, the librarian and classroom teacher may consider how to create lessons and projects that address the higher levels of the taxonomy. Multifaceted projects involving stages of activity are appropriate, as are self-selected topics and activities.

INSTRUCTIONAL PROCESS

The traditional process of didactic instruction is seldom appropriate for gifted students. Rather, researching topics of interest and using more of an inquiry approach are appropriate. Group discussion is a helpful means of instruction, as are simulation activities. Science labs and social studies lessons based on group processes and inquiry, such as a compare-and-contrast assignment, are important to gifted students.

Inquiry Instruction

Inquiry instruction could be considered the opposite of direct instruction. Rather than telling information, the teacher poses or helps the students pose questions. Asking questions in an inquiry lesson is very different from posing questions for evaluation and testing purposes. The questions are not about material already taught but questions for which the students have not been told the answers. Inquiry instruction is best used when the teacher or librarian has learning concepts, abstractions, or patterns as the goal of the lesson or when an affective response is the main point. Some examples of topics that could be taught through inquiry instruction are classes of arthropods, the advantages and disadvantages of socialism, causes of the Gulf War, and attitudes toward persons with disabilities.

Instructional decisions must be made prior to the lesson:

1. What is the objective for the lesson?
2. How will the lesson be opened so that the learner will be interested and past knowledge will be activated?

3. What particular model of inquiry best suits the objective?
4. How will student knowledge be assessed?
5. How will this lesson be followed up in the future?

For the first decision, the librarian will determine the focus of the lesson by considering the content and determining if the content aims for the student's becoming aware of a concept or understanding a concept, comprehending an abstraction, discovering a pattern among data or figures, or prompting an affective response. The goal for the lesson should be written out as part of the instructional plan. The opening activity, decision 2, should focus on motivating the students to want to learn more about the topic. The librarian might display a set of artifacts, sing a song, act out a simple skit, read from a classic book, or pose a riddle. Several models of inquiry may be used for decision 3: concept attainment, concept formation, and the research process (described in separate sections that follow). For the fourth decision about student evaluation, the librarian may decide to have students write a paragraph or a poem describing what they have learned or have a small group work to create an oral report, which is then presented by one group member. The final decision requires the librarian to determine at what point within library instruction the ideas from this lesson will be revisited or to collaborate with the teacher to help coordinate follow-up in the classroom.

Concept attainment

The concept attainment process involves presenting examples and nonexamples of a concept without telling the students what the concept is and having them use their inductive logic to describe and eventually name the concept. This activity may be done as a large class discussion, in small groups, or individually. An example for the library might be in teaching the concept of biography to second graders. Clearly the librarian could simply define the term using a direct instruction format, but the concept of biography may be better retained if the students figure it out for themselves. The librarian may present examples and nonexamples by showing books and reading aloud their titles and stating if it is a "yes" or "no" with respect to the concept being taught. The conversation may go like this:

This book, *The Civil War*, by Robert Paul Jordan is a No.

Lincoln—A Photobiography by Russell Freedman is a Yes.

Lincoln—At Gettysburg by Gary Wills is a No.

With Malice toward None: The Life of Abraham Lincoln by Stephen B. Oates is a Yes.

The Collected Works of Abraham Lincoln edited by Roy B. Basler is a No.

The Story of Ford's Theater and the Death of Lincoln by Zachery Kent is a No.

Abraham Lincoln: A Biography by Benjamin P. Thomas is a Yes.

A small group could then look over the books and come up with ideas about what differentiates the Yes books and No books and what is the same about the books in each category. Through good lead questions, the librarian can help the students understand the concept of biography. Use of this method as opposed to simple telling will help students remember the concept better.

Concept Formation

The librarian can assist students in developing the understanding of a concept by having them determine the differences between properties of objects or events and group objects or events based on common elements and form categories and labels for the concepts. An example of a possible concept formation lesson for the library may be to lay out forty books, four from each hundred of the Dewey decimal system, and have a group of students group these and come up with labels for their book clusters. If the groupings are different from those used in the Dewey decimal system, that is all right; the idea is to help students understand the concept of categories of books. The actual categories may later be taught.

The Research Process

Once students know the basic steps of the research process, they will operate independently most of the time, asking questions when they run into a roadblock. The importance of research skills for gifted learners cannot be overemphasized: Gifted students need a way to get information and ideas sooner than more typical learners. They must be able to move efficiently on their own into areas not yet explored. They need to become familiar with the skills of historical research, descriptive research, and experimental research as tools for future learning and thinking" (Clark, 1992, p. 320).

Gifted students should be exposed to the research process by their midelementary years (third to fifth grade) (Stockton & DuChateau, 1984). Some school librarians begin teaching the research process to gifted students in the first and second grades. These are the basic steps:

1. The student writes out suggested topics and discusses these topics with the librarian. Together they determine if the library contains enough material about each topic, as well as where relevant material may be obtained outside school.
2. The student selects which topic to pursue and writes out questions about it, each question on a separate notecard.
3. As the student reads sources, he or she writes any information relevant to the questions on the back of the notecards. The student is encouraged to record the information in his or her own words, beginning each card with the phrase, "I have learned. . . . "

4. For each reference used, the student completes a bibliography card and codes the information so that the source of the information can be identified.
5. As a rule of thumb, the student should attempt to collect about three references for each question.
6. The note cards are organized into piles by the question the card addresses. This organization becomes an outline for a verbal report, project, or paper about the topic.
7. A rough draft is written. The draft should be written with the sources closed in order to discourage plagiarism. If a different kind of product is being prepared, a plan for developing that product should now be written.
8. The librarian or teacher and student go over the draft together, perhaps repeatedly, and discuss the features of the draft that are well done and what needs to be rewritten.
9. After the co-editing, the final product is prepared.

In step 3, it is advisable to teach students the read, think, and write (RTW) method to assist them in learning how to *not* copy the information straight from the source. The idea is for students to *read* a passage; close the book, marking the page with a bookmark; *think* about what they have just read; and then *write* a note in their own words. This process of actually closing the book should help keep students from plagiarizing (Serpas, 1993).

Another format for the research process is a note chart. Questions are written in columns across the top of the chart, and the references or sources are written down the left side. Notes are then written under the appropriate question and across from the corresponding reference from which the information was taken. A section across the bottom of the chart is reserved for the main idea of each question, which then can be converted into the topic sentence or opening paragraph when put into written form. It is very easy to transfer this chart form into an outline for a report. The chart might be as small as an 8½ by 11 inch sheet of paper or as large as a posterboard. The idea is to be able to visualize all the information collected at one glance. Also, in this way the researcher need not repeat the notation of the same information from a different source unless it is necessary to do so.

There are many more ways to use inquiry instruction. The classic text *Models of Teaching* by Joyce and Weill (1986) is filled with ideas about the use of inquiry methods. Some inquiry activities may be set up at learning centers, where students can process the information individually or with a partner. Any educator will get better results if a variety of instructional techniques is used. Many times, a combination of inquiry and direct instruction within the lesson is the best idea to teach the topic. Often all the steps are not completed in a single class period but extend over multiple lessons.

PRODUCT MODIFICATIONS

Gifted students will likely write many reports in their academic careers; however, other options for final products should also be acceptable. Similarly, varying the audience to whom the product is presented is also motivating.

Students should have choices as to what product may best represent the knowledge they have acquired about the specific topic. Products may be visual, verbal, kinesthetic, or written (Clark, 1992)—for example:

- Models representing the topic such as a diorama of the rainforest or a plaster volcano. (kinesthetic)
- A written dialogue between two historic individuals such as A. G. Bell and Ben Franklin. (written)
- A speech demonstrating a process that has been researched, such as how to cook Louisiana shrimp. (verbal)
- A panel discussion on the topic that a team of students pursued. (verbal)
- A chart that compares the population of three African countries with respect to the religions practiced. (visual)
- A filmstrip produced to depict the process of cheese making. (visual)
- A debate over the use of the death penalty in the home state. (verbal)
- A map of a country that shows the products of the area. (visual)
- A game created to show the audience how to make a simple telephone. (kinesthetic)
- A series of journal entries depicting what life was like on a wagon train moving the family west. (written)
- A letter written to a celebrity or politician asking for attention to certain matters that were researched, such as welfare reform proposals. (written)
- A position paper on a controversial topic such as using adult courts to prosecute juveniles who have committed felonies. (written)
- A video that tells how seeing eye dogs are trained. (visual and verbal)
- A simulation in which students experience how people who use wheelchairs get around. (kinesthetic)
- A speech about the lowland gorillas in the Congo. (verbal)
- A timeline depicting the years in which various explorers mapped out the state. (visual)
- An advertisement about a new product that the student developed. (visual)
- A flowchart depicting the decisions the student makes as he or she proceeds through the research process. (visual)

It is easiest to assign a basic report, but if a written report is the product frequently required, then the students will soon tire of it. By varying the products, interest and motivation are maintained.

Providing for multiple and authentic audiences is also important for gifted students. Most often the audience consists of the teacher or librarian only and perhaps the parents. Many more potential audiences may be located, such as another class in the school. Maybe for the current report, the principal will agree to be a reader and make comments. If the project involves food, perhaps a member of the cooking staff will agree to make comments. Writing to a celebrity, an author, a politician, an entertainer, the local newspaper editor, or the zookeeper makes the audience real, and the project becomes more believable and purposeful. As the project is developed, the student and librarian need to consider what type of project topic, product, and audience make a good combination. The student wants to feel as if there may be a possible impact for all of his or her hard effort.

TWO EXAMPLES OF PROJECTS

The Stock Market Project

For school districts in northeastern Illinois, the *Chicago Tribune* and Northern Illinois University have pooled their resources and developed materials for a stock market project that can be used by middle school and secondary gifted students from sixth to twelfth grades. Some schools have the students meet after school for a stock club program; others use a special meeting time during the school day.

Students work in teams of two or three. Each group is allocated $100,000 of fake money to invest in stocks of their choosing. The *Chicago Tribune* is sent daily during the project to each team in each school. The students graph the progress of their stocks and search for articles in the newspaper and in the library that could inform them about the companies in which they are interested in investing. Weekly, each team makes a decision about buying or selling their stocks. They need to figure in the broker's fees and taxes and maintain a stock portfolio of their investments, keeping track of their total assets. Northern Illinois University collects data as to which stocks each team is buying and/or selling that week and records the teams in order by their total portfolio value.

This project or contest lasts for several months, about ten weeks, twice during the school year, in the fall and in the spring. The teachers and students who participate truly enjoy this project, as it is very real and they can see the utility of learning this material for their future. This is an excellent project to do with gifted and talented students; it provides a connection to the world beyond the school boundaries and requires a great deal of inquiry and decision making on the part of the students.

Futures Conference

A second project is to predict specific aspects of the future. Students, working solo or in small groups, begin by brainstorming the aspects of the future they want to think about—fashions, computers, houses, transportation, schools, or even things as simple as the wheel. Each individual or group is to write and sign a contract detailing the steps they are going to take to accomplish their task and complete their final product. They are to record characteristics of the topic in the past and in the present, and then predict how this topic will appear or be used in the future.

Students spend weeks researching their topic and preparing a product to show the knowledge they have gained. Many resources are used as the students gather information about the topic. A special conference day is then given over to the displaying and sharing of these products. Students also participate in activity sessions presented by teachers and adults from the community who come to share their knowledge and expertise on a topic, also exploring the past, present, and future. At the end of the conference, students hear what other groups have discovered and give feedback to each other. This activity clearly uses the higher levels of Bloom's Taxonomy as students synthesize information across subject areas and evaluate each other's work.

When modifying the curriculum, all three of the components—content, process, and product—must be considered. Gifted and talented students need opportunities for decision making, and therefore choices in these three categories will increase motivation as well as foster independence.

FOSTERING LITERATURE ENRICHMENT FOR GIFTED READERS

Books open a world of ideas to all segments of the school population, and especially for gifted and talented students. The school library media specialist may find these students to be more likely to come searching for a good book to read; many of them are voracious readers, and encouraging this passion for reading is an important role for the school librarian.

Reading guidance, as defined by Halsted (1988), is "the right book for the right child at the right time." The school librarian can guide students to a good book in several ways: by casually mentioning a book in conversation, by walking around and giving suggestions as students are making selections, through the use of booktalks, or through the distribution of written bibliographies on an author or topic. When pursuing information about what types of books a particular student reads, be sure to pose the question casually and not directly so as not to turn them away. Encouraging them to pursue classics such as *Treasure Island* and *The Adventures of Tom Sawyer* as early as fourth or fifth grade is appropriate. It is important for the school librarian to keep an eye out for gifted and talented students and lead them to good literature that may be not only intellectually appropriate for them but also that stimulates and satisfies their often insatiable curiosity.

Care must be taken to encourage them to read at their intellectual level but also at their emotional level (Halsted, 1988). Many of these students often wish to read challenging books that they may not be emotionally ready to handle. If some literature is read too early in their development, they may then forgo these same excellent books when they are emotionally ready and miss some important understandings. For example, a fifth or sixth grader may have the ability to read and comprehend the vocabulary in *Schindler's List* (Keneally, 1993) but not be ready to deal emotionally with the traumatic events of this story. Assisting students to make wise decisions about their reading choices is an important aspect of this role.

A CASE STUDY

One school district found it necessary to use the services and materials of the library media center to assist in the development and presentation of curriculum for one gifted and talented student. When he entered kindergarten, Adam could read; he had taught himself at the age of eighteen months. After a battery of tests was administered, it was discerned that he could read and comprehend on a ninth-grade reading level and add, subtract, multiply, and divide in his head with two-place decimals. It was evident that this child would need a specialized curriculum to meet his needs.

The school librarian was asked to become involved and collaborate with classroom teachers in the development of curriculum for this special needs student. Projects were developed for Adam that would extend topics in the basic curriculum. Thus, he was learning the same curriculum as the regular education students, but went into more depth in each designated area of study. The library media center became the focal point for much of Adam's learning. For example, when the class was studying space in third grade, Adam was directed by the library media specialist in researching beyond the textbook and even the encyclopedia. He researched information about astronauts by directly communicating with NASA through the use of telecommunications and a computer modem located in the library media center.

After going to space camp one summer, another project, writing a computer program, was planned by the librarian and his sixth-grade classroom teacher. Utilizing resources and technology in the library media center for several months, Adam developed a space survival simulation for his classmates to do. He practiced his presentation on videotape, critiquing himself and reworking and rewriting for improvement. He then took the computer program back to share and teach to his class. The tough part was for him to learn to teach the information and bring it down to a level his classmates would understand.

As a result of these types of collaboration, the library media specialist became involved in Adam's instruction in many ways, especially as they got to know each other over the years. The librarian became aware as Adam traveled through the grades in school of how he learned, as well as what he already knew, and as a result was an important asset in planning projects and curriculum for him. Thus, she often became a liaison between Adam and his teachers. In many ways she also became a counselor for Adam, helping him to deal with social skills, such as learning tolerance of others not as quick to get the answer as he was. The library media center became a second home to Adam, where he could feel safe and good about himself.

Being left on his own continuously in the library media center was not a strategy that the library media specialist wanted to promote. Developing a structure or framework for Adam's studies was imperative, because although he was extremely bright and capable, he did not have the wisdom of experience. This is not to say that choices were not also important. Bright children often are intelligent enough to know that they do not have control. Giving them choices within a framework is an important way to give them some control over what they are learning, as well as learning to make decisions and develop a feeling of worth.

The library media center held much for Adam; but just as in the "space" example mentioned earlier, it also is a connection to the outside world. When preparing a project on antique cars for the districtwide "Futures Conference," using something as simple as the telephone to call a car dealer became a lesson in the importance of extending beyond the school environment to the community to access information. This particular car dealer led him to an antique car dealer, who subsequently became a mentor to Adam, sharing his expertise, knowledge, and a love for antique cars with him. This wonderful relationship started from the school library media center telephone. The library media center and all it has to offer became an integral part of this special needs student's education.

REFERENCES

Bryant, M. (1989). Challenging gifted learners through children's literature. *Gifted Child Today* 12(4): 45–48.

Clark, B. (1992). *Growing up gifted: Developing the potential of children at home and school*. New York: Macmillan.

Ganapole, S. J. (1989). Designing integrated curriculum for gifted learners: An organizational framework. *Roeper Review*, 12(2): 81–86.

Gardner, H. (1993). *Multiple intelligence: The theory in practice*. New York: Basic Books.

Greenlaw, M. J., & McIntosh, M. E. (1988). *Educating the gifted*. Chicago: American Library Association.

Halsted, J. (1988). *Guiding gifted readers: From preschool through high school*. Columbus, OH: Ohio Psychology Publishing Company.

Joyce, B., & Weill, M. (1986). *Models of teaching*. Englewood Cliffs, NJ: Prentice–Hall.

Keneally, T. (1993). *Schindler's list*. New York: Simon & Schuster.

Kessig, M., & Zsiray, S. W. (1989). Library media centers: Playgrounds for the gifted. *Gifted Child Today* 12(4): 26–28.

Kulik, J., & Kulik, C. (1984). Synthesis of research on effects of accelerated instruction. *Educational Leadership* 42(2): 84–89.

Parker, J. P. (1989). *Instructional strategies for teaching the gifted*. Boston: Allyn & Bacon.

Renzulli, J. (1978). What makes giftedness? Reexamining a definition. *Phi Delta Kappan* 60: 180–184, 261.

Serpas, R. (1993). *The research process*. Effingham, IL: Illinois Library Media Association Conference.

Stockton, B., & DuChateau, M. (1984). Working with gifted and talented children. *Catholic Library World* 55(8): 346–351.

13 Libraries as Laboratories for Learning: Integrating Content, Learners' Needs, and Experience into the Curriculum

Amy Otis-Wilborn and Terry McGreehin

It was trip day again in Ms. Frizzle's class. Everyone was excited. We were going to the planetarium to see a sky show about the solar system. . . . As usual, it took a while to get the old bus started. But, finally, we were on our way. As we were driving, Ms. Frizzle told us all about how the Earth spins like a top as it moves in its orbit. It was just a short drive to the planetarium, but Ms. Frizzle talked fast. . . .

When we got to the planetarium, it was closed for repairs.

"Class, this means we'll have to return to school," said the Friz. We were so disappointed! On the way back, as we were waiting at a red light, something amazing happened. The bus started tilting back, and we heard the roar of rockets.

"Oh dear," said Ms. Frizzle.

"We seem to be blasting off!" (*The Magic School Bus: Lost in the Solar System*, 1990)

And so begins an adventure with Ms. Frizzle, deemed the "weirdest teacher in school." The breadth and depth of information that is packed into each of the five adventures created by author Joanna Cole and illustrated by Bruce Degen take on special meaning as her students are immersed in direct, albeit imaginary, experiences that pull not only their minds but also their bodies into learning adventures. While Ms. Frizzle serves as the all-knowing expert for her students, author Joanna Cole acknowledges her own collaboration with Dr. Donna L. Fresch from the Center for Radar Astronomy at Stanford University and John Stoke, an astronomical writer/producer at the American Museum–Hayden Planetarium.

Joanna Cole, alias Ms. Frizzle, exploits many of the basic instructional strategies educators acknowledge as important to student learning. First, she situates her stories in schools and classrooms, a context with which learners can identify. Second, she uses elements of absurdity and humor to entice and motivate learners. Third, scientific information is linked with direct experiences and in response to learners' own questions and curiosities. Finally, Cole organizes and displays information in a variety of formats. Most are produced by the learners themselves and include notebook pages with lists of facts, illustrations, graphs, charts, narratives, and dialogues. The teaching and learning context Cole creates integrates science content, background knowledge of the learners themselves, and meaningful experience.

The instructional scenario in the Magic School Bus story, *Lost in the Solar System*, reflects characteristics of an integrated curriculum, enhanced by the contributions of other professionals, each adding important expertise and perspective. Librarians and teachers can collaborate to develop integrated curricula that enhance learning in students with special needs (henceforth referred to as learners). Collaboration between these two professionals enlarges the potential content of study, creates opportunities for learning that is all learner centered and authentic contexts, and presents opportunities for meaningful integration of cognitive and linguistic experience.

RETHINKING CURRICULUM CONTENT AND PROCESS

Integrating various aspects into the curriculum is not a new idea, but it has gained support and attention over the past several years and grows out of current knowledge about teaching and learning (Pappas, Kiefer & Levstik, 1990; Zacharias-Lewinsky, Koenig, Otis-Wilborn & Messenheimer-Young 1992). One argument for rethinking curriculum is based on what has been learned through observation and study of how children learn. Children are "meaning makers," not empty vessels ready to be filled up with knowledge. Learners construct their own meanings based on a personal interaction between information and experience (Brooks & Brooks, 1993; Goodman, 1990). This constructivist view of learning places teachers in the role of a facilitator or guide who is responsible for creating an instructional context that capitalizes on learners' previous knowledge and experience base. Teachers arrange this mix of information and experiences to facilitate learners' access to content knowledge and help them manipulate this knowledge in meaningful ways.

Another reason for rethinking curriculum stems from dissatisfaction with the traditional separation of curriculum content into discrete or isolated units, such as reading, math, science, and social studies, which removes the natural links that exist among disciplines in everyday life. Educators and employers alike are troubled by outcomes revealing that although students may know factual information, they evidence difficulty in using this information to solve real problems (Brooks & Brooks, 1993). Some learners can generalize or transfer the information they learn to real-world situations; others, including those who experience identified learning problems, find this task more difficult. Information and experiences are made meaningful to learners when they are situated within a holistic and authentic context that capitalizes on the links joining various content areas.

A third argument in support of an integrated approach to curriculum is that a curriculum in its more standard form emerging from text books and curriculum guides, is premised on the notion that one model fits all learners. This approach defines, delineates, and ultimately limits the information to which students are exposed. Additionally, there is a rigidity in curriculum content and process that prevents students from exploring questions relevant to their own developing knowledge bases. Standard curriculum models neglect to acknowledge that learners begin their learning in different places. Some follow a prescribed step-by-step sequential curriculum, adding building blocks one on top of the other, but most children come with a different set of blocks arranged in unique ways and resulting from sensory limitations, difficulties in processing and interpreting information, or experiential differences. Based on these and other differences, learners come to school with their own unique constructions of meaning.

An analogy may be useful in clarifying these variations in learning. House construction begins from under the ground with the basement and moves above ground with bricks laid or cement poured for the foundation. From that point on, building proceeds in a variety of ways, which are not always from the bottom up. The frame or outline of the house is built, parts of the house are dropped in from all directions, such as windows or the roof; parts of the inside are built before the outside is complete; networks of plumbing and wiring are inserted. There are logical patterns that builders use to construct a house, but these are not from the bottom up or outside in; rather, they depend on a number of factors, including the budget of the home buyer, weather, and the availability of materials.

Children's learning is just as patterned yet idiosyncratic. Each child comes to the teaching and learning context with a set of unique twists and turns based on individual background factors and experience. The goal of all professionals who support children's learning is to assist children in finding their way toward building a "house" that is functional and strong enough to withstand the test of real life. There are standard processes in building houses and teaching children, but it is important to consider that each presents unique characteristics that must be recognized and facilitated in the instructional context. What we know about teaching and learning challenges traditional approaches to curriculum development and implementation.

INTEGRATING THE CURRICULUM

An integrated approach to curriculum development and implementation breaks down the rigidity of traditional approaches and creates a holistic instructional experience that builds on and fills in learners' knowledge frameworks. Models for developing integrated curricula, which are aligned with a constructivist perspective of learning, incorporate the following basic views regarding content, learners, and experience into curriculum planning and implementation (Pappas, Kiefer & Levstik, 1990).

Content. Priority is given to the development of conceptual understandings as opposed to factual or procedural knowledge. Concepts are the networks of information and ideas that integrate various kinds of experience (Brooks & Brooks, 1993; Bruner, 1977).

Learners. Learning is more likely and enduring when the instruction is learner centered and within authentic context, that is, directed by the learner's background knowledge, needs, and interests and within a setting meaningful to the learner and his or her worldview (Brooks & Brooks, 1993; Dudley-Marling & Searle, 1991).

Experience. Cognitive and linguistic processes (thinking and communicating) are viewed as both goals and vehicles in the learning process. Conceptual understandings are developed through thinking and communicating (Dudley-Marling & Searle, 1991).

Libraries represent networks of ideas and information and are natural laboratories for thinking and communicating. Content that is accessible for analyzing and synthesizing into learners' own conceptual frameworks presents a challenging cognitive task. Speaking, reading, writing, and listening are integrated into the process of utilizing the library as a resource. These cognitive and linguistic experiences, however, are presented at the most complex level of experience. In order to build concepts that are meaningful, teachers and librarians must understand the role that experience plays in learning, whether in libraries or classrooms.

BUILDING CONCEPTS THROUGH EXPERIENCE

Bruner (1977) offers a useful taxonomy for viewing the relationships of experience, language, and learning. He asserts three levels of experience that provide the means for a child's interaction with information: enactive (direct experience), such as Ms. Frizzle's trip through the solar system; iconic (experience mapped onto representations that link the experience with visual/graphic symbols), as detailed in diagrams, pictures, and charts depicting relationships of various aspects of the solar system; and symbolic (experience mediated through language), shared in conversations with Ms. Frizzle and students' written reports. According to Bruner, these three types of experience, while hierarchical, are also interactive in nature. A very young child relies primarily on direct or enactive experiences in learning. These direct experiences are continually linked with various linguistic and nonlinguistic communication. Depending on the content or task, adults and children alike use all three levels of experience in learning.

As the child becomes more adept at receptive and expressive uses of language in communication (symbolic experience), the need for true enactive experiences in developing conceptual knowledge decreases. Experience mediated by language becomes the primary means for the acquisition of concepts. Early enactive experiences, however, provide the base for utilizing such communication "experiences" to build increasingly more complex concepts (Andrews, Otis-Wilborn & Messenheimer-Young, 1991). When this process is applied to school teaching and learning, teachers link direct experience with iconic (e.g., pictures, diagrams, illustrations) and symbolic (oral language, printed materials) representations. Successfully integrating the three levels of experience provides an instructional setting that can meet the needs of students at various points of development. Building students' experiential base facilitates their growth as learners and explorers.

Students' use of the library and their interaction with print resources is one of the most potent sources of symbolic experience. It is within this context that ideas are accessed, dissected, analyzed, and synthesized into understandings and knowledge. The ways in which students organize their conceptual knowledge into ordinate and subordinate categories influences how they explore new information. Their communicative competence in asking questions, clarifying concepts, and sharing information with others affects their ability to access the thoughts of others in their exploration of new information. Additionally, students' ability to associate new ideas in organizing and reorganizing their conceptual knowledge is a function of symbolic experience.

The kinds of cognitive and linguistic tasks described above often create barriers for learners with special needs: access to information, processing, and communicating about new information and ideas. For a hearing-impaired child, inaccessibility to incidental messages often restricts the development of his or her conceptual base (Yoshinaga-Itano & Downey, 1986). For students with learning disabilities, organizing information from various sources, visual and auditory, can create misunderstandings and frustration for students. Students who are difficult to motivate or find it difficult to concentrate have particular trouble answering other people's questions. These students are more likely to engage in study when given an opportunity to pose their own questions and follow their own line of inquiry.

The curriculum for all learners, and especially learners with special needs, must be learner centered (Brooks & Brooks, 1993), that is, focused on the interests and development of individual learners. Additionally, learners need to connect information and ideas with real purpose. The library is an authentic context for learning when paired with student inquiry. There is an implicit assumption that, in addition to developing concepts and cognitive and linguistic abilities, another goal is to make the library a meaningful part of students' lives—a lifelong resource.

DEVELOPMENT OF AN INTEGRATED CURRICULUM: THE SOLAR SYSTEM

With the three basic parameters regarding content, learners, and experience in mind, a description of a collaborative approach for designing and implementing a solar system unit for elementary-aged hearing-impaired students is presented. The unit uses *The Magic School Bus: Lost in the Solar System* as its base. Woven into the description of the collaborative process are learners' understandings and expectations regarding the library. Many of the understandings and misunderstandings are shared to illustrate the need to integrate work in libraries with work in classrooms—a case for collaboration. The more collaborative the venture is between librarian and teacher, the more linked and holistic the curriculum becomes, enhancing learners' conceptual development.

The Conceptual Framework

Building the conceptual framework for the solar system unit in this example began with identifying basic concepts and developing an understanding of the concepts learners brought with them to the teaching and learning context. While the content of instruction is traditionally most identified with the notion of curriculum, in this example of an integrated curriculum, concepts serve as the foundation for the content included in the curriculum. Concepts are thought of as understandings or "big ideas" (Routman, 1992) around which more traditionally defined content is wrapped. Taba, Durkin, Fraenke, and McNaughton (1971), in their model of social studies curriculum, targeted three broad concepts for the elementary program: interdependence, evolution and change, and cultural diversity. The development of these concepts was depicted as an increasingly complex spiral extending upward from students' first year in school. The spiral signifies a learning process through which concepts are introduced and revisited throughout the learner's education. Hence, concepts develop in breadth, depth, and complexity over time. Bruner (1977) explains:

> The basic ideas [concepts] that lie at the heart of all science and mathematics and the basic themes that give form to life and literature are as simple as they are powerful. To be in command of these basic ideas, to use them effectively, requires a continual deepening of one's understanding of them that comes from learning to use them in progressively more complex forms. The spiral curriculum [facilitates this because] it turns back on itself at higher and higher levels. (pp. 12–13)

Broad concepts that are given emphasis across a variety of content help learners bring related ideas together, developing even deeper, more complex conceptual frameworks and understandings. Figure 13.1 illustrates the interaction of the child, the curriculum, and language and literacy in the development of increasingly complex concepts.

Using this notion of conceptual development, the teachers built the solar system unit around the three concepts Taba et al. (1971) proposed. In order to make broad concepts relevant to the study of the solar system theme, conceptual statements were developed as the first step toward flushing out potential content of the curriculum unit:

Interdependence: The solar system is made up of millions of parts that work together in identifiable and predictable patterns that, in turn, affect the individual parts.

Evolution/change: Understandings of the physical properties and perceptions/beliefs about the solar system change over time.

Cultural diversity: Across time and across cultures, people have integrated the solar system and its elements into their daily lives.

After the broad concepts are identified, the teacher and librarian brainstorm to generate potential topics of study that will contribute to students' development of the three broad concepts. Figure 13.2 displays the results of brainstorming and illustrates how collaboration between professionals can expand the potential topics of study.

Learners bring their own framework or schema of certain content to the teaching and learning context. This schema (or network of ideas) is based on background knowledge and personal experience. Many learners, including those with special needs, come with schemata on particular topics that are incomplete; that is, pieces of the picture may be missing.

Developing an understanding of the conceptual frameworks that students bring with them provides an important and relevant source of information in determining curriculum content and direction. This is accomplished by working with learners' questions, which helps to determine starting points that are meaningful to learners.

This process brings purpose and context to the curriculum. In Ms. Frizzle's class, students generated a number of questions about the solar system and reflected a fairly extensive background on the solar system. The special needs learners in our student group generated similar questions:

Ms. Frizzle's Students	**Special Needs Students**
What makes night and day?	What makes up the solar system?
Why are spaceships launched with rockets?	Of what are the planets made up?
What is gravity?	Can people live on other planets?
Why do people feel weightless in space?	How hot is the sun?

Figure 13.1
Interaction of the Child, the Curriculum, and the Language and Literacy

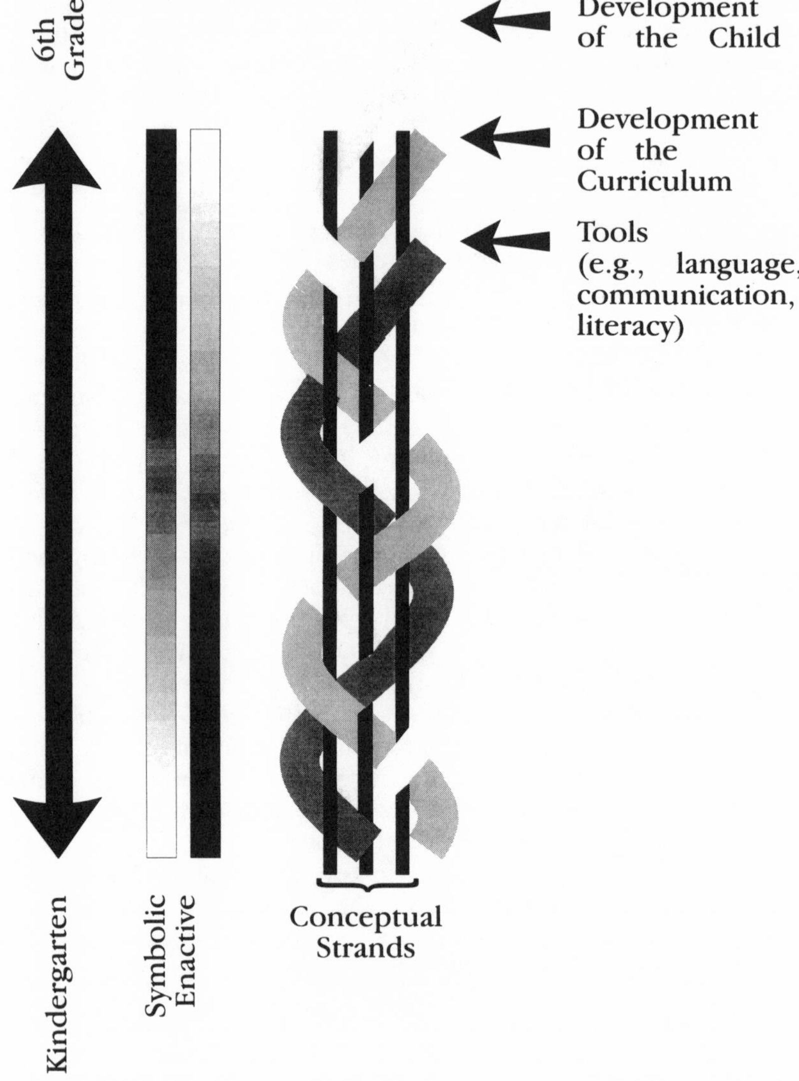

Figure 13.2
Results of Brainstorming Integrated Content Ideas

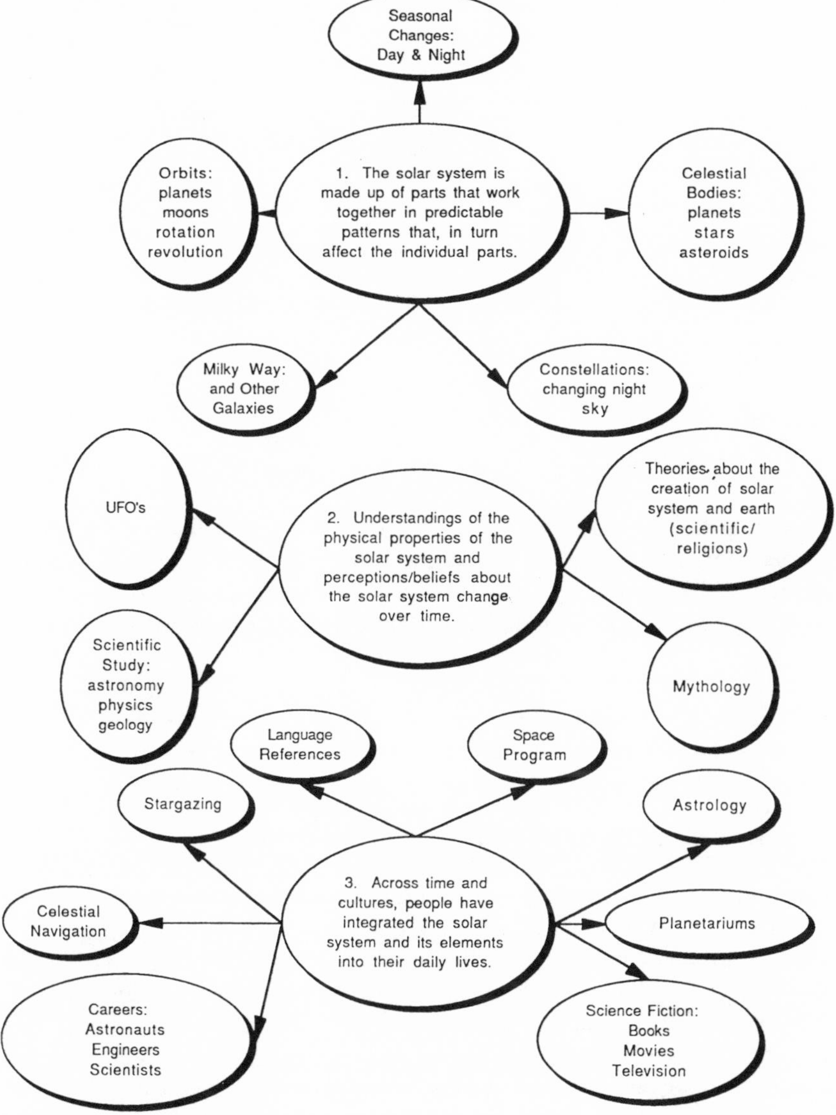

What makes the moon shine?

How big is the sun?

How hot is the sun?

Why is it so hot on Venus?

Why aren't Mars's moons round?

Is there life on Mars?

Why is Mars red?

What are the inner planets?

What are asteroids?

What is Jupiter's great red spot?

What are Saturn's rings?

How long is a year?

Is Pluto a real planet?

Do all planets have a moon like the Earth?

What's the air like on other planets?

How far away are the planets?

How long does it take to get to other planets?

What is an asteroid?

Do plants and trees grow on other planets?

Of what is the sun made?

What type of stuff (equipment) do astronauts need to take with them on a trip into space?

How big are the planets?

Similarities and differences in the questions come from the students' prior experiences and background knowledge. Both sets of questions reflect students' interest in the physical aspects of the solar system—distance, size, and composition. Additionally, students are curious about life on other planets—plant and human. These are the same questions that have driven scientists and astronauts for years. The questions show the natural need of the students to understand the unknown better. With a good sense of students' knowledge base, learning experiences are developed.

Linking Levels of Experience

An integrated approach to curriculum provides learners with opportunities to link past experience with new experiences and expand their knowledge base. In Bruner's (1977) model, experience was divided into three levels, beginning with enactive or direct experience, moving to enactive or graphic/pectoral experience, and finally to symbolic experience associated with oral and printed language. While developmentally learners build competence in operating from one level to the other, learning entails a constant interaction of these three levels of experience. The extent to which students can link concepts across levels contributes to their cognitive and linguistic development. In the arrangement of daily activities, the librarian and the teacher can work together to link levels of experience.

One of the concepts in the solar system unit associated with the interdependence of the various parts of the solar system was the distance between and arrangement of the planets. This was also reflected in student questions. Learners interacted with this concept and the associated factual information at the three levels of experience in the solar system story:

Enactive: Traveling in space, the clock reflected the actual time that passed.

Iconic: Diagrams of planets in the solar system, a mobile depicting distances of the solar system.

Symbolic: Reports that describe the arrangement and distance of the planets; charts that indicate numeric information explaining the distances.

Ms. Frizzle planned to take her students to the museum, which would have provided students mostly with iconic and symbolic levels of experience. However, her unplanned trip through the solar system was the source of enactive, direct experience for students.

In the solar system unit developed for the elementary learners, the classroom teacher worked to bring concepts to the least complex level of experience possible. Certainly taking a trip through the solar system was impossible, so the following activities were undertaken to illustrate on various scales the distances between planets and their arrangement in space:

- Scaled representations were hung in the room to show the students how far each planet is from the sun and which planets are closest to and farthest from the sun and other planets.
- Various scales were used in calculating distances between planets and the sun. Scales were grounded in measures with which students were familiar (e.g., distance from Milwaukee, Wisconsin to Chicago, Illinois; New York to California).
- Students examined various ways that distances were depicted and measured in reference materials in the library.
- In popular literature and television, such as "Star Trek" and "Deep Space Nine," students searched for ways in which distance between celestial bodies was measured and described.
- Students used the various scales and measures they discovered in their own stories and reports of space travel.

The library facilitated linking the various levels of experience by working with students to identify resources that depicted the relationships between planets in pictures (video or still), diagrams, and text that presented factual information. The collaboration between the teacher and librarian supported students' learning of conceptual and related factual information because they were united in their focus.

While the library represents a variety of resources, learners recognized the library only as a resource for books and specifically facts. Students were aware of the various formats and modalities in which information could be found, but they were not cognizant of how these were related to each other in providing a bigger, more detailed picture. When students were asked, "Why do you go to the library?" their answers included, "read books," "check out books," "use computers," "learn how to read so I won't be dumb", "find out stuff," "do homework", and "get information."

Authentic Use of the Library

Two aspects of context that relate to the integration of libraries into the curriculum through collaboration are important to consider: the context of the school library itself and the context of learners. An overriding goal and one of our assumptions is that learners view the library as a functional part of their lives. For this to become a reality, however, learners must see the relevance of the library and the role of the librarian as a resource that extends beyond the school library. The fact is that school libraries often reflect a very different image to learners than does their community library, a difference found in interviews with learners who were involved in the solar system unit. The scheduling of library hours was arbitrary and rigid. The library period was once a week. A class visited the library as a group, often with an undefined goal. In contrast, the motivation for visiting a community library is predicated on a need—to answer a question, find a good book, or find a quiet place to read or work.

Another contrast between school and community libraries is in the routines associated with using the library. In the school library, learners must adhere to sets of rules and procedures that are developed to make it easier to serve classes rather than individuals. This may entail checking out all of the books at once rather than books to individual students. Additionally, students are not required to use library cards. Other routines that look very different include seating arrangements for classes and group instruction. These routines are convenient for the librarian and teacher but restrict learners from developing typical library routines, communications, and procedures.

Students' ability to generalize what they learn at school is dependent on their ability to practice in authentic settings. Some learners with special needs are less equipped to generalize tasks outside the school setting because the context outside the school library is often different. Learning is most productive when students are involved in the process, having direct and repeated involvement in the language and action of library routines.

This perspective fosters integration of authentic library routines into the learning process. When tasks are authentic, the library is seen as a tool rather than a subject. To use the library in this way, however, there are important competencies that learners need. Every school librarian works hard to assist students' learning to use the card catalog, find fiction versus nonfiction, understand the organization of titles and areas of the library, use equipment such as microfiche and perhaps computers, audio, and video resources. In many school libraries, the librarian is responsible for developing training sessions for students at the beginning of each year to demonstrate how to use the library. This process presents skills to students as discrete behaviors that are unrelated to a context in which they might be used meaningfully or authentically. The concept of "authentic" requires that learning have immediate and real use to a student; long-lasting learning is less likely when separated from content and purpose. Learning to use the library must occur within a problem-solving context—in search of information and answers to real questions and/or needs generated by the learners themselves.

Using the library as a tool enhances learners' knowledge. Sparse background knowledge on a given topic or theme is reflected in misunderstandings the learners may illustrate or in their difficulty in organizing knowledge into logical conceptual categories. This can interfere with typical approaches to teaching learners use of the library as a tool. One student in the solar system group chose to become the class expert on the planet Neptune. Upon entering the school library, he went immediately to the card catalog, as instructed by the teacher and librarian, and looked up "Neptune." Because there was no book with the title "Neptune," the student concluded no information was available. The student's framework restricted him from exploring other paths for information. These paths could best be developed in the context of the student's search. Creating a concept map with student-generated ideas would prompt other directions in the search for information on Neptune. This student had a grasp of isolated library skills that were procedural in nature. He was not equipped to draw on and organize his developing conceptual knowledge base to assist him. The library, when used to accomplish real tasks, actually can enhance students' conceptual knowledge base.

BREATHING LIFE INTO LIBRARIES

One does not need to convince librarians or teachers of the "life" that is a part of the library. However, the attitudes of the special needs learners in this solar system group indicated that the library did not represent a vibrant and exciting place to explore. All learners, but particularly those who have difficulty learning through traditional instructional means, can utilize the content and process associated with the library to support their learning. Many adult hearing-impaired individuals emphasize the importance of print as a primary source of their information; access to information through oral communication or even signed communication is incomplete and without critical detail. Learners who have difficulty processing and organizing content need the guided challenge of developing strategies for searching for information in meaningful contexts. Finally, an excitement for learning can be engendered in learners who exhibit behavioral or motivational problems by expanding instruction beyond the traditional classroom context, materials, and content. Libraries represent not only a depository for information but a context in which cognitive and linguistic learning can be supported.

Real integration of content to expand and fill in conceptual understanding, needs and interests of learners, and meaningful purpose should be the goals of collaboration of teachers and librarians in school instruction. This integration requires a level of collaboration between these professionals where teachers and librarians merge and even transfer aspects of their professional roles to each other and their students. Teachers facilitate students' search for resources, and librarians become involved in developing the conceptual knowledge base of individual learners. The process of planning and implementing integrated instructional units brings the life of the classroom and the library closer together. One result of this process is that new areas of expertise emerge for all those involved; everyone becomes a learner.

In the story of Ms. Frizzle and her students' study of the solar system, their travel in space comes to an end. What they learned through direct experience is summarized in reports, charts, and models when they return to school. Communication of this experience to others, however, has students wondering if anyone will believe how exciting it really was!

[In the car riding home from school.]

Student: We went to outer space today.

Mom: Of course you did, dear.

[Checking out a book on stars at the library.]

Student: And there was Ms. Frizzle, floating among the asteroids!

Librarian: (What an imagination!)

[Eating dinner at home.]

Student: We could have been lost in space forever.

Dad: Eat your salad, honey. (Cole, 1990, p. 36)

Librarians and teachers can be the agents that help link learners with experience, information, and purpose. The knowledge gained becomes the building block for lifelong learning. Librarians, as well as teachers, have this goal for their students.

REFERENCES

Andrews, S., Otis-Wilborn, A., & Messenheimer-Young, T. (1991). *Beyond seeing and hearing: Teaching geography to sensory impaired children*. Indiana, PA: National Council for Geographic Education.

Brooks, J. G., & Brooks, M. G. (1993). *In search of understanding: The case for constructivist classrooms*. Alexandria, VA: Association for Supervision and Curriculum Development.

Bruner, J. S. (1977). *The process of education*. Cambridge, MA: Harvard University Press.

Cole, J. (1990). *The magic school bus: Lost in the solar system*. New York: Scholastic.

Dudley-Marling, C., & Searle, D. (1991). *When students have time to talk: Creating contexts for learning language*. Portsmouth, NH: Heinemann.

Goodman, Y. (1990). *How children construct literacy*. Newark, NJ: IRA.

Pappas, C. C., Kiefer, B. Z., & Levstik, L. S. (1990). *An integrated language perspective in the elementary school: Theory into action*. White Plains, NY: Longman.

Routman, R. (1991). *Invitations: Changing as teachers and learners, K–12*. Portsmouth, NH: Heineman.

Taba, H., Durkin, M., Fraenkel, J. M., & McNaughton, A. (1971). *A teacher's handbook of elementary social studies: An inductive approach*. Menlo Park, CA: Addison-Wesley.

Yoshinaga-Itano, C., & Downey, D. (1986). A hearing impaired child's acquisition of schemata: Something's missing. *Topics in Language Disorders* 7(1): 45–57.

Zacharias-Lewinsky, T., Koenig, S., Otis-Wilborn, A., & Messenheimer-Young, T. (1992). Language and literacy in early childhood: Camping, canoes, and adventure for profoundly hearing-impaired children. *Volta Review*, 94(4): 359–364.

14 School Library Media Specialists and Professional Development

Caren L. Wesson

Like students, teachers are lifelong learners. They continue to need professional development in order to keep abreast of new methodologies and new theories about teaching and learning.

School library media specialists must approach professional development from three perspectives. First, they must be dedicated to their own growth (Keegan & Westerger, 1991). Perhaps no other area of education has more flux than the library. The technological advances and the information explosion will indeed keep school library media specialists active as they attempt to remain current. The second perspective deals with the supportive role of school library media specialists with respect to their colleagues' continued growth. They not only keep a professional library for their colleagues' use, but also participate in a variety of professional development activities. The third perspective is the role of the school librarian in helping to prepare future school librarians. Connections across generations is an important professional development contribution. In this chapter, these three perspectives on professional development will be explored. Unique connections to working with children with special needs will be highlighted throughout.

PERSONAL PROFESSIONAL DEVELOPMENT

Even more so than other educators, school library media specialists have a continuing obligation to seek out new information pertinent to their jobs. Of obvious concern is the need to keep abreast of developments in technology useful in school library media centers, among them the interactive videodisc, the CD-ROM, and remote database/telecommunications. At the literary end of the spectrum, the school library media specialist needs information about new literature and materials appropriate for the curriculum of the children who use the center, including students with special needs. In order to gather this information, the specialist needs to engage in a number of activities, including belonging to professional organizations and reading the journals affiliated with these organizations, attending conferences, observing at other sites, and meeting with other teachers. Another major means of professional development is action research projects.

Professional Organizations

Several national and international organizations that the school library media specialist typically joins are the Association for Educational Communication and Technology, the Society for School Librarians International, the International Association of School Librarianship, and the most prestigious, the American Library Association (ALA) and its most significant division for school library media specialists, the American Association of School Librarians (AASL). Upon receiving membership with ALA at an initial individual cost of thirty-eight dollars a year, members receive the journal *American Libraries.*

By far, the most esteemed and useful organization for serving children across the range of special needs is the Council for Exceptional Children and its divisions, including the Division for Learning Disabilities, the Council for Children with Behavior Disorders, and the Division for Mental Retardation. The annual fee is seventy-five dollars, which also covers two journals: *Exceptional Children,* which publishes research, policy papers, discussion papers, and reviews of literature, and *Teaching Exceptional Children,* with practitioner-oriented articles geared toward ideas for curriculum and instruction of special needs students. Other organizations of interest are the Council for Learning Disabilities, the Association for Severely Handicapped, and the A. G. Bell Society, for educators working with hearing-impaired students. The organizations tied to specific disabilities should be explored as the need arises given the school's population. The journals from these organizations are helpful in providing ideas for instruction of special needs students.

Conferences

A number of national and state conferences are conducted exclusively for school library media specialists. The ALA holds two national conferences yearly in June and December, and the AASL holds one every other year in November. For information on state conferences, contact the local state organization.

Special education conferences are helpful for school library media specialists. These conferences could assist in the generation of ideas for interventions for working directly with the special needs students, as well as ideas for working with the teachers and parents. A major thrust of special education conferences is collaboration. The special education conferences that a school library media specialist may want to consider attending include the Council for Exceptional Children's (CEC) annual international conferences or the annual state CEC conference. At these conferences, there are often sessions relevant to literacy development and research/study skills of special needs students, which may be of particular interest to the school library media specialist. Many local conferences have sessions that can be related to working with special needs students. Lately, there have been a number of conferences focused on the at-risk population and on students from various cultural backgrounds.

Attending these conferences has a number of benefits for the school library media specialist: the enthusiasm generated by new information and ideas, practical ideas that can be readily implemented in the library, and networking with other professionals with similar roles and/or interests. Sometimes the best ideas are not those heard in sessions but those shared informally between sessions.

Observing in Other Sites and Visiting with Other Teachers

Visiting other school libraries that serve special needs students can stimulate new ideas. A variety of aspects about the site may be studied. The physical layout, the selection of materials, the methods used to teach library skills, and collaborative relationships with other teachers may be of interest. To get the most out of the visit, the host librarian needs to be willing to think aloud, openly sharing the logic behind decisions made and sharing that information without too much mental editing. Thinking aloud is also of benefit to the host librarian as it provides the opportunity to make ideas more explicit. Similarly, school librarians may visit special education classrooms or inclusive general education classes. The more educators truly understand the roles each plays, the more clearly they will communicate and their collaboration will improve.

An alternative to a site visit is meeting with other librarians informally after school or even over the telephone. Two formats are useful in these kinds of situations. One is simple random conversation in which one idea leads to another and a general roundtable discussion is held. A second format is to have specific agenda items or questions of concern to school librarians. Districts that are technologically advanced can use bulletin boards via telecommunications. It is imperative that library media specialists continually communicate with others in their field. Overall, the point is to develop a network of resources.

ACTION RESEARCH

A major new trend in teacher professional development is use of action research. The librarian selects a problem or a particular aspect of his or her role that needs improvement and then seeks to determine a way to change the identified aspect and a means of measuring improvement in that area. For example, if the librarian is concerned that the special education students are often remiss in returning their books on time, that may be the focus of the action research project. He or she may choose a specific class with which to conduct the action research project, which includes an intervention designed to improve the return rate, and another class to maintain in the old manner. In having these two groups, the librarian will have a basis of comparison. The data collected may simply be the percentage of students from each class who return books on time over a three-month period. The intervention for the target class could be a number of procedures. For example, the librarian may develop a specific reinforcement procedure for this class, so that when students return books on time they get a star on a chart. When they receive ten stars, they get a book to keep. Another idea is to send home a reminder to the parents of the children in the target class the day before library class.

Action research may be conducted with an individual student. Often special needs students respond well to an intervention designed specifically for them. The intervention should be determined by the librarian; sometimes action research works best when the person considering alternative ideas has someone off whom to bounce the ideas. Thus, an informal discussion with a colleague may be helpful. Sharing these projects is an important aspect of this process.

SUPPORTING PROFESSIONAL GROWTH OF COLLEAGUES

Another way in which school librarians are involved in professional development is by supporting the professional growth of their colleagues (American Library Association, 1988; Miller, 1991; Thompson, 1991) through organizing and ordering professional materials that benefit colleagues and by offering to share knowledge through inservices, consultations with colleagues, and collaborative teaming.

Teachers are busy people who have many duties to perform, roles to play, and goals to attain. They need support from a variety of sources to keep abreast of the latest educational trends. Special education teachers are no different. School districts usually have someone whose job is to help keep teachers current. Sometimes this is the curriculum director; other times this role is performed by building principals or an instructional leadership director. Whoever performs this role must have the school library media specialist as a working partner.

Professional Materials

Most schools have, as part of the library or housed in a separate area such as a teachers' work area, current educational literature. This literature must be purchased, organized, and maintained by the school library media specialist. The resources to be included in the professional development section of a school library media center cover a large range. Local curricular materials that are not kept by every teacher need to be available. For example, when a secondary teacher needs to know what was covered in sixth-grade world history, the district's goals for sixth-grade social studies should be readily available.

Professional journals should be included in this section of the library. Each building will have its own special set of needs with regard to the specifics of which material is important for its staff. An elementary school might want to order *Elementary School Journal, Reading Teacher, Teaching Exceptional Children, Learning, Instructor*, and *Arithmetic Teacher*. A middle school's journal section might include the *Middle School Journal, Teaching Exceptional Children*, and *Contemporary Education*. Similarly, secondary school libraries may house journals such as the *Journal of Research in Science Teaching, Phi Delta Kappan*, and *Curriculum Inquiry*. Considering the information gathered from the survey and the budget allowance, the school library media specialist can acquire a professional periodical library that reflects the needs of the staff. If there are budget constraints, the district may order one copy, which can be routed and shared by several buildings. In order to determine which journals are appropriate for the school, the library media specialist may want to conduct a simple survey that lists possible journals and asks the teachers to check the ones they think they would read. The survey might include a short description of each journal, or perhaps a collection could be put together for the teacher's perusal before voting for the ones they deem most useful. Given the budget and using this information to prioritize, the librarian may select the ones to order. The library media specialist may also photocopy the contents pages of popular journals and place them in staff mailboxes to spark interest in a particular topic or article. Teachers who want to read a specific article may then leave a note for the librarian to obtain a copy.

Books related to education are important elements in the professional development section of the library. Again, budget considerations are important in ordering, and a survey may be helpful. Perhaps once a year, the librarian can assemble a list of possible books to be ordered and ask the teachers to indicate which ones they are likely to read. In order to assemble such a list, the librarian may want to visit the local bookstores and check the educational section, as well as the nearby college or university bookstores, which house educational texts. From a perusal of these shelves, a good list of possible materials to be ordered may be developed. Texts about special needs students should be included in this set. Of course, reviews in journals such as *Booklist* and *School Library Journal* and suggestions obtained upon attending conferences are valuable tools for locating resources for the school library media center's professional library as well. Soliciting ideas from colleagues and looking through publisher catalogs are other ways to develop the list. Professors from local colleges and universities may also offer suggestions.

Donations from colleagues are useful for this section of the professional library. As teachers take classes, they may acquire books that they are willing to share by storing them in the school's professional development library. In this way they still have access to these books without having to store them personally.

A final storage function that can be accomplished in this section of the library is the housing of catalogs of educational materials. Many teachers receive numerous materials catalogs, but no one teacher gets them all. Many general educators may benefit from seeing special education catalogs and vice versa. In order to maximize the potential of all these catalogs, they may be stored in the professional development library. A simple file drawer with the catalogs organized alphabetically would suffice to make these materials current and accessible. Teachers might get in the habit of sticking any catalogs into the librarian's mailbox after they have perused them and completed order forms or filed the information on their "wish list." The librarian then makes the catalogs available to everyone.

Inservice, Consultation, and Collaboration

Inservice

Often the librarian is in the unique position of knowing about technological advances such as the CD-ROM and interactive videos (Barron & Bergen, 1992). These advances are often the subject of the conferences the librarian attends. To develop a complete inservice plan with regard to technology will take input from a number of individuals, including the principal and teachers. Some teachers still need to learn the basics of using a computer, others need to be made aware of the software available, while others need only advanced use information. If via committee or survey, a general consensus of the overall needs of the faculty can be ascertained, the librarian may have a planning or presenting role in the inservices on technology. Surveying not only the technological inservice needs of staff members but also the abilities of those already knowledgeable is important. Asking these staff members to share their expertise with their colleagues in a building inservice is an excellent way to collaborate.

Another area that is usually the specialty of the school library media specialist is children's literature. So many excellent children's books are published annually that teachers need advice on the ones that are important for the students they teach. Recently, there has been a great outpouring of books focusing on children of color. *Can't Sit Still* by Karen Lotz, *You're My Nikki* by Phyllis Rose Eisenberg, *Grandpa's Face* by Eloise Greenfield, and *Dear Willie Rudd* by Libba Moore Gray provide a multicultural perspective to the literature that teachers may use. Similarly, books about special needs children are important for teachers to learn about. Some newer titles in this area are *Alex Is My Friend* by Marisibina Russo, *I'm Somebody, Too* by Jeanne Gehret, and *The Lion Who Had Asthma* by Jonathan London. The librarian can share these and other titles through booktalks for teachers on specific topics or thematic units used schoolwide. (See Chapter 3 for more information on booktalks.)

Another option is for the library media specialist to organize short yearly inservices about literature. Perhaps taking a half-hour of a staff meeting or offering an optional before- or after-school inservice are ways of providing teachers with the opportunity to learn about the new literature. A special display for new books may be helpful, as may a monthly list of books received that is distributed to the staff.

Another domain within the school librarian's expertise that needs to be shared with other teachers is resource-based learning (RBL), or helping students learn to use resources to extend their learning base (Haycock, 1991). Resource-based learning differs from resource-based teaching, which refers to a teacher-centered instructional model in which teachers use multiple resources to gather the content of the lesson. In RBL, the students are the ones who use multiple resources. The teacher's role becomes one of facilitator. The librarian may teach students what the resources are and how to use them.

The three basic objectives for students in RBL are the ability to manage and use information to solve problems, the skills to communicate effectively, and the capacity to form interrelationships (Thompson, 1991). The underlying assumption of RBL is that students must be socialized into the role of lifelong learner. Teachers still play an active role in this type of instruction, through three basic functions (Haycock, 1991). First, teachers have the responsibility for structuring an environment conducive to RBL. Second they guide student learning through a combination of techniques, including coaching, questioning, and prompting. The third role for the teacher is to monitor student progress with respect to RBL. (More information about the assessment aspect may be found in Chapter 2.)

A team approach of librarian and classroom teachers is efficacious in teaching RBL. The school librarian first shares background knowledge about RBL with the teachers, and then they jointly plan activities that address objectives from the classroom through RBL for all students, with the exception of those who are severely disabled. Brewik (1991) points out that all children need access to RBL and information literacy. He states that the lack of systematic attention to these issues will be felt by students such as those in special education: "The impact, as usual, will be felt most quickly and most deeply by those who are already socially, educationally, and economically disadvantaged. The gap between the haves and have-nots will widen as a new information elite emerges" (p. 7).

Consultation

When an individual teacher rather than the entire staff needs information, a simple consultation model will suffice. A consultation model is a slightly more formalized model of teachers helping teachers. There are a number of formats under which teachers help each other personally. If no system for teacher-to-teacher assistance is in use in the school, one may be created by asking teachers to identify the areas they feel most knowledgeable about and producing a list of these skills and areas of expertise. (This kind of list may not be necessary in smaller-sized buildings, but when the staff is larger than twenty-five, it is impossible to know the strengths of each person.) Asking teachers to identify their strengths is a professional development activity in and of itself because it requires reflection. Teachers must become comfortable with tooting their own horns. The librarian is likely to include technology, children's literature, and other personal favorites among his or her areas of expertise. Perhaps study skills, report writing strategies, thematic lesson plans, and drama in the classroom are other areas the librarian may be willing to share with other teachers.

One overall emphasis within professional development is making better use of local resources. The answer is often right in front of the teachers; it is a matter of recognizing the strengths of those within the school. An organized list of staff strengths and resources may have positive, far-reaching consequences. One staff planned an inservice program within their school by developing mini-classes on nine different technologies demonstrated and taught by fellow staff members who offered to share their knowledge and expertise on such topics as CD-ROM encyclopedia, automated card catalog, videodisc, and Macintosh software applications. Peer coaching—two teachers spend time with each other, sharing feedback, advice, and suggestions—can follow the declaration of teaching strengths and weaknesses. Trust between the two teachers, journal recording of their shared work, and time to work together are essential elements of this model.

Collaboration

The school librarian can share expertise by offering to plan and teach collaboratively with the classroom teachers. An open invitation to all teachers and capitalizing on friendships initially may foster situations in which a co-taught lesson or unit is initiated. As two or more educators collaborate (Haycock, 1991), they learn from each other. The expertise of each team member is shared with the others.

Perhaps a third-grade teacher wants the students to learn about using basic reference materials while studying several countries in social studies. The librarian and teacher work together to identify which reference materials will best be used and taught within this unit. Through collaborative planning, they decide to teach the children how to use the atlas and encyclopedia. They plan a series of lessons, with the culminating project being a map and one-page report of a country to be completed by each child. Another example is of a team of four sixth-grade teachers who want their students to research a type of energy source, write a paper, and plan an experiment that demonstrates the energy. One goal for the project is that each student uses multiple references, such as nonfiction books, encyclopedias, and magazine articles. Teaching students to find relevant information becomes the focal point for the librarian's instruction.

At the high school level, a theme such as World War II may be selected by the sophomore-year teachers. Again the school librarian may be helpful in identifying appropriate materials and determining which specific information skills need to be taught within this unit. This may be taught as a cross-disciplinary unit with art, music, literature, math, history, and science all brought in. Different types of resources need to be used in each area. Thus, this unit may be a synthesis of previously taught resource skills that had previously been used in isolation.

Clearly, collaboration is a key concept as schools continue to restructure. The librarian can set the tone, provide a model, and generally encourage collaboration. As special needs students become more involved in inclusive programs, they will be included in these collaborative team taught lessons. The teaching team will need to keep individual needs in mind and accommodate through changing instruction, modifying assignments, and adding motivational aspects. (See Chapter 1 for specific ideas.)

As professional development becomes a priority in a school, the doors are opened, and the sharing of educational issues and tips about teaching becomes an expectation. Everyone benefits from this kind of openness and trust building. As the librarian is such a central figure in a school, he or she may take on heavier roles in assisting colleagues than a classroom teacher might. Clarifying the role description with the principal will help the library media specialist set priorities and make decisions about what functions should receive the most time and attention. Overextending oneself should be avoided.

PRACTICE TEACHERS IN THE SCHOOL LIBRARY

As the role of the library heightens in schools, the need for more and better trained school librarians will lead to increased college activity in preparing these professionals. Recruiting individuals into the field is also part of the job. As new people are prepared, they need a site in which to practice and mentor librarians from whom to learn. Working with a student teacher librarian is rewarding and challenging, but the reality is that student teachers in library science are rare. The more likely scenario is that a general educator will have a student teacher who has an interest in the library and wants to spend time there. Regardless of full- or part-time status of a student teacher librarian, the cooperating librarian role requires some conceptual and affective understandings.

First, the cooperating librarian needs to be aware of the expectations of the student teacher librarian. The university supervisor should make expectations very clear through discussions and written communication. The cooperating librarian should have answers to the following questions.

- What is the ultimate goal? To take over the entire operation of the library for three weeks? Two? Not at all?
- Do the expectations include teaching several units to classes such as a study skills or a creative drama unit?
- What kind of evaluation must be filled out at the end of the experience?
- How much collegial interaction is expected?
- How do we get started in having him or her learn about how this library is run?
- How often will the university supervisor visit?
- What kind of record-keeping system should be used to track the student teacher librarian's progress?
- Is there a schedule for what teaching responsibilities are expected week to week?
- Is this the final experience before graduation or an earlier practicum?
- What are expectations with respect to teaching special needs students?

Once the student teacher librarian is on site, establishing a relationship and an open channel of communication is of primary importance. Most often people in this position are afraid of their cooperating teacher and afraid of failing. They have attended years of college to arrive at this point and now know it is all on the line; their years of work may be for naught if they are unsuccessful in this culminating experience. So, making the person feel comfortable while still indicating high expectations, is first on the list of what to accomplish.

Second, if the answers to the above questions are not available, then it is up to the school librarian and the student teacher librarian to answer them. It is best to have as many answers as possible early in the experience so that no one appears to be changing the rules midstream. The two may want to work together to answer these and other nitty-gritty questions, like "What do you want me to do in the next fifteen minutes?"

A typical sequence of activity for the student teacher is to have about an hour of the librarian's uninterrupted time in which a tour of the facility, including the entire school, and a description of how the librarian functions within this school, is provided. Next, the student teacher will spend about two days primarily in observation of both the librarian and the students, with the librarian demonstrating good teaching and librarianship. Then the student teacher is assigned simple tasks, some of which involve the students and others of a clerical nature. By the beginning of the second week, the student teacher may be working and planning for work with one or two individual children and one small group requiring instruction in the library. Perhaps special needs students are involved at this point, and the librarian will share information about teaching some of the individual students. Reading to a class is likely to be an early activity. By the fifth or sixth week, the student teacher may be in charge of several classes.

As the student teacher librarian takes on increasing responsibilities, the librarian needs to conduct systematic observations and provide informal feedback from time to time. The worst thing a cooperating librarian can do is leave the student teacher librarian in the dark about how he or she is doing. Honesty is paramount. Delivering the first negative feedback at the end of the semester is inexcusable. A positive side effect of having a student teacher in the library is that usually the librarian learns a lot about himself or herself as well as getting fresh ideas from the student teacher. This is a professional development situation for all participants. Being in someone else's view makes people more cognizant of their own teaching and that alone can help foster improvement. Thus, this experience has positive outcomes for all.

CONCLUSION

Teachers are also obligated to view themselves as lifelong learners. As such their own professional development must be attended to as they continue to learn how to improve their teaching. Attending conferences, self-reflection, action research, collaboration, and mentoring new librarians are all ways to pursue professional development. It is not enough to keep doing the job and consider that professional development. Professional development activities must be purposeful and planned. These types of activities keep teachers and librarians fresh, motivated, and effective.

REFERENCES

American Library Association. (1988). *Information power: Guidelines for school library media programs*. Chicago: American Library Association, and Washington, DC: Association for Educational Communications and Technology.

Barron, D., & Bergen, T. (1992, May). Information power: The restructured school library for the nineties. *Phi Delta Kappan*, 521–525.

Brewik, S. (1991). A signal for the need to restructure the learning process. *NASSP Bulletin*, 1–7.

Haycock, C. (1991). Resource-based learning: A shift in the roles of teacher, learner. *NASSP Bulletin 75*(535): 15–23.

Keegan, B., & Westerger, T. (1991). Restructuring and the school library: Partners and the information age. *NASSP Bulletin*, 9–14.

Miller, N. E. (1991). School library media specialists: Working for the information age. *NASSP Bulletin*, 43–48.

Thompson, J. C. (1991). Resource-based learning can be the backbone of reform: Improvement. *NASSP Bulletin*, 24–28.

Annotated Bibliography

INTRODUCTION

American Association for School Librarians & Association for Educational Communications and Technology. (1988). *Information power: Guidelines for school library media programs.* Chicago & Washington, DC: American Library Association & Association for Educational Communications and Technology. This text delineates professional standards and guidelines for school library media centers and the programs they should provide in schools today. In particular, the roles and responsibilities of the school library media specialist are addressed, along with a mission statement. Other facets discussed are leadership, planning, management, personnel, resources, equipment and facilities. The importance of this publication is pervasive as information sources and new technologies become more and more significant in educating students today.

CHAPTER 1

Pugach, M., & Wesson, C. (1990). Supporting the participation of exceptional students in today's classrooms. In E. Meyer (Ed.), *Exceptional children in today's schools.* (pp. 75–106). Denver: Love Publishing Co. Pugach and Wesson describe the disadvantage of pull-out programming for children with special needs. In terms of social drawbacks, they suffer from lack of membership in one group, ostracization and the stigma of separation. In the academic domain, students who are pulled out of their general education classrooms have a disjointed curriculum and contradictory instruction. Although teachers try to work in a carefully organized manner, there is often not enough time for communication. The chapter offers practical ideas for having disabled students stay and be successfully taught in general education classrooms. The benefits of this inclusive education model are also provided.

CHAPTER 2

Loetscher, D. (1988). *Taxonomies of the school library media program*. Englewood, CO: Libraries Unlimited, Inc. The intent of this book is to look at the emerging role of the school library media center and the school library media specialist. Methodologies for examining this developing role and ways in which to evaluate the attainment of the new goals are provided. An examination of the student's and the administrator's role with regard to the school library media center are also discussed, as well as the impact of resource-based teaching on the school library media center. The various features of the school library program are presented, along with a sample of evaluation instruments from several school models throughout the United States. This text presents to students, classroom teachers, administrators, and school library media specialists the possibilities of how a school library media center can and should function, and the services it should provide.

Vavrus, L. (1990). Put portfolios to the test. *Instructor*. 100(1): 48–53. Portfolios have become a major trend in education and school curriculum. Vavrus provides a definition of portfolios and answers some of the questions most commonly asked about them. Discussed is the importance of understanding that a portfolio is not merely a folder of a student's work, but "a systematic and organized collection" that reflects student growth on a continual basis. Self-evaluation is an important component according to the author, as is involvement of teachers, students, and parents in the selection of work to be placed in the portfolio.

CHAPTER 3

Baker, A., & Greene, E. (1987). *Storytelling: Art and technique*. New York: R. R. Bowker Company. This book is an excellent source of information on the ancient art form of storytelling. A history of this art form is given, along with suggestions on selecting stories that are "tellable" and appealing. Basic steps in learning and preparing a story are presented, as well as suggestions for storytelling in special settings with special needs children. Ideas for the presentation itself, such as adjusting and adapting to audience feedback and being aware of the listening mood and different age groups of the audience. A section is devoted to children as storytellers and another to the planning and publicizing of story hours, workshops, and festivals. An appendix is provided with sources of stories for telling.

Bauer, C. (1983). *This way to books*. (Illustrated by L. Gates). New York: H. W. Wilson Company. *This Way to Books* is a collection of ideas, programs, techniques, and activities developed to involve children in books and literature. These suggestions revolve around thematic units and are somewhat unconventional in their attempt to entice children into reading. The author suggests using toys, puppets, crafts, music, costumes, and banners. One section of the book gives suggestions for storytelling with a collection of story programs set around themes and another gives examples of four traditional booktalks. Examples of using poetry with children and games or crafts related to particular stories are also presented, along with ideas for exhibits utilizing such things as bulletin boards and chalkboards to encourage children to appreciate good literature.

Sierra, J. (1991). *Fantastic theater: Puppets and plays for young performers and young audiences.* New York: H. W. Wilson Company. With today's educational trend toward literature-based curriculum, *Fantastic Theater* is a valuable resource. This book focuses on the development of critical thinking skills and cooperative learning skills through the exploration of expression and the production of dramatic presentations. Thirty plays derived from a variety of cultures are provided in a flexible format for children to perform or for adults to perform for children. This book is for the beginning puppeteer as well as the more advanced puppeteer, with ideas on how to dramatize through pantomime or more formal presentations. Suggestions are given for creating puppets, stages, props, scenery, narration, music, and sound effects. Directions with reproducible or traceable patterns for shadow and rod puppets are also provided.

Trelease, J. (1989). *The new read-aloud handbook.* New York: Penguin Books. Jim Trelease has been a proponent of reading aloud to children for over ten years since he published the first edition of his handbook in 1979. Now in its third edition, it is also available in other editions in Great Britain, Australia and Japan. Having been an artist and writer for *The Springfield Daily News* and a lover of children's literature, Mr. Trelease presents parents and teachers with wonderful suggestions on why and when to read aloud to children. He also discusses the stages of reading aloud and some of the do's and don'ts. The importance of sustained silent reading as a partner to reading aloud, and developing a home library as well as a relationship with the local public library, are also addressed. Most importantly, a treasury collection of books to read aloud is provided in annotated bibliographic form, along with grade levels and the number of pages.

CHAPTER 4

Howard, M. Ed (1980). *Puzzled about educating special needs learners? A handbook on modifying vocational curricula for handicapped students.* Madison WI: Wisconsin Vocational Studies Center. This handbook provides information and specific techniques that have proven to be effective with the special populations. It also provides examples of how to develop a cooperative working relationship among the vocational instructor, special needs instructor, parents, and the community employers in order to better serve special needs students.

Sarkees, D., & Scott, J. (1985). *Vocational special needs.* (2d ed.). Homewood, IL: American Technical Publishers, Inc. The intent of this book is to look at how to successfully mainstream the special needs student into vocational education classes. Special needs learners have a legal right to enter vocational programs; however, the vocational educator and the special needs educator need to work collaboratively in order for this student to meet with success. This book provides the practical application of strategies that enable the instructors to achieve their goals. The authors emphasize how vocational programs can enhance training and employment opportunities for the special needs learner.

CHAPTER 5

Batshaw, M. (1992). *Children with disabilities: A medical primer*. (3d ed.). Baltimore: Paul H. Brooks. A basic reference work, this volume reviews the causes and characteristics of disabilities which affect young children. Chapters on cerebral palsy, autism, and other disorders are descriptive and clear. The introductory section on genetic abnormalities and normal child development are well-written and informative. This overview is useful for parents and professionals.

Friedberg, J. B. (1992). *Portraying persons with disabilities: Nonfiction. An annotated bibliography of nonfiction for children and teenagers*. (2d ed.). Providence, NJ: R. R. Bowker. The authors of *Accept Me As I Am* (Bowker, 1985) have updated their earlier work with this entirely new source. It includes four major sections covering children and teens' nonfiction dealing with physical problems, sensory problems, cognitive and behavior problems, and various disabilities. Within each of these sections, books are listed alphabetically by author, with full ordering information, reading level, and review sources. Full content information is given, followed by a critical analysis of the work. Books cited are indexed by author, title, and subject. The introductory sections are excellent for background information. The authors provide a foundation for collection development with the first chapter on the criteria for selection. The second chapter provides a historical perspective of the social issues, attitudes and trends concerning the subject of disability. Also included is a timeline of events which have influenced persons with disabilities. A third chapter, containing a bibliography of reference books on various disabilities and on persons with disabilities, is useful as a guide in developing a good reference collection about disabilities.

Moore, C. (1990). *A reader's guide for parents of children with mental, physical, or emotional handicaps*. (3d ed.). Rockville, MD: Woodbine House. Written by a parent and updated twice, this "list of lists" is a basic source for information about disabilities, public policy, and advocacy, and as a guide to journals, magazines, newsletters, and directories about disabilities. It is an important tool for librarians, teachers, and parents. It is a selection tool for books on special needs and also includes a comprehensive referral list, "Where to Write for More Information."

Robertson, D. (1992). *Portraying persons with disabilities: Fiction. An annotated bibliography of fiction for children and teenagers*. (3d ed.). Providence, NJ: R. R. Bowker. This is a valuable guide in the selection process. It updates

Bowker's *Notes from a Different Drummer* (1977) and *More Notes from a Different Drummer* (1984), the landmark sources for children's and young adult's books about disabilities. Annotated entries cover titles published between 1982 and 1991. The introduction includes background on awareness and sensitivity, and provides selection criteria for fiction about persons with different abilities. Arranged by topical chapters, the book is fully indexed by title, author, and subject, making it useful in several ways. Specific disabilities can be checked in the index. A good source for background information about disabilities is found in one of the introductory chapters. Full descriptive and evaluative annotations will help in the selection process.

Vellman, R. (1990). *Meeting the needs of people with disabilities: A guide for librarians, educators, and other service professions*. Phoenix: Oryx. This book provides a detailed overview of people with disabilities and includes extensive chapters on school libraries and special education. Extensive listings of support agencies and resource materials make this an essential volume for a professional collection.

CHAPTER 6

Ouzts, D. (1991). The emergence of bibliotherapy as a discipline. *Reading Horizons*. 31(3): 199–206. This article looks at the role of the reading teacher in carrying out bibliotherapy procedures. Children today are experiencing a myriad of problems that could adversely affect their social and emotional development. Steps are offered on how to administer an interest inventory to begin the bibliotherapy process, as well as criteria for book selection.

Pardeck, J., & Pardeck, J. (1990). Using developmental literature with collaborative groups. *Reading Improvement*. 27(4): 226–237. This article offers a creative means of using collaborative groups in bibliotherapy sessions to meet individual developmental reading deficits. Four group skills useful for collaborative groups are identified, suggestions for follow-up activities are provided. Suggestions to evaluate individual improvement in reading comprehension are discussed.

CHAPTER 7

Ahrentzen, S. (in press). Socio-behavioral qualities of the built environment. In R. Dunlap & W. Michelson (Eds.), *Handbook of environmental sociology*. Westport, CT: Greenwood Press. This chapter looks at some recent empirical and conceptual advances in understanding the influence of the built environment upon social behavior. It focuses on the built environment as an influence upon the social performance of people and the social meaning of places. A model for classifying these environment–behavior relationships is presented, and this model can be applied by architects and others to assist in learning what is important to the owners and future users of any setting.

Davis, C., & Lifchez, R. (1987). An open letter to architects. In R. Lifchez (Ed.), *Rethinking architecture: Design students and physically disabled people.* Berkeley: University of California Press. Physical accessibility is not only a matter of gaining admittance, but also a quality of experience—how one feels about a place and interprets it, or how one orients within it. In this chapter, the authors reflect upon the rising numbers of persons with disabilities living within the community, and argue that the architecture profession has not kept up with these demographic and socioeconomic changes. The result is environments that are not suited to the needs of these individuals. It is important that those in the architecture profession learn to understand this "quality of experience" and strive to design with it in mind. As the chapter concludes, the authors provide several methods to facilitate such learning.

Zeisel, J. (1981). *Inquiry by design. Tools for environment-behavior research.* Cambridge: Cambridge University Press. This book helps in using environment-behavior research to make better design decisions. The author illustrates many research techniques used in this still-emerging field, and provides several examples to demonstrate the strengths of each technique. The opening chapters include a review of the design process and the research process, and how these can work together. Later chapters include such topics as observing physical traces and environmental behavior, using focused interviews, and using standardized questionnaires.

CHAPTER 8

Male, M. (1994). *Technology for inclusion: Meeting the needs of all students.* Boston: Allyn and Bacon. This textbook is an update of Dr. Male's previous book, *Special Magic*. The philosophy is clearly focused on using technology to enhance inclusion and the educational opportunities of all students. Emphasis is placed on recognizing appropriate applications of technology across the life span, providing appropriate physical, sensory and cognitive access, and collaboration between professionals and families. Numerous product profiles and practical how-to features are also discussed.

Lewis, R. (1993). *Special education technology: Classroom applications.* Pacific Grove, CA: Brooks/Cole Publishing. This book provides a comprehensive introduction to instructional and assistive technology that educators are likely to encounter in schools. Extensive product profiles, illustrations, user snapshots, and resource lists make this an invaluable resource for professionals and parents interested in using technology with students with special needs.

CHAPTER 9

Coleman, J. (1990). Characteristics of at-risk youth and the library's role in dropout prevention. *Tech Trends.* 35(4): 46–47. This reviews the literature related to at-risk youth and highlights the role of the library as a source of assistance in dropout prevention. In this vein, the author discusses two primary roles of library media specialists: information specialist and instructional consultant. As an information specialist, the library media specialist can use his/her expertise to assess and meet the informational needs of a school's faculty and students. This may assist in helping students connect with an area of interest and become more empowered learners. As an instructional consultant, library media specialists can use their exposure to the spectrum of learners across the grade levels to provide a broader perspective in educational problem-solving and a richer understanding of school-wide curriculum. As pointed out by the author of this article, the role of the library media specialist is often overlooked when addressing the needs of at-risk learners.

Wood, J. (1992). *Adapting instruction for mainstreamed and at-risk students*. New York: Merrill. This text provides an overview of the identification and placement procedures used for special needs students. It includes a discussion of prereferral, referral, assessment, and eligibility determination procedures. The text also includes techniques for adapting instruction, techniques for adapting the physical environment, and techniques for facilitating the social and behavioral success of special needs learners in the mainstream. Although this text is not specifically designed for library media specialists, the information contained in the text is relevant and important to all educators who serve students with special needs.

CHAPTER 10

Deshler, D., Alley, G., Warner, M., & Schumaker, J. (1981). Instructional practices for promoting skill acquisition and generalization in severely learning disabled adolescents. *Learning Disability Quarterly*. 4: 415–421. This article outlines instructional procedures that promote the acquisition and generalization of newly acquired skills. When implemented, these procedures (developed at the University of Kansas Institute for Research in Learning Disabilities) increase the effectiveness of the teaching of strategies and skills to students with severe learning disabilities. The importance of this article is the validation of the specific set of instructional procedures that ensure maximum skill acquisition and generalization.

Ellis, E., Lenz, B., & Sabornie, E. (1987). Generalization and adaptation of learning strategies to natural environments: Part 1: Critical agents. *Remedial and Special Education*. 8: 6–20.

Ellis, E., Lenz, B., & Sabornie, E. (1987). Generalization and adaptation of learning strategies to natural environments: Part 2: Research into practice. *Remedial and Special Education*. 8: 6–23. These companion articles present a comprehensive examination of the issues surrounding the generalization of newly acquired skills by adolescents with mild disabilities. In that generalization rarely occurs spontaneously, these authors have presented a four-level model of generalization that emphasizes direct instruction in generalization skills by various mediators (e.g., teachers, peers, students).

CHAPTER 11

Stainback, W., & Stainback, S. (1987). Facilitating friendships. *Education and Training of the Mentally Retarded*. 22: 18–25. This article addresses the importance of teaching mentally retarded students the specific skills to develop friendships, citing friendships as an important component in the education of the total child. A definition of friendship is provided along with a discussion of each skill necessary in the development of friendships. Some examples of these skills are: establishing areas of compatibility; sharing and providing support; trustworthiness and loyalty; and conflict resolution. The article concludes with ideas for teaching these skills, specifically discussing the method of coaching.

Johnson, D., & Johnson, R. (1987). *Learning together and alone: Cooperative, competitive and individualistic learning*. (2d ed.). Englewood Cliffs, NJ: Prentice-Hall. In this book, the Johnson brothers describe the appropriate use of the three goal structures; cooperative, competitive, and individualistic. How these goal structures tie in with learning processes and instructional outcomes is also addressed. They include details on how to structure a classroom so that each goal structure may be used, but they recommend that 70% of instructional time be in cooperative structures with each other goal structure receiving 15% of instructional time. Three chapters are then devoted to setting up the specific components of cooperative learning including student acquisition of collaborative skills erecting positive interdependence, and processing of groups' cooperative learning skills. Lastly, they address teacher concerns including low and high achievers, classroom management, and disruptive students.

CHAPTER 12

Clark, B. (1992). *Growing up gifted: Developing the potential of children at home and school.* New York: Macmillan Publishing Company.This text discusses a wide spectrum of topics related to teaching the gifted and talented, from definitions of giftedness in the forms of intelligence and creativity to at-risk gifted students who may be underachievers, handicapped, female or from a low socioeconomic or culturally diverse background. Also included is a section on the early childhood development of gifted children, which addresses the prenatal and social–emotional development of these children, the preschool years, and parenting. A history of schools' gifted programs and an explanation of modern programs from the early years through the secondary level is discussed. The importance of differentiating and integrating the curriculum is addressed, as well as the criteria and problems in identifying gifted and talented students. A chapter is also devoted to the importance of meeting the affective as well as the cognitive needs of these special needs students.

Greenlaw, M., & McIntosh, M. (1988). *Educating the gifted*. Chicago: American Library Association. *Educating the Gifted* is an excellent sourcebook as it provides extensive selected and annotated bibliographies at the conclusion of each chapter. The various chapters briefly address such topics as:

a historical perspective of gifted education and definitions of the terms gifted and talented; an identification process from nomination, to screening, to selection, to validation; counseling of these students; programming; academic curriculum; and parenting.

Halsted, J. (1988). *Guiding gifted readers: From preschool through high school.* Columbus, Oh: Ohio Psychology Publishing Company. Encouraging gifted children to read good literature is the focus of this book. The text discusses ideas for guiding gifted students from preschool age on through the high school years. How to utilize bibliotherapy to affect the emotional development and how books can further the intellectual development of these students is included. Ideas on reading guidance, formats for discussing books and the importance of using the library at an earlier age than the average child are presented, as well as a discussion of the different literature genres as they can be applied to gifted children. An annotated bibliography of books that gifted children can and should read is arranged by suggested grade level and listed under five affective categories: *identity; aloneness; getting along with others; developing imagination (for younger students) or using abilities (for older students);* and *drive to understand.*

CHAPTER 13

Andrews S., Otis-Wilborn, A., & Messenheimer-Young, T. (1991). *Beyond seeing and hearing: Teaching geography to sensory impaired children.* Indiana, PA: National Council for Geographic Education. This monograph is part of a *Pathways in Geography* series to support the teaching and learning of themes, concepts, and skills in geography at all levels of instruction. This monograph focuses specifically on teaching and learning in students who have visual and hearing impairments. Two chapters provide background information about the effects of hearing and vision impairments on learning. The other chapters in the monograph describe a process for curriculum planning and implementation that emphasizes the important roles of experience and communication in teaching and learning. These authors provide a rationale supporting an integrated experience-based curriculum model to enhance developing conceptual understandings in geography for all students. In the final chapters, a unit based upon *Paddle to the Sea,* a book by H. C. Holling, is presented which provides specific examples of the curriculum planning process and learning experiences that integrate experience and communication.

Dudley-Marling, C. & Searle, D. (1991). *When students have time to talk: Creating contexts for learning language.* Portsmouth, NH: Heinemann Publishers. This is a small book with a very powerful message. The authors share with readers a logical and understandable argument supporting the central role that communication plays in classroom learning. Their premise is that language is a tool and not a subject. Additionally, Dudley-Marling and Searle describe specific ways in which classroom teachers and other educational professionals, including librarians, can create situations that promote teacher-to-student and student-to-student talk which can enhance the development of students' understanding and use of a) the language specific to academic content (science, math, etc.) and b) the language that promotes positive social interactions. For example, chapters describe how to extend conversations, "talk around the edges," evaluate communication, and work with students who experience difficulty in communicating.

CHAPTER 14

NASSP Bulletin, May 1991. 75 (535). This issue of the *NASSP Bulletin* focuses on the restructuring of schools and school library media centers. Authors, including Brewik, Keegan and Westerger, and Haycock, discuss concepts such as resource-based learning, the information age and the school library media specialist, and the role of the school library media specialist in the restructuring of schools. This issue of the *NASSP Bulletin* explores the possibility of the school library media center as the hub of the school with the coming of the information age.

Index

About the Contributors

DAVE L. EDYBURN is a faculty member in the Department of Exceptional Education at the University of Wisconsin–Milwaukee. Dr. Edyburn's teaching responsibilities involve preparing teachers to use technology in instruction. His research interests focus on designing and evaluating technology-enhanced learning environments.

MARY ANN FITZGERALD has been a special education teacher for Milwaukee public schools for two decades, serving as both a diagnostic and a consulting teacher. At the University of Wisconsin–Milwaukee, she has taught many classes in learning disabilities, issues and trends in special education, mainstreaming, and general special education. She currently works as a facilitator of inclusive education programs in which special education students are taught in general education settings. She works directly with teachers and students.

JANE GLODOSKI is a consulting teacher for the Milwaukee Public Schools. She helps teachers and students work together to include special needs students in general education settings.

ANN HIGGINS HAINS teaches preservice and inservice classes and research seminars in early childhood education for children with special needs at the University of Wisconsin–Milwaukee. Her research interests include parent-professional collaboration and the use of technology in early childhood special education classrooms.

DEBORAH JILBERT has taught secondary learning disabilities for a number of years. She currently works as a vocational specialist helping students with special needs at the Waukesha County Technical College. She is interested in helping students bridge the school to work gap.

MARGARET J. KEEFE is a school library media specialist and teacher of gifted children in the Wheeling Community Consolidated School District #21 in Illinois. She previously taught for ten years in the classroom at the first and second grade levels. She is interested in making the school library media center the hub of the school as curriculum becomes more and more integrated with the research process and technology. She also uses her bilingual abilities at Robert Frost Elementary School, which serves a diverse population.

ROBERT P. KING has worked with a vast variety of special needs populations in public school and hospital settings. He is currently a professor at Cardinal Stritch College, Milwaukee, Wisconsin, where he directs and teaches in the program to train teachers who work with emotionally disturbed students. His research interests include working with adjudicated youth and alternative therapies for working with emotionally disturbed youth.

TERRY MCGREEHIN teaches at Plymouth Children's Center, an early childhood education and child care program in Milwaukee. She explored the use of integrated curriculum as an undergraduate student and in her work with young children at the children's center.

WILLIAM J. MURRAY is a doctoral student in the School of Architecture and Urban Planning at the University of Wisconsin–Milwaukee and works as a behavioral psychologist for a national health-care company. He is interested in creating empowering environments with and for individuals with disabilities.

AMY OTIS-WILBORN is a professor at the University of Wisconsin–Milwaukee, where she also serves as the director of the Center for Teacher Education. She works primarily with preservice and practicing teachers in the areas of language and literacy teaching and learning and teaching students with hearing impairments. Her research interests include teacher education, integrated curriculum, and education of students with hearing impairments.

LULA PRIDE is Assistant Director of Indian Prairie Public Library in Willowbrook, Illinois. Ms. Pride, who has an M.L.S. from Louisiana State University, has over twenty years of professional experience in academic and public libraries. From 1988–1991, she was Director of Project SLICD, Statewide Library Information for Caregivers of the Disabled, a disability information service in Illinois that was recognized by the American Library Association and the National Organization on Disability as a national model. She continues with her special interest in community based information and referral, and has published local organizational directories for two suburban Chicago libraries.

M. LEWIS PUTNAM is a researcher at the Washington Research Institute, Seattle. He taught at the University of Wisconsin–Milwaukee, where he specialized in methods for teaching adolescents with learning disabilities. His research interests include the identification of setting demands on students in school and the generalization of students' skills across settings, instructors, and tasks.

LOIS SCHULTZ is the Youth Services Consultant for school library media specialists and children's librarians in public libraries for the Suburban Library System, a regional library system in suburban Chicago. Ms. Schultz has her M.L.S. from the University of Illinois in Champaign-Urbana and has worked as a school librarian and as a children's librarian in a public library in the Dayton and Montgomery County Public Library in Ohio and the Downers Grove Public Library in Illinois. She was Assistant Professor in the graduate library school at the University of Illinois and has also taught as an adjunct professor at Northern Illinois University. Courses she has taught include reference, selection, administration, audiovisual, school library management, children's services, and selection of library materials for children and young adults.

DEBORAH L. VOLTZ is an assistant professor in the Department of Exceptional Education at the University of Wisconsin–Milwaukee, where she teaches classes in special education, learning disabilities, and mainstreaming. Her research interests include collaboration between special and general educators and accommodating student diversity in urban general education settings.

CAREN L. WESSON, was a professor in the Department of Exceptional Education at the University of Wisconsin–Milwaukee. She taught courses in general special education, general education, learning disabilities, emotional disturbance, and research and issue seminars. In recent years her research interests included collaboration between special and general educators and the inclusion of special needs students in general education settings.

Atlanta-Fulton Public Library